Parliamentary Roles in Modern Legislatures

This book gathers the most influential authors on role research and legislative studies to examine the different roles that MPs are playing in modern-day legislatures. It provides a comprehensive and critical overview of current research on legislative roles, summarises previous research, presents a large variety of methodological approaches and also explores the latest developing approaches to role theory.

The concept of political roles has become increasingly relevant for understanding contemporary political systems. Parliamentary, legislative and representative roles are professional roles that provide a way of connecting the individual legislator to their institution that can also explain a legislator's attitude and behaviour. Drawing upon case studies with as much as 40 years of data that include Germany, the Netherlands, UK, Austria, Hungary, Australia, New Zealand and the European Parliament, this book examines the link between representative roles, different institutional settings and parliamentary behaviour. It argues that the roles MPs play depends on whom they think they should represent: between their voters, their party, the people of their country and also themselves, conflicts of loyalty can occur. This book provides a framework to analyse MPs' choices by searching both the reasons for their views about representation, and the consequences of those views in parliament.

Parliamentary Roles in Modern Legislatures will be of strong interest to students and scholars of government, legislative studies, political parties, comparative politics, political sociology and deliberative democracy.

Magnus Blomgren is a Senior Lecturer at the Department of Political Science at Umeå University, Sweden.

Olivier Rozenberg is Associate Research Professor at Sciences Po (Paris) where he works in the Centre d'études européennes.

Routledge/ECPR studies in European political science

Edited by Thomas Poguntke

Ruhr University Bochum, Germany on behalf of the European Consortium for Political Research

The Routledge/ECPR Studies in European Political Science series is published in association with the European Consortium for Political Research – the leading organization concerned with the growth and development of political science in Europe. The series presents high-quality edited volumes on topics at the leading edge of current interest in political science and related fields, with contributions from European scholars and others who have presented work at ECPR workshops or research groups.

1 **Regionalist Parties in Western Europe**
Edited by Lieven de Winter and Huri Türsan

2 **Comparing Party System Change**
Edited by Jan-Erik Lane and Paul Pennings

3 **Political Theory and European Union**
Edited by Albert Weale and Michael Nentwich

4 **Politics of Sexuality**
Edited by Terrell Carver and Véronique Mottier

5 **Autonomous Policy Making by International Organizations**
Edited by Bob Reinalda and Bertjan Verbeek

6 **Social Capital and European Democracy**
Edited by Jan van Deth, Marco Maraffi, Ken Newton and Paul Whiteley

7 **Party Elites in Divided Societies**
Edited by Kurt Richard Luther and Kris Deschouwer

8 **Citizenship and Welfare State Reform in Europe**
Edited by Jet Bussemaker

9 **Democratic Governance and New Technology**
Technologically mediated innovations in political practice in Western Europe
Edited by Ivan Horrocks, Jens Hoff and Pieter Tops

10 **Democracy without Borders**
Transnationalisation and conditionality in new democracies
Edited by Jean Grugel

11 **Cultural Theory as Political Science**
Edited by Michael Thompson, Gunnar Grendstad and Per Selle

Parliamentary Roles in Modern Legislatures

Edited by Magnus Blomgren and
Olivier Rozenberg

Routledge
Taylor & Francis Group

LONDON AND NEW YORK

First published 2012
by Routledge
2 Park Square Milton Park Abingdon Oxon OX14 4RN

Simultaneously published in the USA and Canada
by Routledge
711 Third Avenue, New York, NY 10017

Routledge is an imprint of the Taylor & Francis Group, an informa business.

British Library Cataloguing in Publication Data
A catalogue record for this book is available from the British Library

Library of Congress Cataloging in Publication Data
Parliamentary roles in modern legislatures/edited by Magnus Blomgren and Olivier Rozenberg.
    p. cm. – (Routledge/ECPR studies in European political science; 78)
Includes bibliographical references and index.
1. Legislators. 2. Legislative bodies. 3. Legislators–Europe.
4. Legislative bodies–Europe. I. Blomgren, Magnus. II. Rozenberg, Olivier, 1976–
JF511.P358 2012
328–dc23
                                                    2011035716

ISBN: 978-0-415-57568-3 (hbk)
ISBN: 978-0-203-12649-3 (ebk)

Typeset in Times New Roman
by Wearset Ltd, Boldon, Tyne and Wear

Contents

Figures and tables

Figures

Tables

Contributors

Rudy B. Andeweg, Professor at the Department of Political Science, Leiden University, Netherlands.

Heinrich Best, Professor at the Department of Sociology, Jena University, Germany.

Magnus Blomgren, Senior Lecturer at the Department for Political Science, Umeå University, Sweden.

Anika Gauja, Senior Lecturer at the Department of Government and International Relations, University of Sydney, Australia.

Gabriella Ilonszki, Professor at the Institute of Political Science, Corvinus University of Budapest, Hungary.

Marcelo Jenny, Lecturer at the Department of Government, University of Vienna, Austria.

Wolfgang C. Müller, Professor at the Department of Government, University of Vienna, Austria.

Julien Navarro, Senior Lecturer at Université catholique de Lille, France.

Olivier Rozenberg, Associate Research Professor at Sciences Po, Centre d'études européennes, Paris, France.

Kaare Strøm, Distinguished Professor at the Department of Political Science, University of California, San Diego, USA.

Lars Vogel, Research Assistant at the Department of Sociology and the Collaborative Research Centre 580, Jena University, Germany.

Thomas Zittel, Professor at the Department for Social Sciences, Goethe-University Frankfurt am Main.

Foreword

Donald D. Searing, University of North Carolina at Chapel Hill, USA

There is a revival of scholarly interest in the roles that politicians play in parliaments, and Blomgren and Rozenberg's excellent volume is a landmark contribution to this work. The golden era of political role analysis was grounded in sociological theory. It faded away, especially in the United States, during the 1980s and 1990s. The current restoration relies instead on neo-institutionalism. It is energized by widespread interest, especially in Europe, in links between structure and agency, institutional change, and multi-level governance. For this restoration, and for this book, two neo-institutional approaches have been influential: my own motivational approach, which is in the spirit of March and Olsen's contributions, and Kaare Strøm's strategic behavior framework, which is in the tradition of rational choice. Chapters in this book draw on ideas from both, and several seek to bridge them.

What are roles?

Role analyses were always mired in conceptual confusion, often about absence of agency and definitions of roles. The agency question is largely settled, for we all now recognize that institutional rules constrain the thinking and behavior of purposive politicians who are at the same time negotiating to achieve their individual aims. This neo-institutional foundation is shared by the motivational and strategic behavior frameworks. Nonetheless, there are still outstanding issues, beginning with role definitions. Blomgren and Rozenberg's own definition – "patterns of attitudes and/or behavior that result from being a member of parliament" – points to three issues that structure this book's chapters.

One is to what extent should our understandings of roles reflect the understandings of the politicians we study? Some argue that the everyday descriptive categories that politicians use are impediments to generalization and should be replaced by theoretically standardized concepts. Others feel we must work with these categories, at least in the first instance, because such categories are central to the motivations of the actors whose behavior we are trying to explain. This is a deductive–inductive disagreement and, in practice, a matter of emphasis. Blomgren and Rozenberg suggest splitting the difference because "it only makes sense to talk about parliamentary roles ... if MPs' views about being MPs are considered one way or another."

The second issue, related to the first, is associated with the most widely studied parliamentary role types of the twentieth century, delegates and trustees, whose roles were often defined by a specific attitude toward representation: whether MPs should be guided primarily by the views of their constituents, or by their own judgments. The question here is whether a single attitude constitutes a role, or whether roles are better understood as patterns or configurations. Of course a single attitude measure may be tapping a full-blown role in the minds of politicians which, according to Blomgren and Rozenberg, is more likely to be the case today, because ideas about delegate and trustee modes of representation have become familiar in the political cultures and parliaments of contemporary liberal democracies.

The last issue, which sounds more abstruse, but which is critical for the strategic behavior approach, is whether it makes sense to define roles in terms of behavior alone, that is to say, to leave attitudes (e.g. norms, goals, preferences) outside the definition. Blomgren and Rozenberg seem to be of two minds about this, on the one hand agreeing with Andeweg that norms in particular are integral to the concept, and should therefore be included in the definition, on the other seeing virtues in the parsimony of keeping them out.

The motivational approach, which emphasizes politicians' understandings, defines roles as complex configurations of attitudes and core behaviors: "particular patterns of interrelated goals, attitudes and behaviors that are characteristic of people in particular situations." Its strength is also its weakness: an inductive complexity that requires considerable research costs in time and money and also complicates cross-national analysis. By contrast the strategic behavior approach, which focuses on constructing universalistic accounts, defines roles parsimoniously as patterns of strategic behavior only: "regularized patterns of [strategic] behavior ... in common and repeated activities on which others depend." And, likewise, its strength is also its weakness: a parsimony in defining roles as strategic behavior which may be so parsimonious that its constructs are no longer recognizable as roles.

Why are roles important?

The roles of politicians are important because these are the routines through which political leaders educate, govern, reform, and represent citizens in contemporary liberal democracies. It would seem impossible to define and explain such political systems adequately without taking account of politicians' roles. Yet there have always been powerful traditions in the social sciences, and especially in comparative politics, eager to convince us that political leaders' careers and decisions are determined by broad structural forces and trends, thereby depreciating their significance, either by excluding politicians from explanations or treating their contributions as constants.

Neo-institutionalists reject the one-directional claim that the behavior of political leaders is determined by systemic factors and institutional settings. Institutions circumscribe behavior but do not dictate it. Structure and agency are interdependent, not institution-dominant. Roles constrain but also enable. "Let us remember, then," John Stuart Mill wrote, "in the first place, that political institutions ... are the work of men, owe their origin and their whole existence to human will. Men did not wake on a summer morning and find them sprung up. Neither do they resemble trees, which, once planted, 'are aye growing' while men 'are sleeping.' In every stage of their existence they are made what they are by human voluntary agency."[1]

Responsibilities and roles

Roles are the means through which politicians play their parts in looking after the political system's essential tasks or responsibilities. They regularize and economize politicians' efforts and, from the perspective of the regime, make key aspects of their performances dependable much of the time, albeit not rote and not determined.

As Jenny and Müller in the present volume observe, our studies of politicians' roles have concentrated on a limited number of aspects of a limited number of representational and legislative tasks. We have not explored roles related to many other essential duties that put politicians in a variety of different arenas outside parliament from media events to meetings with civil servants, interest groups, and contacts with ordinary citizens. The principal responsibilities that politicians have in liberal democratic political systems, and examples of a few of the roles associated with them, are as follows: (1) accountability (e.g. policy advocates): scrutinizing, critiquing, and evaluating governments, ministers, civil servants and colleagues; (2) representation (e.g. constituency members): redress of grievances, opinion representation; (3) regime building (e.g. parliament men): protecting key liberal democratic institutions and principles, and educating citizens and other elites about them; (4) governing (e.g. ministers – "politicians" or "administrators"): forging a sense of common purpose and tending the machinery of government by deliberating, deciding, compromising, managing.

This book suggests many new questions, and new perspectives on old questions, for research on roles. Some are systemic and focus on constraints: how do electoral systems, multi-level governance, or political party affiliation affect the choice and interpretation of representational roles? How do formal and informal accountability rules teach, reinforce or undermine integrity? Or Andeweg's intriguing question: to what extent are role conceptions situation-specific? Other fresh perspectives come from organizational psychologists who have recently begun to study politics as an occupation.[2] They look at politicians' roles in the context of entire careers from apprenticeship occupations like public relations through post-parliamentary linked occupations like lobbying, and they are more likely to focus on the enabling side. What constitutes career success? What motivations and skills are needed to succeed in particular career pathways and in particular roles? What part does mentoring and career management play in successful role performance?

Habits, strategic thinking, and the logic of appropriateness

In three thoughtful chapters, Blomgren and Rozenberg provide a wide-ranging review of theoretical, conceptual, and empirical issues. I will comment here on several considerations that have particular relevance to the strategic behavior framework.

Defining roles as routinized strategic behavior is an innovative step that helps bring roles into the rational choice paradigm. It is also a move that several contributors to this volume fear may cast out traditional understandings of roles as practices with strong habitual as well as strategic components. Part of the problem lies in confusion over distinctions among habits, strategic thinking, the "logic of appropriateness," and purposive behavior. Although habits have been the most opaque of these ideas, recent experimental work in social and cognitive psychology and neuroscience can shed some light here.[3]

Habits are behavioral routines that have been repeated frequently in the past in stable contexts. The greater the repetition, the greater the likelihood that such routines will exhibit the psychological characteristics of habits. With habits, past behavior is usually the best predictor of future behavior. Examples of habits that are embedded in politicians' roles might be "constituency members" processing constituents' requests for help with pensions, or walking down the corridor and through their party-designated division lobbies to vote "automatically" with their parties on most matters most of the time. Habits contrast with more instrumental behavior, which is usually more personally important to people, whose intentions are the best predictors of what they do. In these more purposive cases, the issues at stake are more likely to be novel or complex thereby requiring more thoughtful guidance. Habitual routines are very common because they offer important cost-effective benefits in cognitive economy and performance efficiency. It is estimated that, in general, between 50 and 95 percent of role-related behaviors may have strong habitual features. The proportion is undoubtedly smaller for politicians because they encounter much novelty and complexity in their work.

Several characteristics of habitual behavior pose problems for conceptualizing politicians' roles as strategic behavior routines, for strategic thinking and routinized behavior may be an unusual combination. Thus, in habitually performed behavioral routines, the actors' regulation of their behavior is conducted with minimal or sporadic monitoring. They don't think very much, let alone strategically, about what they are doing. They may even be thinking about other things. Moreover, when behaviors are performed habitually, actors may not be aware of discrepancies between these behaviors and their personal goals. In other words, they may be acting against their personal self-interest. This is one of the ways that the normative components of roles push members to act in their collectivity's interest rather than in their own.

The "logic of appropriateness" is March and Olsen's neo-institutionalist interpretation of the psychology of politicians' roles, which sits somewhere between the ideal-type antipodes of "automaticity" in habits and "calculated utility" in strategic thinking. Politicians, in their view, see themselves as members of institutions who ordinarily want to do what is appropriate in specific types of situations. They have positions in institutions, these positions are associated with roles, and the roles have institutionally established expectations. This mode of thinking is purposive: unlike with habits, politicians think a great deal about what the appropriate thing to do would be and why – even if they don't always do it. This thinking is purposive but not usually strategic: politicians are not calculating their expected utilities. And they are prepared to follow rules, at least for the time being, that are antithetical to their selfish self-interests. March and Olsen believe that the "logic of appropriateness" is the most common practice for the greatest number of role situations. But even if this claim is as much of an overestimate as are comparable claims about the omnipresence of habits, taken together, role thinking in terms of habits and in terms of the logic of appropriateness seems likely to occupy too large a portion of the psychology of roles to be ignored by definition.

Again, the strategic behavior framework defines roles as repeated patterns of particular types of strategic behavior. It is the repetition that turns the strategic behavior into something that sounds like a role. But the problem is that frequently repeated behavioral routines also sound like habits, which are incompatible with the adjective "strategic" as used in the strategic behavior framework. Strategic thinking is most likely to be prominent in experiences like role choice, or, in important non-routine judgments such as when a "ministerial aspirant," who wants to attract positive attention from the whips, considers subjects on which to speak in the Chamber, or when a "specialist" considers complex alternatives in public policy or institutional reform. The strategic behavior framework as applied in rational choice research designs is particularly good at spotting constraints, institutional rules that interact with politicians' motivations to shape their behavior. This has been its major contribution to the study of legislatures. But when it comes to roles, it may have to be more broadminded about the nature of "purposive" behavior, or be satisfied with studying only those aspects of role behavior that approximate its motivational model.

Preferences, goals, and other motivations

Blomgren and Rozenberg observe that the motivational and strategic behavior frameworks appear to differ most in their palates of preferences.

The motivational approach treats preferences as both exogenous and endogenous. In other words, politicians enter parliament with their own personal motivations, which include career goals (relatively conscious and strategic) as well as emotional incentives (more psychological and motivational). As they negotiate, play, and switch roles over time, they modify their existing goals and even their emotional incentives in order to adapt to situations and achieve their evolving aims. For instance, when "ministerial aspirants" find that they have no hope of achieving office, their desire for office is likely to fade as they look for other roles to play. Emotional incentives, which the motivational approach identifies as key energizing forces, have been avoided by most legislative researchers in favor of cognitive career goals, which are easier to see and connect with institutional contexts.

By contrast, the strategic behavior framework treats preferences as exclusively exogenous. In other words, politicians enter parliament with dominant personal preferences that are not significantly affected by their experiences in the institution. Among their personal preferences, two are posited as dominant: reelection and desire for office. This might seem to exclude from consideration goals such as doing public service or pursuing common interests, as well as emotional incentives like "status," which close observers of politicians have long considered central to politicians' careers. Kaare Strøm suggests, however, that when these two dominant motives are not so dominant, behavior may be driven by all sorts of other motives. So even here the two approaches may not be as discordant as they seem; and Blomgren and Rozenberg have some good ideas about how to reconcile them in the contexts of bounded rationality and neo-institutionalism.

Country studies and cross-national studies

The revival in studies of politicians' roles is more focused on cross-national research designs than was its predecessor. It wants to discover regularities across contemporary liberal democracies in types of roles, in choosing roles, and in their consequences. Blomgren and Rozenberg suspect that such commonalities are more likely to be found in representational than in legislative roles because representation is a universal responsibility whereas many legislative roles are fitted into particular institutional arrangements. Several chapters in this book offer evidence that some legislative role types, such as policy advocates, party delegates and ministerial aspirants may be widespread in a number of liberal democracies, and that some patterns connecting these roles with institutional rules and motivations may travel fairly well too.

On the whole, however, there seems to be great variety in politicians' roles across even relatively similar parliamentary contexts. This suggests that single country studies should continue to be attractive for the potential power of their explanations and that, as Ilonszki demonstrates in this volume, there is much to be gained through pursuing one-country longitudinal studies as well, for here the nature of the roles we are investigating is more constant than it is cross-nationally, which is an advantage for explanation and prediction. The cross-national perspective directs out attention to important systemic questions that we would otherwise overlook even studying one country's parliament over time, and most empirical chapters in this book address such questions. For example: What conditions explain different distributions of role types in different parliaments? How do different distributions of role types channel what different parliaments do?

The strategic behavior and motivational frameworks both see psychology as the route to regularities. The difference between them is that the strategic behavior approach has already "discovered" its psychology in several posited goals and is seeking cross-national patterns in how these goals interact with formal rules. This is its advantage for cross-national research over the motivational framework which is better suited to in-depth country studies or studies of international institutions like the European Commission.[4]

Conclusion

The research programs that we left behind in the 1980s produced many new ideas and welcome data, but they were also mired in conceptual confusion and disappointing empirical results. Today's motivational and strategic behavior approaches are clearing out some of the underbrush and introducing more systematic and empirically promising research designs.

The motivational framework synthesizes the formally dominant sociological perspective with its economic counterpart by linking institutional norms with the purposive behavior of individual politicians. Its strengths lie in the greater potential validity of its explanations, its weaknesses in generalizability. The strategic behavior framework incorporates roles into its paradigm by redefining the role concept and providing a motivational account that better fits microeconomic theory. Its strengths lie in its greater generalizability, enabled by its greater parsimony, which, however, places limitations on validity, on explaining what is actually going on in the world.

How much should we invest to redeem this neglected subject in which we lost interest long ago? Will our neo-institutional constructs and early empirical results convince us of the importance of looking vigorously again at the roles of politicians, this time from a somewhat different perspective? There is also a normative reason for seeing how far we can go. The quality of leadership in liberal democracies is judged by how well a nation's politicians are performing roles associated with the basic responsibilities entrusted to them. As political scientists, we ought to be able to offer publics and politicians convincing standards for understanding and judging these role performances, standards grounded in empirical research and justified by democratic theory.

Notes

1 Mill, John Stuart (1958). *Considerations on Representative Government*. New York: Bobbs Merrill: 58.
2 Silvester, Jo, Wyatt, Maddy, and Randall, Ray (2011) "Predicting politician performance: Applying work psychology to political roles." Centre for Organisational Psychology, Department of Psychology, City University, London.
3 Wood, Wendy, Quinn, Jeffrey, and Kashy Deborah A. (2002) "Habits in everyday life: Thought, emotion, and action," *Journal of Personality and Social Psychology*, 83, 6: 1281–97.
4 Hooghe, Liesbet (2001) *The European Commission and the Integration of Europe: Images of Governance*. Cambridge: Cambridge University Press.

Preface

We met each other in the midst of our doctoral studies on the ECPR conference in Turin 2002. We both independently presented papers dealing with the link between the traditional democratic national institutions and the growing importance of the EU system. How parliamentarians view their role as democratic elected representatives was an important part of this analysis. It helped us to understand how legislatures work and discuss prospects as well as limits for future democratic European institutions.

Six years later, in 2008, we arranged our own ECPR workshop in Rennes, and this time parliamentary roles were the focus of the event. We realized gladly that our invitation attracted a number of high-profile scholars from around the world and this made us certain that the concept of roles is returning to the scientific agenda. Even though we would have wanted to give room in this volume to all participants at this workshop, this has obviously not been possible. However, we want to express our gratitude to Audrey André, David Arter, Kelly Blidook, Gabriela Borz, Karen Celis, Olivier Costa, Sam Depauw, Kris Deschouwer, Silvia Erzeel, Richard S. Katz, Matthew Kerby, Eric Kerrouche, Peter Mair, Shane Martin, Araceli Mateos, Christine Neuhold, Federico Russo, Thomas Saalfeld, Marco R. Steenbergen, Bram Wauters, and Andreas Wuest, who attended and/or presented papers on this workshop and contributed to the highly interesting discussion on roles, representation and democracy.

This kind of book is not cheap to produce. We gratefully acknowledge the support of the Swedish Riksbankens Jubileumsfond which, through its grant to the project "Constitutional Reform 2010: Political Parties and the Rules of the Game" (P2007–0370:1-E Bergman), made this research possible.

Some of the participants of the Rennes workshop present their research in this book and we are certainly happy about this. They have, with patience and sincerity, really made the editing process of this book enjoyable and stimulating. Now that it is finished, we hope that it was worth waiting for. We also hope that we have succeeded in our effort to show the width and variation in the current research on parliamentary roles, as well as point out some important lessons for future projects. The sole judge of this is of course you – the reader of this book.

Magnus Blomgren and Olivier Rozenberg
Umeå and Paris, August 2011

1 Introduction

Magnus Blomgren and Olivier Rozenberg

This book deals with the comparative analysis of legislative roles within modern legislatures. Be they legislative, parliamentary or representative roles, this concept refers to patterns of attitudes and/or behavior that result from being a Member of Parliament (MP). Since the 1960s the analysis of different legislative roles has constituted a specific field of legislative studies in North America and Europe. Various – and to a large extent opposing – theoretical schools have used the concept of role to analyze things as diverse as the influence of MPs' backgrounds on their activity, MPs' ability to conduct collective tasks, or their capacity to adapt to different institutional settings. Legislators' views of their constituents and how they should be represented have been particularly important in many studies. Very often, legislative roles have been defined on the basis of MPs' degree of independence from their voters and party.

The study of legislative roles has generated a huge amount of research in the past, and much of it is based on remarkably elaborate empirical work. However, this strand of research became unfashionable in legislative studies around the 1980s. This was partly a result of a general decline in the use of the concept of role in the social sciences more generally. Because of the divisions between the different theories using this concept, studies of roles failed to produce a homogenous theory. Instead, concepts using the word 'role' as a noun or adjective (such as role-making, role-taking, role strain, role conflict, among many others) were developed, which ran the risk of obscuring the initial concept. In legislative studies more specifically, attempts to connect MPs' views about representation to their activities as representatives turned out to be disappointing. In other words, it was difficult to identify sets of attitudes associated with being an MP that were at once comprehensive, coherent, consequential, and mutually exclusive.

Although legislative roles clearly went out of fashion, several elements indicate that they may be coming back in. Three points can be quickly developed, from the most specific to the most general. First, certain studies that were published during the period when the role concept was at its least popular appear to have become quite influential today. This is especially the case for Donald Searing's seminal work (1994), and of the collective book edited by Thomas Saalfeld and Wolfgang C. Müller (1997). In Europe at least, these studies have been followed by several on-going collective and comparative research projects, questioning the way MPs view their work. Beyond its diversity, what is common to this new strand of research is that it appears to be more interested in understanding empirically how representation actually works, than in applying macro-theories.

Second, the 'neo-institutional' turning point in political science has given legitimacy to the conceptualization of institutions as sets of enabling or constraining rules. By elaborating on the relation between agents and structure, the concept of roles allows us to capture the process by which institutional rules can enable or constrain MPs. Roles are constraining insofar as they are associated with a given social status or institutional position. But they are also potentially enabling because they are performed, and because they provide comprehensive patterns that allow MPs to organize their work, and sometimes to make tough decisions. In this respect it might be possible to integrate the role concept into a rational choice framework.

Third, the recent renewal of interest in legislative roles is most probably linked to the current difficulties in so-called advanced democracies. It is not too risky to say that there is something broken in the state of political representation. The unpopularity of political elites, sudden electoral shifts, progression of the extreme right and of populist leaders, low electoral turn-out, and so forth: the picture is obvious to most. If we look at legislatures more specifically, the growth of non-elected decision-making bodies, from independent national agencies to various EU institutions, indicates that the legitimacy of political representation through elected, public and pluralist bodies is increasingly challenged – if not openly questioned. In this context it may be useful to study how MPs perceive these changes. The fundamental question of whether the fact that MPs are elected has an impact on their attitudes and behavior has actually never been so relevant.

Questioning roles

This book is therefore an attempt to capture the current revival of roles in legislative studies. The return of the role concept raises many questions, since the role concept is more complex than a simple metaphor from the stage, both because this research tradition carries a heritage of disappointment, and because both theoretical and empirical studies using roles are diverse and sometimes divergent. The remainder of this introduction sketches these questions before presenting the outline of the book.

Which definition?

The first and most important issue has to do with the definition of legislative roles. Is it possible to agree on a common definition? Should parliamentary roles be divided between representative roles (i.e. roles based on the representational link, such as *trustees* or *delegates*) and legislative roles (i.e. roles based on parliamentary activities, such as *constituency members* or *policy specialists*)? A conceptual clarification is obviously welcome here and the past fascination for neologisms (mis)using the word 'role' should be avoided. At a more general level, when speaking about roles we assume that MPs face collective and coherent sets of norms and expectations, which to a large extent rely on conceptions of political representation. Diverging views arise when discussing the reasons for the development of these norms and the MPs' reactions to them.

Which causes?

The second set of questions concerns roles as dependant variables. How can we explain both the formation of roles within legislatures and the role-taking process by legislators? One group of explanatory variables focuses on social, societal, and political elements that exist outside of legislatures. These variables look at the type of constituency (socially as well as politically), the personal background of legislators (again, the social as well as the political), and the type of elections (candidate selection, voting rules, personal vote, etc.). Another group of variables concentrates on the legislature, that is the type of political system (determined according to a number of criteria established in comparative research: type of state, type of regime, bicameralism, agenda-setting power, committees' strength, etc.) on the one hand and the socialization of legislators on the other hand. The career path within assemblies may especially influence the role-taking process. Reasons for taking a role and the changing of roles are therefore numerous. As a result, MPs may have to cope with conflicting roles.

Which consequences?

Roles can also be defined as independent variables. The effects of roles are analysed mainly in the form of legislators' individual behavior and attitudes, but they can also be studied in their collective behavior, i.e. the parliament's performance. If we take a broad definition of legislative roles, the question is therefore: are MPs' activities coherent with collective expectations resulting from their position within the legislature? If we adopt a more precise definition of representative roles – as most studies do – the question is: do MPs' views about their work and especially about their constituents, have a systematic impact on their behavior? Or on their political opinions? Or on their capacity to fulfill collective tasks such as legislating, voting, debating, informing ministers, helping voters and so forth?

Most contemporary legislative studies no longer look at legislative roles per se, but typically consider roles as one variable among others when trying to explain the behavior and activities of legislators. For instance, the time spent within the constituency doing surgery work can be a result of a number of things: the type of constituency (for example the geographic distance from the parliament), the electoral safety of the seat and the period in the career of the legislator. However, it can also be a result of the individual MP's view of how legislators should behave, which is usually associated with representative roles. Yet this simple example shows how difficult it is to operationalize the role concept; firstly there are alternative ways of conceiving roles, and secondly the way legislators view their job may not be independent from the other aforementioned variables. Studying roles therefore means identifying roles and their possible effects, but it also means constantly questioning the validity of this concept. If MPs' views of their work depend only on the electoral safety of their seats, it is more or less useless to employ the role concept when explaining the time they spend in their constituencies. However, if the way they view their work is not constrained by the electoral safety of their seat, then roles might bring a heuristic added value to the analysis.

Which methodological and empirical strategies?

This above argument indicates how crucial the choice of methodological and empirical strategies is when studying legislative roles. The connection between empirical designs that use roles as either dependent or independent variables is a delicate issue. Scholars that try to explain role-making and role-taking assume that roles do have consequences for behavior and attitudes – otherwise why should these practices be studied? In other words, scholars who look at roles as dependent variables tend to consider, more or less implicitly, that roles do have consequences. Yet it is the task of studies looking at roles as independent variables to determine whether this is the case. The same problem applies in reverse – scholars who try to assess the effects of roles alongside other explanatory variables may neglect the connections between a given role and those variables. In other words, considering roles as independent variables runs the risk of missing the complex relation between roles and the institutional position of the agent.

More concretely, studying roles means first identifying them and attributing them to specific groups. This line of research draws on qualitative interviews and quantitative surveys, studies of parliamentary discourses and opinion, and ethnographic observations, among others. Each method certainly has its own advantages; however, a major problem from a comparative and cumulative perspective is that each strategy tends to promote a particular definition of what legislative roles are. Consequently, a minimal agreement as to what roles are probably does not exist. As several chapters in this book suggest, the traditional distinction between *trustees* and *delegates* receives an ambiguous reception today. On one hand, it is severely criticized for being both over-simplified and too abstract, but on the other hand, the chapters make it clear that fifty years after it was formulated, the distinction between *trustees* and *delegates* is still essential for the discussion on roles.

One important aspect of the methodological discussion concerns comparison. Most previous studies on legislative roles were single case studies. There are reasons to hope that this is changing with the current revival of legislative roles, and this raises new challenges and questions. Are shared or similar roles played all over advanced – and less advanced – democracies? Is the concept of representative roles a useful tool for comparing legislatures? Is it possible, with the role concept, to divide legislatures according to new categories?

Which theory?

Functionalist theorists used roles in order to show the coherence within legislatures. Likewise, interactionist theorists used the concept in order to highlight the great capacity of MPs to adapt to different types of encounters. To a large extent, such theoretical arguments have become dated in social sciences and this has contributed to a certain decline in the use of the role concept. As rational choice theory tends to be dominant in legislative studies, the issue of the coherence between roles and rationality needs to be raised. At first sight, the strong sociological legacy of the concept leads one to conclude that roles have to do with diffusing collective norms rather than promoting individual interests. Yet the capacity of legislators to select roles and to play them in various ways makes one think of roles in terms of a rational strategy. Is it useful to conceptualize for instance vote-seeking MPs as playing a role? What exactly is the individual benefit for an MP from playing a role? Coherence? Cost-saving? Identification? To some extent, rationalist interpretations of roles have been challenged by studies that portray the motivations of politicians in more detail and in some cases even their emotions. Between reason and emotion, how should we theoretically understand roles?

The theoretical debate is not limited to the question of the rationality of roles however – it raises other crucial questions. How are roles changing over time? How do roles contribute to the fulfillment of collective function within parliaments? How do MPs learn their roles? What can be considered restrictive in the role-taking process? What is the relation between how MPs see their roles and what voters expect? To what extent do legislative roles participate in the recruitment function of legislatures (for example the selection of ministers)? To what extent are MPs conscious of playing a role? Is there a dominant role in the role set of each legislator? And, last but not least, how do ongoing changes in legislative roles reflect the global evolution of representative democracies? For instance, are constituency MPs more numerous today than in previous years? Does the relative decline of public trust towards politicians and institutions result in the selection of more autonomous-trustee MPs or more dependant-delegate MPs?

Outline of the book

The following chapter of the book, by the two editors of this volume, presents an analytical review of the role concept in legislative studies. It distinguishes between a functionalist and an interactionist tradition and discusses the reasons for their decline. Then the chapter argues that the neo-institutional turning point in political science has brought legislative roles back on the agenda. In this perspective, the writings of Donald Searing and Kaare Strøm are presented and compared in order to assess the coherence of this epistemic comeback.

In Chapter 3, Heinrich Best and Lars Vogel study roles as a dependent variable. The goal is to determine the background characteristics that may explain the choice of a specific role, and to discuss the determinants of change in German legislators' role adoption. Pre-parliamentary socialisation and party affiliation appear as particularly important in that respect. Best and Vogel rest on a unique large-scale panel survey.

In Chapter 4, Rudy B. Andeweg questions both the behavioural consequences of role orientations, as well as the relevance of the traditional delegate/trustee category. The chapter attempts to revise these concepts by distinguishing between representation 'from below' and 'from above'. By studying the behavioural consequences of the role orientation, Andeweg takes the opposite approach to the preceding chapter and regards roles as an independent variable. To meet that end, he analyses longitudinal survey data on Dutch parliamentarians from the last forty years.

In Chapter 5, Kaare Strøm presents an up-to-date version of his 1997 paper that was published in Müller and Saalfeld's volume mentioned above. In the chapter, Strøm defends, as well as elaborates on, the thesis that roles should be regarded as rational strategies. In his view, parliamentary roles should be understood as behavioral patterns or routines of democratic legislators, which can be understood as strategies that politicians adopt in situations of uncertainty and scarce resources.

This strategic approach is tested and supported by Thomas Zittel in Chapter 6. Zittel uses roles as a dependent variable and studies whether the electoral system or party socialisation, affects the propensity to feel like a party delegate, district delegate or trustee. From a theoretical standpoint, the electoral system is associated with rational strategies, and the duration as party member is used as a proxy for long-term socialization and norms adoption. In order to support the strategic approach, Zittel rests on the interesting potential offered by the mixed German electoral system.

In Chapter 7, Anika Gauja uses a fundamentally different perspective, both theoretically and methodologically, in order to compare representative roles in Australia, New Zealand and the United Kingdom. The study rests on in-depth interviews to analyse the conflict between representing the party, the constituency and/or the whole country. In the three parliaments under study, the contrast is particularly striking between the domination of party cohesion and the legitimacy of a trustee style of representation. In order to understand this contrast, Gauja focuses particularly on the different answers brought by parliamentary party groups.

In Chapter 8, Marcelo Jenny and Wolfgang C. Müller seek to map the roles played within the Austrian Parliament by following a research design based on comparing MPs activity and their views. A cluster analysis of data on MPs behavior enables Jenny and Müller to identify five mutually exclusive types of MPs. Then the identification of each MP's role is compared to his/her views on representation collected through interviews. This approach allows the researcher to interpret the meaning of the behavioral categories, and also to test the potential discrepancy between what MPs say and what they do.

The two last chapters investigate more closely the question of change, and specifically the effect of institutional change on legislative roles. In Chapter 9, Gabriella Ilonszki studies the effects of the numerous changes of the Hungarian political system for the two last decades on MPs' views. She assesses various theoretical models in order to explain the relatively stable constituency focus of Hungarian MPs. The legacy of a specific political culture is specifically acknowledged. Throughout the chapter, Ilonszki adopts a positional approach to roles: that is, a conception of roles based on the position occupied by MPs locally, in their party and before being elected.

The other case of institutional innovation is given by the empowerment of the European Parliament. In Chapter 10, Julien Navarro follows Donald Searing's path and elaborates a motivational typology of the roles played in Strasbourg on the basis of qualitative interviews. After having identified mutually exclusive roles, he tests their coherence on MPs' behaviour as well as their views on Europe and democracy. He also investigates the predictive power of these categories on the subsequent political career of the Members of European Parliament.

In the concluding chapter, we return to the different contributions in order to gauge their theoretical as well as methodological diversity. In that perspective, the relations between roles, behaviour and rationality appear particularly central. Second, we connect the debate about roles with several major issues in legislative and comparative studies, such as electoral engineering, multi-level governance, the increase of non-legislative activity, and gender and minority representation. These different aspects enable us to conclude that parliamentary roles can be a relevant way to evaluate current political phenomena. Both MPs' views on their job and the division of labor between them, say something about the current state of political representation.

References

Müller, W.C. and Saalfeld, T. (1997) *Members of Parliament in Western Europe*, Oregon: Frank Cass.

Searing, D.D. (1994) *Westminister World. Understanding Political Roles*, Cambridge: Harvard University Press.

2 Legislative roles and legislative studies

The neo-institutionalist turning point?

Magnus Blomgren and Olivier Rozenberg

Although not a unified theory, the concept of 'roles' is central in sociology. It aims to make sense of the uniformity and regularity of individual behavior that results from a position in society and/or from the incorporation of collective norms. Ann Weber (1995: 1134) defines a role as 'a set of norms (obligations or expectations) attached to an individual's social position, occupation, or relationship status'. The definition makes clear that role is a notion that links individuals to their social environment. Roles are played by individuals and can be understood as strategies (Turner 1992). Furthermore, they depend on social status and are identified by others. The notion has been used in different theoretical perspectives, following the initial, and to a certain extent contradictory, developments of the philosopher George H. Mead (1934) and the anthropologist Ralph Linton (1936) in the 1930s. The sociological theories that have used the concept of role are numerous: functionalist, symbolic interactionist, structuralist, organizational, and cognitive (Franks 2007). Yet, since roles may explain the persistence of the social order – and more importantly for us – of political institutions, it can be argued that the concept of roles has a strong functionalist dimension. However, the functionalist conception of roles appears to be outdated today, particularly regarding the role-taking process. Selecting a role is now seen as a less restrictive process: individuals negotiate role 'prescriptions' rather than passively internalizing obligations (Giddens 1979: 117). Consequently, roles may evolve over time.

In political science, the field of legislative studies is probably where the concept of role has been most successful. 'Parliamentary roles', 'legislatives roles', and 'representative roles' are all expressions referring to roles played by Members of Parliament (MPs). Following Ann Weber's definition, it can be said that legislative roles refer to the norms (obligations or expectations) attached to being an MP. Given the great heterogeneity of the theories using the concept, it is far from easy to give a more precise definition. By way of an attempt, however, we could say that legislative roles:

1 are comprehensive patterns of attitudes and/or behavior shared by MPs,
2 enable MPs to be distinguished or identified as a group, and enable us to distinguish between them, and,

3   have to do with MPs' own conception of their job overall, and their vision
     of their voters in particular.

In contrast with the sociological uses of role theory (Hindin 2007), the analysis
of legislative roles is more focused on how MPs regard themselves, and less on
social expectations on them. There are three key reasons that roles have been
widely used in legislative studies.

First, references to roles stem from the similarities between a political assembly and a theatre. As noted by Thomas Saalfeld and Wolfgang Müller (1997: 1),
'the terminology of roles is borrowed from the stage'. In fact, there are a number
of reasons why MPs play roles. First, roles express the divison of labour between
MPs: some of them are good orators, others are specialised in amending legislation, others are preparing to be appointed ministers. Second, roles also account
for the wide range of activities and settings that an MP is called upon to face.
Much like an actor playing Hamlet in the spring and then King Lear in the fall,
an MP may act act differently in different contexts, with his/her constituency,
his/her parliamentary group and lobby organizations, for example. Beyond the
metaphor of the stage, a more general reason for applying the concept of roles to
legislatures is the apparent stability of these roles. As the same patterns of behavior seem to apply for decades, or even centuries, there are reasons to conclude
that MPs conform to specific shared expectations.

Second, roles represent a strategic move beyond a narrow institutional perspective, to open the black box of legislatures. They have been a way to get
behind the formal rules and procedures and look at the politicians themselves,
rather than the system. The concept of roles has opened up new ways of grouping MPs, providing an alternative to the institutional categories of opposition/
majority, front/backbenchers and even Democrats/Republicans. What some have
called the behaviorist turning point in legislative studies has also been characterized by a strong methodological shift. Researchers began to follow legislators
closely, to observe not only their position and activities, but also their views on
issues and especially the way they understand their work. Consequently, since
the 1960s, methodological approaches using both large-N quantitative studies
(questionnaires) and in-depth interviews have been developed, for example in
US state legislatures (Wahlke *et al.* 1962; Barber 1965), at the Congress (Matthews 1960; Davidson 1969; Mayhew 1974), in Canada (Kornberg 1967), or in
France (Cayrol *et al.* 1973; Converse and Pierce 1979).

Finally, the concept of roles enables us to study some of the more complex
aspects of political representation in empirical terms. This is important because
an essential dimension of legislators' identity lies in the fact that they are elected,
and analytical frameworks using role concepts usually – but not always – rely on
the representative's relation to his or her constituents. This dimension is very
specific to legislative roles. By way of comparison with other professional roles,
we might note that there are several kinds of priests and different ways of conceiving the priesthood. Likewise, there are also different types of government
ministers. Compared with priests or ministers, however, what distinguishes a

legislator is the (scientific) assumption that their roles are based, in one way or another, on the nature of representation. Thus, in most studies, legislative roles predominately reflect the relationship between MPs and their constituents – either as seen by the MP or according to more objective elements (voting systems, district magnitude, candidate selections, and so forth).

It is worth studying MPs' views on the nature of representation and the way it influences their attitudes and activities because political systems bring about contradictory expectations regarding this link (Bogdanor 1985: 300). The idea that representatives should behave like – and even look like – voters is rooted in democratic expectations. However, as stressed by Bernard Manin (1997: 163), among the principles of representative government there are some aristocratic principles, such as the 'partial autonomy of representatives'. Thus, even if we agree with Hanna Pitkin in *The Concept of Representation* (1972), that 'Representing [...] means acting in the interest of the represented, in a manner responsive to them', questions arise when we begin to examine the consequences of this position. One view is that the representative should act just as the represented would act. Another view is that the representative should act according to his or her enlightened judgment, even though this might, from time to time, contradict the will of the represented. During the twentieth century, the increased significance of parties introduced a third element into the relationship between voters and legislators. Although this book is not about representation as such, the normative conflict regarding this representational link has theoretical as well as empirical consequences for the study of roles. MPs' attitudes towards their constituents are all the more difficult to capture – quantitatively or qualitatively – when citizens, politicians, and political scientists share different expectations of what this link should mean.

Despite the specific meanings and questions associated with parliamentary roles, the approach in legislative studies has followed the global trends related to the use of roles in social sciences. The first part of the chapter returns to the twofold legacy – functionalist and interactionist – in the research on legislative roles, and considers the reasons for their progressive decline during the 1980s. This might not be surprising, given the ebbing of the role concept in social sciences, but it might make the recent situation seem more so. Indeed, the second part of the chapter argues that with the renewal of interest in institutions and rules within political science, legislative studies have begun to re-discover the concept of roles. In order to assess the homogeneity of a current neo-institutional approach to legislative roles, we discuss in detail a motivational/psychological approach theorized by Donald Searing (1994) and a strategic/rational approach outlined by Kaare Strøm (1997).

The legacy of research on legislative roles in political science

Role analysis in legislative studies has partly resulted in the identification of different families of legislators. Donald R. Matthews (1960) for example, identified four key roles in the US Senate: *professionals* (55 percent), *amateurs* (34 percent), *patricians* (7 percent) and *agitators* (4 percent). Roger H. Davidson (1969) categorized congressmen according to the roles of *tribunes, ritualists, inventors, brokers,* and *opportunists*. However, the concept of role has usually been understood, not simply as a part played in the parliament but also in reference to a specific theoretical framework. Thus, the pioneering study of four United States state legislatures, in *The Legislative System* by John C. Wahlke, Heinz Eulau, William Buchanan and Leroy C. Ferguson (1962), had a tremendous effect on legislative research all around the world during the 1960s and 1970s. The equally important study of the US Congress, in *Home Style: House Members in their Districts* by Richard Fenno (1978), is today regarded as a classic in research on legislatures. These two volumes represent two opposite approaches to the study of parliamentary roles, one functionalist and one interactionist. In order to understand the history of research on legislative roles we need to return to the arguments presented in these studies and reflect theoretically and methodologically on their differences and their effects on political science.

The functionalist tradition

In studying four US state legislatures (California, New Jersey, Ohio, and Tennessee) and by interviewing almost all their members, Wahlke *et al.* (1962) set out to use role theory to uncover the underlying political processes and the informal channels within different institutions. For that purpose, the authors believed that it was important to carefully map legislators' norms of behavior, rather than their individual goals or the institutional rules they operate under. According to their view, roles were intimately connected to institutional positions and relevant behavior:

> The concept of role associated with a position of membership in any institutionalized group refers to precisely those behavioral uniformities of regularities which constitute the institution. [...] If one is interested in the structure and functions of an institution, it would seem proper to ascertain and analyze those forms of behavior which are central and constitutive to the institution as such.
>
> (Wahlke *et al.* 1962: 10)

They describe the origin of different roles as a combination of personal characteristics and 'ecological characteristics of political units' (Wahlke *et al.* 1962: 22). These two elements create what they call the individual's legislative role potential. Ecological characteristics include, among other things: ethnic and socio-economic character, party composition, political organization, and level of voter interest.

Wahlke and his colleagues use the notion of roles rather creatively by elaborating a complex conceptual framework with various kinds of roles – 'core roles', 'clientele roles' and 'incidental roles' – related to the actors with whom MPs interact (for details, see Saalfeld and Müller 1997: 4–8). But the impact of their work has mainly been concentrated on what they define as 'representational roles' (see for example: Eulau and Karps 1977; Kuklinski and Elling 1977; Loewenberg and Kim 1978; Converse and Pierce 1979; Clarke and Price 1981; Müller and Saalfeld 1997; Rao 1998). This field of research distinguishes between *trustee*, *delegate*, and *politico*, which are concepts formulated by Wahlke *et al.* (1962: 272–80). Members of a large number of legislative assemblies around the world have been questioned about these role concepts, and we can see that in their basic form these typologies are straightforward enough. *Trustees* follow their own judgment and conscience, and are influenced by what we might call a Burkean representative ideal. The trustee acts as a free agent in that 'he [sic] claims to follow what he considers right and just, his convictions and principles, the dictates of his conscience' (Wahlke *et al.* 1962: 272). The *trustee* is not bound by any mandate, either by a party or by the constituency. Edmund Burke argued in his famous speech to the electors of Bristol in 1774 that 'Parliament is a deliberative assembly of one nation, with one interest, that of the whole – where not local purposes, not local prejudices, ought to guide, but the general good, resulting from the general reason of the whole' (Pitkin 1969: 175–6). *Delegates*, on the other hand, see themselves as having a mandate from someone. They are obliged to follow instructions, even in cases where it is contrary to their own convictions. The *delegate* is an elected representative and should therefore follow those responsible for his or her election. Finally, the role of the *politico* combines the *trustee* and the *delegate*, taking on either one of these two roles depending on the circumstances. This may be done either simultaneously, with the possibility of a role conflict, or consecutively, for instance, he sees himself as a *delegate* in local issues, but a *trustee* in other issues.

However, how you represent something or someone says nothing about what or whom you represent. This is an important analytical distinction. Wahlke *et al.* discriminate between the *focus* and the *style* of the representative (Wahlke *et al.* 1962: 269). A representative's *style* concerns whether they consider themselves bound by the instructions of those they represent or as a free agent; that is to say as a *delegate*, a *trustee*, or a *politico*. *Focus*, on the other hand, refers to the extent to which a representative is guided in their decisions by a concern for general or more specific interests. This means that their representative *style* might be a free agent (*trustee*), but their representative *focus* remains the concerns of a specific group in society. Two further concepts have attracted much interest regarding the focus dimension. The *areal role*, concerns the representative's focus on the welfare of the political unit as a whole or the welfare of a specific constituency. Second, the *party role* tries to capture the importance of the political party.

These two dimensions – style and focus – constitute fundamental aspects of the role system. To demonstrate the connection between them Eulau *et al.* (1978: 118) analyze the answers from 197 respondents from four US state legislatures. One hypothesis is that respondents who focus more on overall state interests (areal focus) do not have any clear state-clientele to refer to, and therefore are more likely to describe their representational style as that of *trustee* rather than *delegate*. As shown in Table 2.1, this turns out to be verified. None of the state-oriented representatives (i.e. those focused on the overall interest of the state and not on the electoral district) is associated with the *delegate* style.

Furthermore, Table 2.1 shows that it is possible to be district-oriented and still more or less be a *trustee*. That is, the legislator might define him or herself as clearly representing a specific interest (district), but at the same time reject instructions from that specific interest (*trustee*). A third conclusion is that representatives who are associated with the politico-style of representation tend to be less distinct when it comes to their areal focus, i.e. they are simultaneously oriented towards the state and district. It is important to remember, however, that this does not say anything about why certain roles appear in a particular context, or if these have any effect on the representatives' behavior. This is only a strategy to map out the system of roles in certain institutions.

There has been an immense effort to conduct studies that explain why representatives adopt certain roles, or that use roles as independent variables in explaining behavior. It is essentially impossible to give a complete picture of the wide range of work inspired by *The Legislative System* (for a more comprehensive review, see Jewell 1983). However, some empirical conclusions are worth mentioning. One argument has been that a representatives' adaptation to a role depends on a process of socialization. For example, the age at which a representative engages in politics is believed to be important. Allan Kornberg (1967) indicates that self-started Canadian MPs with early socialization were most like to act as trustees. Yet, other studies conclude that there is no connection between socialization and the kind of representative role adopted (Prewitt *et al.* 1966).

The socialization argument seems to be more relevant when it comes to direct personal experience of legislative work. Indeed, a number of studies indicate that representative roles develop with legislative experience. In an American context, Bell and Price (1975) show that the *trustee* role becomes more pronounced over time and that the party role and interest group role develop primarily during legislative work. The volatility of the role orientation during an MP's time in office is further developed in a later study of Canadian MPs, where the conclusion is that depending on their particular career goals (e.g. ambitions to be party leader, cabinet member or Prime Minister) the role orientation of the representative takes different directions over time (Clarke and Price 1981). More ambitious MPs tend to downplay contact with the constituency.

Table 2.1 Areal-focal and representational role orientations in four US states (in %)

Representational role orientation	District-orientated (n = 89)	State-district oriented (n = 64)	State oriented (n = 44)
Trustee	37	55	84
Delegate	36	8	–
Politico	27	37	16
Total	100	100	100

Source: Eulau *et al.* (1978: 124).

The bulk of this kind of research was done on US representative institutions, and there are reasons to believe that the conclusions would be slightly different in a European context. The role of the party organization attracts particular attention in this comparison. In the work of Converse and Pierce on the French National Assembly, the *delegate* role was more pronounced than in the analysis of US legislatures. Political parties essentially turn out to be the most important source of mandate for French representatives (1986: 674). Much more recently, a new investigation of French MPs has confirmed how crucial party affiliation is. Costa and Kerrouche (2007) show that left-wing and right-wing MPs still consider their roles differently. In spite of the fact that the two groups are increasingly socially similar, those on the right tend to see the job as a personal vocation and those on the left as a task undertaken for the party.

The limits and decline of the functionalist approach

It is one thing to establish how representatives define themselves, but the crucial question is whether or not there is a connection between role conceptions and how representatives behave. This connection was to a certain extent assumed in the literature, but it has been difficult to connect various role concepts to actual behavior. For example, a number of studies have tried to determine whether *delegates* act in accordance with the expectations in their districts. Hedlund and Friesema (1972: 744) show that the adoption of roles does not provide an adequate mechanism for insuring that constituent opinions translate into legislative action. Yet, it has been shown that *delegates* are more aware of popular opinion in their districts, and actually tend to act according to voters' expectations on issues with high salience (Kuklinski and Elling 1977; McCrone and Kuklinski 1979). This tendency does not however influence their voting more broadly, i.e. on issues with low salience. This point is put intelligently by Cavanagh in the following terms: 'in the absence of any instructions to mandate a course of action, the representative becomes a trustee by default' (1982: 128).

Since the beginning of the 1980s, the use of the functionalist approach to role theory declined substantially. This was a result of a general reorientation in social sciences and an effect of problems inherent in the theory itself. That is, theoretical expectations were not clearly demonstrated by empirical research, and the idea that parliamentary roles were helping legislatures to fulfill global functions seemed all the more naïve. These more general difficulties of this approach may be dissected into a number of specific problematic aspects. The first problem concerns the source of representative roles, i.e. roles as a dependent variable. Even though a vast number of studies have tried to explain why representatives identify with a certain role, it has not been possible to make any general conclusions regarding these relationships (Jewell 1983: 310). Furthermore, the theoretically complex system of variables that was thought to influence various role identifications, made it difficult to duplicate studies in different institutional contexts. This made it even harder to draw solid conclusions as to why certain role orientations are more common in some settings than in others.

A common critique was also that the *trustee–delegate–politico* typology was perceived as biased towards a US conception of democracy, since 'There is not much 'responsible party' representation in Congress' (Page *et al.* 1984: 741). In a European context the question would be whether a representative is bound by instructions from his or her party organization, rather than from the constituency. Rudy B. Andeweg (1997) argues that the most severe problem with using models 'imported' from the US for the understanding of political roles is the inadequate incorporation of political parties.

The second problem concerns the meaning of the concept of roles; what do roles really capture? One problem here has been the conceptual pluralism in role research, which created confusion rather than clarification. In practice this has worked against the goal of creating a common 'language' as a tool for understanding different roles (Biddle 1986; Searing 1994: 7). Paradoxically, however, the simplified distinction between *trustee* and *delegate* turned out to be rather sterile for several reasons. Those roles that did not exist in the minds of politicians appeared to describe a range of (academic) ways of conceptualizing parliamentary representation, rather than two cohesive patterns of norms and behavior. As Kent Price put it, 'unless the legislators conceive their positions in terms of the trustee–delegate–politico role typology, the concept is not a meaningful phenomenon' (1985: 169). This criticism as to what roles really mean opened up a debate that undermined the fundamental theory of representative roles (see also Francis 1965). For example, it suggested that the process of representation is much more complex than the theory implies (Cavanaugh 1982) or that being a *delegate* is a question of information-seeking and uncertainty-reduction rather than role-playing (Alpert 1979). From a more conceptual standpoint, recent developments in political theory also support the view that the binary distinction between *trustee* and *delegate* obscures the complexity of the representative process as a collective decision depends of the aim of legislators (pluralist or not), the source of their judgment (self-reliant or not) and the degree of their responsiveness (Rehfeld 2009).

The third problem concerns the efficiency of roles as a conceptual tool for explaining individual as well as collective behavior. Is behavior a part of the definition of a role, or is it a mediating mechanism between institutional rules/expectations (independent variable) on behavior (dependent variable)? In *The Legislative System*, Wahlke *et al.* argue that:

> [the concept of role] postulates that individual legislators are aware of the norms constituting the role and consciously adapt their behavior to them in some fashion [...] To study the role of legislators, then, is to study particular sets of norms which underlie relevant legislative behavior.
>
> (Wahlke *et al.* 1962: 9)

However, this supposes the ability to make a clear distinction between attitudes and behavior. Is what you do an expression of your role or vice versa? Or is role identification merely the expression of an aspirational ideal? Is behavior influenced by other concerns? These problems were not helped by the fact that attempts to connect various role orientations to patterns of behavior resulted in disappointment. Donald Gross presents the discouraging conclusion when looking at the connection between a representative's tasks and role concepts, 'representative style [...] is generally unrelated to many of the legislative behaviors one would hypothesize that it would be related to' (1978: 370).

Even though the functionalist approach to role theory was dominant for several years, it was isolated in trying to understand how a representative's attitude and identification influenced his or her behavior. A very different way of approaching this issue is found in what has been called the interactionist approach.

The interactionist approach or the Fenno tradition

To *represent* is a verb. It is not state of mind or self-defined label – it is something you do. Following the same reasoning, to have a legislative role is first and foremost to *play* a role. In order to understand representation and legislative role-taking, we need to understand how politicians learn, negotiate, and cultivate their roles in actual situations, be it in the House or within the constituency. Inspired by the symbolic interactionism elaborated by Mead (1934) and followed by prominent sociologists like Goffman (1959), some studies tried to analyze how legislators constructed their roles according to the institutional setting in which they were placed. Amongst these studies are, notably, Ralph Huitt's case study of a senator portrayed as an outsider (1961), and John Manley's in-depth analysis of the chairmanship of the powerful Committee on Ways and Means in the House of Representatives (1970). But the most influential work certainly originates from the American political scientist Richard Fenno, who wrote two important volumes during the 1970s. The first book analyzes activities in the committees of the US Congress (Fenno 1973) and the second, which is entitled *Home Style* and is perhaps more important for our purposes, follows the district activities of eighteen legislators of the US House of Representatives over a nearly eight-year period (Fenno 1978). In this book Fenno tried to investigate – 'by looking over their shoulder' – what it was that representatives saw when they returned to their home district. His argument was that in order to understand their actions in Washington, we need to understand how these representatives relate to those they are representing. The home district and Washington are intertwined through the actions of representatives, but they are also two completely different worlds. Fenno's work was indeed the culmination of a slow but steady rise in dissatisfaction with the narrow focus on roll call votes in the US.

With the help of his explorative approach, Fenno concluded that the representative's view of the home district, and their actions there, changed over time. He makes a distinction between two phases: *expansionist* and *protectionist*. The first stage is to solidify a core group of supporters that constitutes the backbone of an election campaign; it is then possible to cultivate the support of additional groups within the district. However, at some point this expansionism ceases and becomes protectionism, where the representative focuses on maintaining his or her support rather than finding additional groups. To a certain degree, this might be a different way of saying that the role (in functionalist terms) changes over time, from a style that is less *delegate* and more *trustee*; a pattern that is recognized in other studies previously mentioned. Over time, a representative becomes more confident in his or her role and does not have the same need of signals from the constituency. Furthermore, according to Fenno, a representative's leverage to choose home style depends on contextual aspects of the district. A district that is perceived as homogeneous gives the representative a narrower opportunity to choose his or her style than a heterogeneous district does. This means that different milieus give a representative a range of opportunities for personal characteristics to define their home style. Furthermore, Fenno argues vigorously that representation is not a one-way street. To represent is not only to act in accordance with the will of the represented, it is also to convince, argue and justify certain behavior. In this sense, not only do Congressmen bring the home arena to Washington, but also the other way around. Thus, Fenno provides a more complex picture of representation than the *delegate–trustee* dichotomy implies. These styles '...persist side by side because the set of constituent attitudes on which each depends also exist side by side' (1978: 161).

Fenno also emphasizes the strategic behavior of legislators:

> He [the Congressman] differentiates among them [the represented] in terms of their political support for him and, in some cases, their political loyalty to him. If, therefore, we start with the Congressman's perception of the people he represents, there is no way that the act of representing can be separated from the act of getting elected.
>
> (Fenno 1978: 233)

That is, representatives act purposefully either to gather additional support or to cultivate that already won on the home arena, and the action taken in Washington is a consequence of this goal. In this sense, Fenno's description of the constituency–representative relationship connects with a much wider and increasingly large literature on politicians as rational agents (Ferejohn and Fiorina 1975; Sinclair 1983; Denzau *et al.* 1985).

That being said, Fenno's most important legacy is not theoretical, but methodological. The appendix of *Home Style* consists of almost fifty pages of description and justification of his strategy of participant observation. At the same time, this is probably the area in which Fenno has been criticized the most. It is costly, both in terms of money and time, to do this kind of research and the value added is questionable. This approach is especially criticized for the lack of generalizability, which is to do with the selection of respondents and the size of the sample (Kuklinski 1979). In Fenno's defense however, it should be said that he is aware of all these problems and argues that the approach is first and foremost exploratory and designed to formulate hypotheses rather than to test them.

The cost associated with the scientific strategy that Fenno represents, is possibly the reason that this approach has attracted a limited number of followers. Quite a lot of work has been done to evaluate and measure the constituency–representative link (Parker 1980; Anagnoson 1983; Taggart and Durant 1985), but much of it is not concerned with discussing legislative roles as such. For instance, Bruce E. Cain *et al.* (1979; 1987), followed Bristish MPs in their constituencies, but they were more concerned with measuring and comparing the personal vote – 'that portion of a candidate's electoral support which originates in his or her personal qualities' (Cain *et al.* 1987: 9) – than with analyzing the symbolic dimension of MPs' encounters. It should however be noted that symbolic interactionism had a big impact in some countries, particularly where political scientists used sociological references in order to escape from the public law legacy. This has been – and still is – particularly the case in France for the study of legislators, but also mayors (Haegel 1994), the President of the Republic (Lacroix and Lagroye 1992) and local governments (Nay 1997).

In practice, the interactionist studies of politics focus on the creation of roles in a variety of social situations, emphasizing the individual meaning that is given to them. Thus, this strand of legislative role research does not follow an approach with pre-set concepts in order to pinpoint the relationship between the represented and the representatives. Instead, the aim has been to emphasize that individual parliamentarians participate in defining their roles and that these roles have many variations, and undergo constant change. This tradition has shed light on the way social interaction shapes roles as well as behavior, but it has suffered from a difficulty in conciliating the uniformity of norms implied by the role concept, and the diversity of institutional settings. Moreover, this school of thought often tends to ignore legislators' ability to develop their own standpoint independently of the social interactions in which they are engaged. As written by Searing (1991: 1246): 'The psycho-logistic cage, in fact, turns out to be sociologistic'.

The constituency link and European studies

Functionalist and interactionist approaches have both contributed to the research on legislative roles; however, as this short overview shows, their ambitions have not been fulfilled. Inconclusive results, conceptual confusion, empirical costs, and parochialism all contributed to a substantial decline in the use of the role concept in legislative research during most of the 1980s and 1990s. The theoretical and methodological developments came to a halt after this, although a number of empirical studies still use roles as the imperative concept. This has particularly been the case for studies focusing on the constituency link – to the point that using the role concept often means empirically investigating how MPs see their duties toward their voters.

One widely documented trend is the rise of constituency MPs. Phillip Norton for example, analyzed British MPs in a number of different studies, and his main conclusion was that the importance of taking care of the constituency had become increasingly prominent as a role (Norton and Wood 1993; Norton 1994). This was then further developed and verified by Michael Rush (2001). Pippa Norris, also analyzing British MPs, concluded that there is a significant relationship between 'members' commitments to [constituency] service work and their legislative behavior' (1997: 46). In other words, those MPs who make this kind of duty a high priority also spend more time in their constituencies. Other works comparing northern European MPs tend to conclude that legislators' role orientations do have consequences for their behavior (Esaiasson and Holmberg 1996; Esaiasson and Heidar 2000). Even when the consequences are harder to determine, this kind of research enables the measurement of possible gaps between discourse and action. Dutch MPs, for example, do recognize that they care about local interests but hardly ever meet ministers to defend them (Thomassen and Andeweg 2004), whereas there are reasons to believe that the opposite is true for their French counterparts (Costa and Kerrouche 2009).

Several recent – and less recent (Bogdanor 1985) – studies have focused on the relationship between electoral systems and MPs' views about representation. This is a traditional question (Miller and Stokes 1963) that has reemerged on the research agenda due to the erosion of political support (Dalton 2004) and the growing recourse to electoral engineering (Norris 2004). However the results of these studies are largely contradictory. McLeay and Vowles, looking at the case of New Zealand, show that there is no substantial difference between MPs' views on constituency representation, even when they are elected in single-member and multi-member electoral districts. Their explanation is that expectations of acceptable legitimate behavior for an MP are 'a product of norms and values of the past' (2007: 92). Other studies are more positive about the causal link between electoral systems and legislators' constituency focus, but they disagree on what exactly is significant in the electoral system: the proportional versus plurality system (Norton 2002), the number of MPs per constituency (Klingemann and Wessels 2000; Heitshusen *et al.* 2005) or the national or local level of the constituency (Thomassen and Esaiasson 2006). These mixed results reveal firstly that, as elected agents, MPs do care about local interests – independent of their electoral system. They also indicate that electoral variables are not sufficient to explain role orientation but that the social background of the MPs also matters (gender, ethnicity, religion, past profession).

Recently, the introduction of the principal–agent theory mixed with an interactive conception of representation (from below versus from above) borrowed from Esaiasson and Holmberg (1996), has led Rudy B. Andeweg and Jacques Thomassen (2005) to propose an original framework for characterizing the constituency link that gets rid of the old *trustee–delegate* split. The operationalization of this framework on Dutch MPs appears to be particularly promising, but the difficulty labeling the new typology ('authorization, accountability, delegation and responsiveness') in terms of roles indicates that this trend in the research is more focused on representation than on legislative roles. Similarly, the 'task definition approach' promoted by Esaiasson, which is focused on the types of interest that MPs seek to defend, 'says nothing about the motives underlying

MPs' view of their task' (2000: 80), and is explicitly opposed to role analysis for that reason.

Apart from the study of the constituency link, there is one particular area in which roles have become an interesting conceptual tool to analyze a swiftly changing political environment, and that is in the European Union. Beginning with the European Parliament, there is an obvious uncertainty as to what representatives should represent: their country/government, national party, European party, etc. The very early study by Hagger and Wing (1979) used a functionalist approach to analyze how Members of the European Parliament (MEPs) relate to their work. Their conclusion was that country of origin is the most important factor in explaining why MEPs adopt various roles. A similar point was made by Bernhard Wessels (1999) and Richard Katz (1999) in studies conducted many years later. Katz also emphasized the connection between role orientations and EU attitudes: MEPs privileging legislation over party conflict are more likely to be pro-European than others. Several empirical studies, with different research designs (Blomgren 2003; Scully and Farrell 2003; Scully 2005), conclude that electoral systems and other 'national artifacts' explain to a large extent the adoption of different roles among MEPs. Other 'agents' in the EU, such as European civil servants or commissioners have also been questioned, in a similar way to the MEPs (Hooghe 2001; Trondal 2002; Checkel 2003; Egeberg 2006). One overall conclusion of these studies is that civil servants bring their views on representation with them when they go to EU institutions, and, some of them at least, are molded into a more EU-oriented view over time. At the national level, legislative roles were also used in order to analyze changes due to the interaction with the supranational level. Wessels (2005) connects role orientations in national parliament with MPs' views about Europe. He concludes that national legislators supporting the participation of national parliaments in policy-making, rather than representative functions, were more likely to agree with strengthening the European Parliament and to oppose intergovernmentalism.

The discrete return of roles in various parts of European studies indicates how useful the concept is for analyzing institutional change, and especially conflicts of loyalty within multi-level systems of governance. It partly explains why research on legislative roles has progressively reappeared on the scientific agenda. More generally, the revival of parliamentary role research should be understood as a result of growing interest in the relationship between institutions and political behavior. Various theoretical schools approach the relationship between structure and agency very differently. The neo-institutionalism inspired by rational choice emphasizes how different institutional rules create and circumscribe different incentives for the agent (Shepsle 1989; Tsebelis 2002). The normative neo-institutionalist approach, on the other hand, emphasizes how institutions prescribe behavior with more or less explicit expectations (March and Olsen 1989). Notwithstanding these important differences, these different schools are both focused on the individual's role within a wider set of institutional mechanisms; simply put, it is the interplay between structure and agency that is the key scientific endeavor (Peters 1999: 141). Consequently, with the neo-institutional approach, legislative studies have become more focused on how legislature's rules affect MPs, especially how they enable or constrain behavior. Roles appear to be particularly relevant when considering the interplay between structure and agent, since they are specific to a given institutional setting but interpreted by individuals. Figure 2.1 presents a very simple conceptual framework related to roles that is shared by neo-institutionalist schools in spite of their differences.

In terms of legislative research, the main question concerns the effects of a given legislature's institutional rules and individual preferences, on MPs' behavior. The concept of role can be seen as interplay between these factors.

As already mentioned, although there were studies on legislative roles published whilst this concept was out of favor in political science research, the theoretical and methodological developments were very scarce. However, two important volumes are exceptions to this. The first is *Westminster's World* by Donald Searing (1994), in which he analyzed interviews with 521 members of the House of Commons conducted in 1971–1972. The second is the collective volume by Wolfgang C. Müller and Thomas Saalfeld (1997), which includes country-specific chapters on Germany, Denmark, Norway, the Netherlands, and Belgium. Even though all these chapters are important in their own right, it is the concluding chapter by Kaare Strøm that has attracted the most attention. Both of these volumes have had an important impact and represent a return of role theories in legislative studies.

Donald Searing's motivational approach

Donald Searing tends to theorize a motivational approach to studying the roles of politicians by placing himself in the tradition of Matthews' (1960) initial study of US Senators and subsequent studies from the 1960s (Barber 1965), 1970s (Woshinsky 1973; King 1974), and 1980s (Payne 1980; Aberbach *et al.* 1981). This approach is based on what used to be called 'purposive roles', that is, roles that are defined according to the purposes of politicians. The main aspect of the motivational approach is the claim that roles should be studied on the basis of how MPs view them.

Searing distinguishes preference and position roles. Position roles refer to the leadership functions at Westminster, such as the Whips. Given the fact that cabinet members belong to the House in the UK some of those roles designate

Figure 2.1 The neo-institutionalist approaches to roles.

executive positions (Parliamentary Private Secretaries and Ministers). By contrast, backbenchers play preferences roles that are less institutionally constrained. They represent two-thirds of the sample and are more illustrative of the motivational approach.

Following up Oliver H. Woshinsky's (1973) distinction between four incentives among French MPs, Searing investigates the psychological background of the roles. By analyzing the reasons for selecting a given role, he does not only look at rational preferences (called 'career goals') but also at 'emotional incentives' developed by each individual and rooted in personality. Even though he claims to consider both reason and feeling, he acknowledges that: 'Emotional incentives are the principal energizing forces in all parliamentary roles' (Searing 1994: 19).

If we then try to assess the general neo-institutionalist perspective (see Figure 2.1) from Searing's conceptual framework, Figure 2.2 is the result. The double arrow between the motivational core and roles accounts for the endogenous and exogenous conception of politicians' preferences. For Searing, motivations are not necessarily exogenous to the political process. Consciously or unconsciously, goals and incentives are reconstructed when acting within a given organization (Searing 1994: 483). Politicians therefore adapt to their institutional environment. Even if it is not clearly stated as such by Searing, it could be argued that such reconstruction is closely connected to playing a specific role.

Even if Searing distinguishes his theory from the functionalist approach, he tends to be functionalist in considering that the 'goals' a parliament is supposed to fill (legislation, control, representation, recruitment…) tend to produce the repertoire of roles: 'What is remarkable is that out of all this flexibility emerges not hundreds of different backbenchers roles, but instead only four distinct roles and their subtypes […]. This reflects the fact that even backbenchers' flexibility is framed by institutional constraints' (1994: 33). What differentiates him from classic functionalist approaches is that the process of selecting and interpreting roles is regarded as central and not fully institutionally determined. Eventually, four roles and ten sub-roles, with their respective career goals and emotional incentives, are identified. The extensive empirical material allows Searing to quantify each of these, as indicated in Table 2.2.

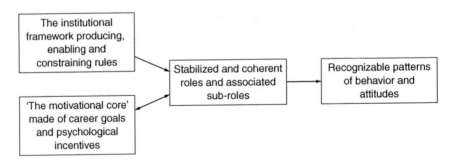

Figure 2.2 Donald Searing's motivational approach to legislative roles.

Table 2.2 Roles and sub-roles among backbenchers at Westminster according to Searing

Roles	Career goals	Sub-roles	Career goals	Emotional incentives
Policy advocates (41% of backbenchers)	Checking the executive	Ideologues (5% of political advocates)	Promoting abstract ideas	Individuality, rectitude, hubris
		Generalists (35%)	Promoting solutions on various topics	Influence, diversity, publicity, game
		Specialists (60%)	Influencing policy in certain sectors	Influence, achievement, self-importance
Ministerial aspirants (25%)	Becoming ministers	High flyers (43%)	Becoming senior ministers	Ambition, status
		Subalterns (23%)	Becoming junior ministers	
Constituency members (25%)	Redressing grievances	Welfare officers (75%)	Solving constituents' personal cases	Sense of competence, sense of duty
		Local promoters (15%)	Solving collective problems	
Parliament men (9%)	Maintaining institutional structures	Status seekers (10%)	Desire to enhance their status	Resentment, status
		Spectators (45%)	Watching the political drama	Vicarious importance
		Club men (45%)	Enjoying the conviviality	Affiliation, avocation, respect

Source: compilation from Searing (1994).

Note

The percentages given in the 'Roles' column indicate the distribution of the 334 backbench MPs. The percentages given in the 'sub-roles' column indicate the distribution of each sub-role within a role category. The sum may be inferior to one hundred given intermediary types. Club men are divided between 'Part Timers', 'Knights of the Shires', and 'Good House of Common Men'.

The most commonly played role in the House is that of the *policy advocate*, but it is highly differentiated between its three sub-roles. *Ministerial aspirants* and *constituency members* are each well identified by their purpose (individual career or constituency work respectively), *parliament men* are less numerous and characterize the pillars of the House.

Motivational roles and behavior

Searing uses in-depth interviews with MPs in order to identify both the repertoire of roles and sub-roles, and to map out which MP is playing which role and sub-role. Creativity, intuition, erudition and above all a comprehensive qualitative approach all appear necessary to achieve this. Yet roles and role-taking are not inferred from actual behavior, but rather on the basis of MPs' general conceptions of their mandate. Having identified the repertoire of roles and assigned a role to each MP, Searing studies the consequences of these roles in terms of action and opinion. In most cases, empirical evidence is provided that motivational roles *do* have consequences. For instance, MPs identified as *constituency members* declare that they do spend more time in their constituency or practice more cross-voting than others. Moreover, role-taking appears to be one of the only statistically significant explanatory variables regarding time spent in the constituency.

Searing argues that this result should not be considered 'tautological', since politicians do not always act in consistence with their self-conceptions. On the contrary, he uses the observed connection between various configurations of roles and MPs behavior, in order to demonstrate the greater relevance of the motivational approach: 'We should, in fact, be very pleased, in the wake of so many studies in which "delegates" did not behave like delegates by voting their constituents' wishes, that we succeeded in generating preference roles like that of the Constituency Members whose players do behave like Constituency Members by tending to their constituents' (1994: 135).

Indigenous roles

Searing delivers a severe critique of the *delegate/trustee* dichotomy, which he sees as being 'constructs that existed in the minds of many social scientists rather than in the minds of many of the politicians we studied' (1994: 13). Instead politicians should be listened to, and the motivational approach suggests that by 'directing our concepts and measures toward roles as politicians themselves conceive of them, we will be in best position to explain the behavior that is inherent in such roles' (1994: 14). Therefore, in many parts of the book, Searing stresses that the label of a given role is commonly used at Westminster, which would demonstrate the relevance of the categorization: 'the fact that backbenchers recognize our four architectonic backbench roles buttresses their plausibility' (1994: 415). The reputation associated with a role within Westminster is also a matter of study. For instance, *constituency members* are frequently criticized by other MPs for their narrow conception of their job, and as a consequence, role-distance may result.

Such a comprehensive approach raises delicate epistemological issues. Firstly, it forces the social scientist to reveal already exiting categories rather than creating one's own. In that sense, the added-value of social science is reduced within the motivational world. Moreover, the Durkheimian legacy would certainly blame such an approach for not maintaining a distance from real world. Is the division of labor as perceived by MPs the most relevant way of studying Westminster? Aren't there other roles, hidden to the actors, which could reveal why MPs act in such or such way?

Secondly, this approach is not exactly followed throughout the book. It appears instead that various roles used by the actors (e.g. *ideologue* or *constituency members*) are mobilized alongside others labels probably created by Searing (e.g. *subaltern* or *status seeker*). It is also likely that existing role labels used by MPs, were not kept by Searing (e.g. *diplomats, inquisitors* or *half-retired*). It is also unclear whether the relation between a given role and its sub-roles is in the minds of the MP or labeled by the author based on similar patterns. Overall, the process of mapping legislative roles is inevitably subjective (and creative). This not a negative remark, nor is it in all probability very surprising, but the inductive process through which the repertoire of roles is created still remains vague. In a way, these aspects lead one to question the connection between identified roles and MPs' behavior. Does a high correlation mean that the repertoire is cleverly established? Or that the categorization of individual MPs to such or such role was particularly relevant? Or eventually that roles have an impact on behavior? The findings of the book appear to be a set of different elements (the repertoire of roles, the categorization of individual MPs and the consequences of the roles) that are impossible to assess and evaluate separately. Moreover, even if it is true that there is no tautology in correlating motivational roles and behavior, the tautological criticism is more relevant when roles are compared with MPs' opinions, given that they were built on MPs' attitudes towards their job.

Thirdly, the 'indigenous' feature of the roles triggers the question of why legislatures produce them and why MPs adopt them. If the roles Searing brings to light make sense for MPs and if those roles give coherence to MPs' attitudes and behavior, then roles do play a central function in strengthening the division of parliamentary labor, and eventually in producing a vision of Westminster's world. As stated by Searing: 'Members are able to understand the performances of their colleagues as variations on familiar roles that help everyone make sense of political life at Westminster' (1994: 33). Parliamentary actors seem to need roles to differentiate and locate each other within the parliamentary machinery. Roles as identifying principles do have both an individual dimension (they express the need for self-esteem), and a collective one (they offer a specific vision of what a legislature is). In this sense, the motivational concept of role not only tells us something about the representative relationship (like for the *trustee/ delegate* split), but also about parliaments as institutions. Parliaments are institutions where the division of labor and the grouping of actors are not only organized through procedures and parties but also through 'composite patterns of goals, attitudes, and behaviors characteristic of people in particular positions' (1994: 369) ultimately based on how MPs emotionally understand their job.

A one-dimensional actor

A last set of remarks concentrates on the fact that, according to Searing, MPs tend to focus on one singular role. This finding is surprising since qualitative in-depth methods usually tend to give a complex picture of political actors, empha-sizing the multiple institutional settings in which they work and the multiple dimensions of their personality. In the field of role theory, the interactionist approach has thus examined how role-taking was dependent on contingent and evolving concrete situations. Contrary to this, interviews conducted in *Westmin-ster's World* tend to reveal that MPs are motivated by one dominant aspect of their job. Searing explains continuously that role homogeneity should be under-stood in terms of predominance rather than uniformity. All MPs need to secure their electoral position but only a quarter of backbenchers are first and foremost motivated by the idea that they should protect their constituents. Very few back-benchers would refuse to enter the cabinet but only a quarter of them openly reveal their ambition during the interviews. Searing also acknowledges that MPs may modify their role when the length of their career creates new incentives and situates them in a different institutional context. Thus, after fifteen years of being unsuccessful, *high flyers* may reconsider their role-orientation and begin to act as *parliament men*. That said, such shifts occur only on very few occasions over the course of a parliamentary career.

Searing's conclusion that MPs tend to prioritize one role appears to be sup-ported by empirical observations (even by a factor analysis). He argues that the mutual-exclusiveness of the role categories has to do with the functional purpose of roles and with MPs' limited energy. In terms of the functional purpose of roles, playing one role rather than several, strengthens the capacity of roles to situate and guide MPs. As explained by Searing: '[Career goals] are particularly likely to be arranged hierarchically and to carry across contexts, for they are developed to serve the "cross-contextual" purpose of guiding the politician's career' (1994: 416). Yet, this functionalist view does not explain how roles succeed in guiding MPs. The other explanation is focused on the limited resources at the disposal of MPs: 'No one has sufficient time and energy to pursue vigorously all backbench roles at once. Everyone therefore gives some roles predominance over others by choosing among them on the basis of their goals' (1994: 81). This explanation is based on the observations that MPs have limited energy and that pursuing a goal efficiently supposes a degree of speciali-zation. However, beside the rational flavor of the demonstration, no reason is ultimately given for explaining why MPs do have a dominant goal.

The importance Searing gives to a psychological account of MPs attitudes and behavior, encourages an explanation of the mutual-exclusiveness of the role categories based on psychology. Searing relies in particular on the political psychologist James Payne who, with his colleagues, stated that: '[...] each politician (with few exceptions) has only one incentive, not a mixture of incentives' (1984: 8). Incentives are thus seen as emotional rather than rational drives. According to theses theorists, the single-dimensionality of the emotional world of politicians has to do with the painfulness of everyday life in politics, with the highly selective feature of political careers and with the uncertain future of political leaders. Having attested that 'Politics is not a cushy, comfortable occupation', they concluded that 'it was an emotional type of drive that propelled individuals to accept the rigors of political life' (1984: 1, 7). The mutual-exclusivity of roles seems to be ultimately accounted for by what we could call a 'psychologist-Darwinism': the work is so demanding that only the most motivated can succeed, and the most motivated are in all likelihood single-minded politicians.

By way of concluding on Searing's work, it can be said that the comprehensive qualitative material gathered for mapping Westminster's roles, obviously makes it difficult to replicate the study elsewhere for the sake of comparison. Nonetheless, in a follow-up study of British MPs, Wood and Yoon (1998) show that the role orientations identified by Searing seem to be very stable. However, Searing's major contributions lie in his effort to clarify and promote the motivational approach and his attempt to develop a heuristic conceptual – and to some extent theoretical – framework, through the rigor of his case-study. Julien Navarro (2009) uses this framework for instance in order to study the recent institutionalization of the European Parliament. One of the two editors of this volume (Rozenberg 2009) also based his study of the Europeanization of the French Parliament on Searing's framework. These studies confirm the parochial features of some of his results: the great variety of *parliament men* for example has been produced by an institution that is several centuries old; the diversity of *ministerial aspirants* is rooted in the high number of cabinet members and so forth. Yet, these studies by Navarro and Rozenberg also indicate just how heuristic Searing's approach is, not only because of the high probability to find *policy advocates, ministerial aspirants, constituency members* and *parliament men* in any legislature, but also because the connections between roles, institutional rules and psychological incentives appear to be – at least partially – independent from national political cultures.

Kaare Strøm's strategic approach

In his short theoretical paper of 1997 and in an up-dated version in this volume, Kaare Strøm discusses Searing's framework and emphases the strategic aspects of role taking. By defining roles as 'strategies for the employment of scare resources toward specific goals' (1997: 155), he connects the literature on roles to the more recent rational choice approach. He argues that 'legislative roles can be viewed as behavioral strategies conditioned by the institutional framework in which parliamentarians operate' (1997: 157). In accordance with the overall neo-institutional framework (Figure 2.1), the strategic approach may be illustrated as in Figure 2.3.

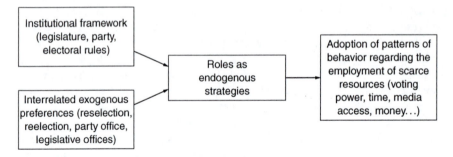

Figure 2.3 The strategic approach to legislative roles.

As indicated in several publications (e.g. Müller *et al.* 2001; Heitshusen *et al.* 2005; Zittel and Gschwend 2008), Strøm's approach has become quite influential. The reason for this is probably the success of rational choice theory in general, but also because of the paper's effort to clarify certain concepts. Roles are defined as endogenous strategies both shaped by institutional rules and by exogenous stable preferences. Furthermore, one of the main benefits of this strategic approach lies in the systematic analysis of the institutional constraints (or lack thereof) that lead to the selection of a given role. These aspects were to some extent neglected by Searing, and Strøm emphasizes the great influence of the rules surrounding the re(s)election of MPs on the strategies they adopt.

Strategic roles?

The main question regarding the strategic approach has to do with the difference between roles and strategies. Although Strøm convincingly argues that roles should be conceptualized as strategies, one might wonder whether it is then useful to continue talking about roles. Is not the concept of roles superfluous if it is synonymous with strategies? Strangely enough, the question is not directly addressed in the paper, but the main answer is probably that roles have to do with patterns of behavior. By postulating that roles are 'behavioral patterns or routines', Strøm implies that efficiently choosing between scarce resources – i.e. acting rationally – leads MPs to systematically adopt specific behavior. This would explain the reference to *roles* and not only to *strategies*, as the very notion of strategy evokes both permanent and contingent adaptation to an evolving situation. Doing surgery work two months before an election is undoubtedly an electoral strategy; doing it on a permanent basis throughout a legislature could be better described as playing the *constituency member* role.

Therefore, conceiving of roles as systematic behavior seems to be central to a rational approach to legislative roles. However, the notion of what is systematic is neither clearly defined nor questioned in Strøm's paper. It could refer to the fact that roles have been played by several MPs and therefore can be conceptualized as *patterns*, or it could mean actions are repeated over time when playing a given role, which can be associated with *routine*. Whether pattern, routine, or both, the essential aspect of the concept appears to rely on the notion of repetition and imitation. MPs playing roles repeat the same strategies day after day and imitate each other.

Bounded rationality?

When it comes to rationality, the analytical consequences of these aspects appear to be particularly promising. On one hand, the question of why these patterns appear can be considered from a rational choice perspective: the systematic feature of roles could be understood in terms of cost-saving, it being rational for a given legislator to follow a behavioral routine because roles save him or her the effort of repeated calculations. For instance, an MP will save time and energy in the sifting of her mail if she has decided to act as a *constituency member*. In this case letters addressed by voters from the constituency will be *systematically* answered, whereas mail from national organizations can be neglected. It would be especially easy to delegate that task. To take another example, a newcomer MP seeking to enter the government, will reduce learning costs if a role orienta-tion of *ministerial aspirants* is at her disposal. By reproducing the behavior of successful politicians – that is by following an existing pattern – she will undoubtedly increase her chance of success. Thus systematic strategies enable actors to rationalize a complicated environment characterized by constant arbi-trations and decision making.

On the other hand, the systematic aspect of roles could also lead to the opposite conclusion. That is, the limitation of the rationality in the entire process. Recalling Max Weber (1978) we might be reminded of the difference between legitimacy through routine and through rationality. Patterns of behavior might help an actor escape from, or constitute a constraint from, purely strategic behavior. In other words, roles can explain why rational MPs do not always behave rationally: because they are embedded in routines ('I do that because I did it') and because they tend to reproduce patterns of behavior ('I do that because others do it'). Even if roles are driven by goals, interpreting them could become an end by itself, rather than the end being the attainment of the initial goal(s). To take the above mentioned example of the *constituency member*, the habit – and possibly the pleasure – of playing such a role could lead an MP to continue interpreting it even when it is no longer strategic to do so. From a purely rational perspective, there is no use in supporting local con-stituents in close-door meetings when there is no prospect of being rewarded for the effort. Yet continuous empirical observations suggest that many *constituency MPs* actually go on playing such roles in all circumstances for a simple reason: they have the habit of doing so. The danger of over-playing a role has also been stressed in the literature, for instance with the example of *ministerial aspirants* neglecting their constituencies. Therefore, if 'institutions are the "rules" that constrain "reason"' as written by Strøm (1997: 156), one might wonder whether roles can be regarded as institutions i.e. whether roles also constrain reason.

Strøm meeting Searing

It is unambiguously true that the writings of Searing and Strøm constitute important theoretical contributions to legislative role research in recent years. However, the first question is whether or not these two approaches are contradictory to each other. They use a common framework with specific interrogations based on two different theoretical perspectives. Searing focuses on the MPs' complex and partially psychological motivations for interpreting a given role. Strøm supports the idea of conceptualizing roles as rational strategies. Searing's framework appears to be very elaborate but difficult to duplicate, whereas Strøm's arguments are to a certain extent an initial attempt that has had a noticeable impact. The differences between them are evident when it comes to the conceptions of what MPs preferences are: exclusively exogenous and strategic in one case, exogenous and endogenous as well as strategic and psychological in the other. Yet these differences should not be overstated. Both frameworks share the idea that roles are produced both by institutional rules and personal preferences, and that they have consequences for behavior. Furthermore, both of these approaches converge in their conclusion that each actor predominately plays a single role, although the justifications for this are explained either rationally or psychologically in the respective theories.

To a large extent, strategic and motivational approaches may thus be conciliated. The rational feature of Strøm's theory rests mainly on the process of adopting a costless strategy within a given institutional setting. The four identified goals of legislative activities appear to be largely axiomatic in this respect: an MP with a seemingly less rational purpose than the four identified (for instance promoting an ideology), could also follow the rational strategy of adopting the role best suited for his/her purpose. Likewise, Searing argues that politicians do not act randomly but that close attention to their motivations reveals the strength of the emotional drive behind strategic goals. Even if reason and emotion are mobilized by different theories, they tend to be intertwined in the minds of political actors. This is clearly the case regarding the sub-role of *specialists* 'where the cognitive goal of influencing the influential is intertwined with the sense of achievement, an emotional incentive' (Searing 1994: 389).

The main difference between the motivational and the strategic approaches fundamentally seems to be focused on their conception of time and role interpretation. Conceiving roles as strategies implies that the achievement of goals is delayed: *constituency MPs* adopt this course of action in order to be re-elected in the future. On the contrary, from a motivational perspective gratification is immediate: *constituency MPs* enjoy acting as *constituency MPs* at the present time. The emphasis placed on immediate gratification is linked with the motivational approach's focus on how MPs interpret their roles. The existence of four backbench roles only indicates how constraining institutional rules are. But within each role MPs have creative leeway as to the way they interpret them – that is in *understanding* as well as *playing* them: 'all of the backbench preference roles we have examined seem less constrained than is usually assumed by either structural or interactionist approaches to the subject. Even the Constituency Member, the clearest backbench role, offers vast opportunities for developing interpretations to suit individual preferences' (Searing 1994: 195). This focus on the way roles are played could account for the bounded rationality of a neo-institutional approach to roles. As indicated in the discussion of Strøm's approach, the systematic behavioral aspect of roles can be understood both as a strategic cost-saving device and as a sociological process of diffusion of collective norms. However, debate has yet to show to what extent these views are contradictory or complementary.

Conclusion

This discussion shows that the history of legislative role research is long and has indeed been somewhat bumpy. Even though a large amount of research has been devoted to analyzing legislative roles, the theoretical and empirical outcomes of this have been limited. In this chapter, we have discussed three of the major reasons for this. The first problem is connected to the role concept as such. Roles are concepts that need to be defined in a way that makes sense and is theoretically and empirically coherent. A lot of effort has certainly gone in to trying to achieve this. However, many of these concepts have turned out to be more important in academic debate than in the 'real world'. For example, in spite of the sound theoretical argument regarding the difference between a *trustee* and a *delegate*, this distinction has been difficult for respondents to comprehend. The result boils down to a methodological problem: do we really know what we are measuring when we ask representatives about these concepts? The second problem arises (and accentuates the first) when it becomes difficult to identify a connection between these concepts and actual behavior. That is, various concepts of roles have been weak as independent variables. The third problem explored here is that there has been a tendency for studies of roles to be limited to single-system analyses. This generally has to do with the ambition to map out the repertoire of roles in a particular legislative system, rather than connect these roles with independent variables such as the electoral system, party system, political culture and so forth. As a result, roles defined as dependent variables have been inadequately analyzed. Of course, there are studies that contradict this description, but as a general critique it still stands.

If this were the end of story, this book would not need to be written. However, growing interest and knowledge concerning the link between various institutional mechanisms and political outcomes, has led to a renewed interest in legislative roles. Guy Peters, looking at what unites all variants of the neo-institutional trend, concludes that 'Perhaps more than anything else, the individual element of policy-making comes into play as the members of the institution interpret what the rules and values of their institutions are' (1999: 150). What Peters is referring to could be regarded as roles. The basic assumption in neo-institutional theories is that institutions influence behavior, which means that roles can be seen as the product of various institutional environments. With the perspective of normative intuitionalism, this means that individuals internalize the explicit or implicit expectations of them as representatives. From this standpoint, roles are seen as an individual's understanding of what is appropriate behavior in a certain situation. From a more rational choice perspective, representatives' understandings of limitations or gratifications produced by various institutional settings can also lead to the adoption of certain roles. The concept of roles may thus be used either way: to analyze legislators' behavior in terms of either appropriateness or strategic calculation. This should mean that the use of the role concept will probably grow in importance because we need something that identifies uniform attitudes among actors in specific institutional settings.

It is important to learn from history, however. Past focus on the repertoire of roles in a single legislature may not be interesting to investigate per se. But if the question is what kind of attitudes a specific kind of legislature produces, compared to other legislatures, the story becomes more interesting. This is because roles say something about the workings of the institutions under investigation. Furthermore, roles might be an important part of the 'stickiness' of institutions, because even though institutions may change for various reasons (for example adjustments of the electoral system), the behavior of the representatives may remain the same – at least for a while. The reason for this is that roles are attitudes that change slowly and their function in institutional development might therefore be crucial. From this perspective, roles are either products of institutions and/or links between institutions and behavior, through coherent attitudes and values. Ultimately, rather than being interesting in and of themselves, legislative roles reveal something about why political institutions are political institutions.

References

Aberbach, J.D., Putnam, R.D. and Rockman, B.A. (1981) *Bureaucrats and Politicians in Western Democracies*, Cambridge, MA: Harvard University Press.

Alpert, E.J. (1979) 'A reconceptualization of representational role theory', *Legislative Studies Quarterly*, 4: 587–603.

Anagnoson, T.J. (1983) 'Home style in New Zealand', *Legislative Studies Quarterly*, 8: 157–75.

Andeweg, R.B. (1997) 'Role specialisation or role switching? Dutch MPs between electorate and executive', in W.C. Müller and T. Saalfeld (eds), *Members of Parliaments in Western Europe: Roles and Behaviour*, London: Frank Cass.

Andeweg, R.B. and Thomassen, J.J.A. (2005) 'Modes of political representation', *Legislative Studies Quarterly*, 30: 507–28.

Barber, J.D. (1965) *The Lawmakers: Recruitment and Adoption to Legislative Life*, New Haven: Yale University Press Ltd.

Bell, C.G. and Price, C.M. (1975) *The First Term: A Study of Legislative Socialization*, London: Sage Publications.

Biddle, B.J. (1986) 'Recent developments in role theory', *Annual Review of Sociology*, 12: 67–92.

Blomgren, M. (2003) *Cross-pressure and Political Representation in Europe: A Comparative Study of MEPs and the Intra Party Arena*, Umeå: Statsvetenskapliga institutionen.

Bogdanor, V. (ed.) (1985) *Representatives of the People?*, Aldershot: Gower.

Cain, B.E., Ferejohn, J.A. and Fiorina, M.P. (1979) 'A house is not a home: British MPs in their constituencies', *Legislative Studies Quarterly*, 4: 501–25.

Cain, B.E., Ferejohn, J.A. and Fiorina, M.P. (1987) *The Personal Vote: Constituency Service and Electoral Independence*, Cambridge, MA: Harvard University Press.

Cavanagh, T.E. (1982) 'The calculus of representation: A congressional perspective', *Political Research Quarterly*, 35: 120–9.

Cayrol, R., Parodi, J.L. and Ysmal, C. (1973) *Le député français*, Paris: A. Colin.

Checkel, J.T. (2003) ' "Going native" in Europe? Theorizing social interaction in European institutions,' *Comparative Political Studies*, 36: 209–31.

Clarke, H.D. and Price, R.G. (1981) 'Parliamentary experience and representational role orientations in Canada', *Legislative Studies Quarterly*, 6: 373–90.

Converse, P.E. and Pierce, R. (1979) 'Representative roles and legislative behavior in France', *Legislative Studies Quarterly*, 4: 525–62.

Converse, P.E. and Pierce, R. (1986) *Political Representation in France*, Cambridge: Belknap Press of Harvard University Press.

Costa, O. and Kerrouche, E. (2007) *Qui sont les députés français? Enquête sur des élites inconnues*, Paris: Presses de Sciences Po.

Costa, O. and Kerrouche, E. (2009) 'Representative roles in the French National Assembly: The case for a dual typology?', *French Politics*, 7: 219–42.

Dalton, R.J. (2004) *Democratic Challenges, Democratic choices. The Erosion of Political Support in Advanced Industrial Democracies*, Oxford: Oxford University Press.

Davidson, R.H. (1969) *The Role of the Congressman*, New York: Pegasus.

Denzau, A., Riker, W. and Shepsle, K.A. (1985) 'Farquharson and Fenno: Sophisticated voting and home style', *American Political Science Review*, 79: 1117–34.

Egeberg, M. (2006) 'Executive politics as usual: role behaviour and conflict dimensions in the College of European Commissioners', *Journal of European Public Policy*, 13: 1–15.

Esaiasson, P. (2000) 'How Members of Parliament define their task', in P. Esaiasson and K. Heidar (eds), *Beyond Westminster and Congress: The Nordic Experience*, Columbus, OH: Ohio State University Press.

Esaiasson, P. and Heidar, K. (eds) (2000) *Beyond Westminster and Congress: The Nordic Experience*, Columbus, OH: Ohio State University Press.

Esaiasson, P. and Holmberg, S. (1996) *Representation from Above. Members of Parliament and Representative Democracy in Sweden*, Aldershot: Ashgate Dartmouth.

Eulau, H. and Karps, P.D. (1977) 'The puzzle of representation', *Legislative Studies Quarterly*, 2: 233–54.

Eulau, H., Wahlke, J.C., Buchanan, W. and Fergusson, L.C. (1978) 'The role of the representative: Some empirical observations on the theory of Edmund Burke', in H. Eulau and J.C. Wahlke (eds), *The Politics of Representation: Continuities in Theory and Research*, Beverly Hills: Sage Publications Ltd.

Fenno, R.F. (1973) *Congressmen in Committees*, Boston: Little, Brown.

Fenno, R.F. (1978) *Home Style: House Members in Their Districts*, Boston: Little, Brown.

Ferejohn, J.A. and Fiorina, M.P. (1975) 'Purposive Models of Legislative Behavior', *American Economic Review*, 65: 407–14.

Francis, W.L. (1965) 'The role concept in legislatures: A probability model and a note on cognitive structure', *Journal of Politics*, 27: 567–85.

Franks, D.D. (2007) 'Role', *Blackwell Encyclopedia of Sociology*, Blackwell Reference Online, retrieved June 30, 2010 from www.sociologyencyclopedia.com/public/.

Giddens, A. (1979) *Central Problems in Social Theory*, London: MacMillan.

Goffman, E. (1959) *The Presentation of Self in Everyday Life*, Garden City: Doubleday.

Gross, D.A. (1978) 'Representative styles and legislative behaviour', *Western Political Quarterly*, 31: 359–71.

Haegel, F. (1994) *Un maire à Paris. Mise en scène d'un nouveau rôle politique*, Paris: Presses de la Fondation nationale des sciences politiques.

Hagger, M. and Wing, M. (1979) 'Legislative roles and clientele orientations in the European Parliament', *Legislative Studies Quarterly*, 4: 165–96.

Hedlund, R.D. and Friesema, H.P. (1972) 'Representatives' perception of constituency opinion', *Journal of Politics*, 34: 730–52.

Heitshusen, V., Young, G. and Wood, D.M. (2005) 'Electoral context and MP constituency focus in Australia, Canada, Ireland, New Zealand, and the United Kingdom', *Americal Journal of Political Science*, 49: 32–45.

Hindin, M.J. (2007) 'Role theory', *Blackwell Encyclopedia of Sociology*, Blackwell Reference Online, Retrieved June 30, 2010 from www.sociologyencyclopedia.com/public/.

Hooghe, L. (2001) *The European Commission and the Integration of Europe. Images of Governance*, Cambridge: Cambridge University Press.

Huitt, R. (1961) 'The outsider in the Senate: An alternative role', *American Political Science Review*, 55: 566–75.

Jewell, M.E. (1983) 'Legislator–constituency relations and the representative process', *Legislative Studies Quarterly*, 8: 303–37.

Katz, R.S. (1999) 'Role orientations in parliaments', in R.S. Katz and B. Wessels (eds), *The European Parliament, the National Parliaments, and European Integration*, Oxford: Oxford University Press.

King, A. (1974) *British Members of Parliament: A Self-Portrait*, London: Macmillan.

Klingemann, H.-D. and Wessels, B. (2000) 'The political consequences of Germany's mixed-member system: Personalization at the grass roots?', in M. Shugart and M.P. Wattenberg (eds), *Mixed-Member Electoral Systems. The Best of Both Worlds?*, Oxford: Oxford University Press.

Kornberg, A. (1967) *Canadian Legislative Behaviour, A Study of the 25th Parliament*, New York: Holt, Rinehart and Winston.

Kuklinski, J.H. (1979) 'Representative–constituency linkages: A review article', *Legislative Studies Quarterly*, 4: 121–40.

Kuklinski, J.H. and Elling, R.C. (1977) 'Representational role, constituency opinion and legislative roll-call behaviour', *American Journal of Political Science*, 21: 135–47.

Lacroix, B. and Lagroye, J. (eds) (1992) *Le Président de la République. Usage et genèses d'une institution*, Paris: Presses de la Fondation nationale des sciences politiques.

Linton, R. (1936) *The Study of Man: An Introduction*, New York: Appleton.

Loewenberg, G. and Kim, C.L. (1978) 'Comparing the Representativeness of Parliaments', *Legislative Studies Quarterly*, 3: 27–49.

Manin, B. (1997) *The Principles of Representative Government*, Cambridge: Cambridge University Press.

Manley, J. (1970) *The Politics of Finance: The House Committee on Ways and Means*, Boston: Little, Brown.

March, J.G. and Olsen, J.P. (1989) *Rediscovering Institutions: The Organizational Basis of Politics*, New York: Free Press.

Matthews, D.R. (1960) *U.S. Senators and Their World*, Chapel Hill: University of North Carolina Press.

Mayhew, D.R. (1974) *Congress – The Electoral Connection*, New Haven: Yale University Press.

McCrone, D.J. and Kuklinski, J.H. (1979) 'The delegate theory of representation', *American Journal of Political Science*, 23: 278–300.

McLeay, E. and Vowles, J. (2007) 'Redefining constitutency representation: The roles of New Zealand MPs under MMP', *Regional & Federal Studies*, 17: 71–95.

Mead, G.H. (1934) *Mind, Self and Society*, Chicago: University of Chicago Press.

Miller, W. and Stokes, D. (1963) 'Constituency influence in Congress', *American Political Science Review*, 57: 45–57.

Müller, W.C., Jenny, M., Steininger, B., Dolezal, M., Philipp, W. and Preisl-Westphal, S. (2001) *Die österreichischen Abgeordneten. Individuelle Präferenzen und politisches Verhalten*, Vienna: WUV Universitätsverlag.

Müller, W.C. and Saalfeld, T. (eds) (1997) *Members of Parliament In Western Europe*, Oregon: Frank Cass.

Navarro, J. (2009) *Les députés européens et leur rôle*, Brussels: Editions de l'Université de Bruxelles.

Nay, O. (1997) 'L'institutionnalisation de la région comme apprentissage de rôles', *Politix*, 38: 18–46.

Norris, P. (1997) 'The Puzzle of Constituency Service', *The Journal of Legislative Studies*, 3: 29–49.

Norris, P. (2004) *Electoral engineering voting rules and political behaviour*, Cambridge: Cambridge University Press.

Norton, P. (1994) 'The growth of the constituency role of the MP', *Parliamentary Affairs*, 47: 705–20.

Norton, P. (ed.) (2002) *Parliaments and Citizens in Western Europe*, London: Frank Cass.

Norton, P. and Wood, D.M. (1993) *Back from Westminster: British Members of Parliament and Their Constituents*, Lexington, KY: University Press of Kentucky.

Page, B.I., Shapiro, R.Y., Gronke, P.W. and Rosenberg, R.M. (1984) 'Constituency, party and representation in Congress', *Public Opinion Quarterly*, 48: 741–56.

Parker, G.R. (1980) 'Sources of change in congressional district attentiveness', *American Journal of Political Science*, 24: 115–24.

Payne, J., Woshinsky, O., Veblen, E., Coogan, W. and Bigler, G. (1984) *The Motivation of Politicians*, Chicago: Nelson-Hall.

Payne, J.L. (1980) 'Show horses and work horses in the United States House of Representatives', *Polity*, 12: 428–56.

Peters, B.G. (1999) *Institutional Theory in Political Science*, London: Pinter.

Pitkin, H.F. (1969) *Representation*, New York: Atherton Press.

Pitkin, H.F. (1972) *The Concept of Representation*, Berkeley: University of California Press.

Prewitt, K., Eulau, H. and Zisk, B.H. (1966) 'Political socialization and political roles', *Public Opinion Quarterly*, 30: 569–82.

Price, K.C. (1985) 'Instability in representational role orientation in a state legislature: A research note', *Western Political Quarterly*, 38: 162–71.

Rao, N. (1998) 'Representation in local politics', *Political Studies*, 46: 19–35.

Rehfeld, A. (2009) 'Representation rethought: On trustees, delegates, and gyroscopes in the study of political representation and democracy', *American Political Science Review*, 103 (2): 214–30.

Rozenberg, O. (2009) 'Présider par plaisir. L'examen des affaires européennes à l'Assemblée nationale et à la Chambre des Communes depuis Maastricht', *Revue française de science politique*, 59: 401–27.

Rush, M. (2001) *The Role of the Member of Parliament Since 1868*, Oxford: Oxford University Press.

Saalfeld, T. and Müller, W.C. (1997) 'Roles in legislative studies: A theoretical introduction', in W.C. Müller and T. Saalfeld (eds), *Members of Parliament In Western Europe*, London: Frank Cass.

Scully, R. (2005) *Becoming Europeans? Attitudes, Behaviour, and Socialisation in the European Parliament*, Oxford: Oxford University Press.

Scully, R. and Farrell, D.M. (2003) 'MEPs as representatives: Individual and institutional roles', *Journal of Common Market Studies*, 41: 269–88.

Searing, D. (1991) 'Roles, rules and rationality in the new institutionalism', *American Political Science Review*, 85: 1239–61.

Searing, D.D. (1994) *Westminister's World. Understanding Political Roles*, Cambridge: Harvard University Press.

Shepsle, K.A. (1989) 'Studying institutions: Some lessons from the rational choice approach', *Journal of Theoretical Politics*, 1: 131–47.

Sinclair, B. (1983) 'Purposive behavior in the US Congress: A review essay', *Legislative Studies Quarterly*, 8: 117–31.

Strøm, K. (1997) 'Rules, reason and routines: Legislative roles in parliamentary democracy', in W.C. Müller and T. Saalfeld (eds), *Members of Parliament in Western Europe*, London: Frank Cass.

Taggart, W.A. and Durant, R.F. (1985) 'Home style of a U.S. Senator: A longitudinal analysis', *Legislative Studies Quarterly*, 10: 489–504.

Thomassen, J. and Andeweg, R. (2004) 'Beyond collective representation: Individual Members of Parliament and interest representation in the Netherlands', *Journal of Legislative Studies*, 10: 47–69.

Thomassen, J. and Esaiasson, P. (2006) 'Role orientations of Members of Parliament', *Acta Politica*, 41: 217–31.

Trondal, J. (2002) 'Beyond the EU membership – non-membership dichotomy? Supranational identities among naional EU decision-makers', *Journal of European Public Policy*, 2002: 468–87.

Tsebelis, G. (2002) *Veto Players – How Political Institutions Work*, Priceton, NJ: Princeton University Press.

Turner, R.H. (1992) 'Role: Sociological Aspects', in D.L. Sills (ed.), *Encyclopedia of Sociology*, New York: MacMillan, Vol. 3.

Wahlke, J.C., Eulau, H., Buchanan, W. and Fergusson, L.C. (1962) *The Legislative System: Explorations in Legislative Behaviour*, New York: John Wiley and Sons.

Weber, A.L. (1995) 'Role conflict and role strain', in H.L. Delgado and F.N. Magill (eds), *International Encyclopedia of Sociology*, London, Fitzroy Dearborn: 1134–7.

Weber, M. (1978) *Economy and Society: An Outline of Interpretive Sociology*, Berkeley, CA: University of California Press, 1st edn, 1922.

Wessels, B. (1999) 'Whom to represent? Role orientations of legislators in Europe', in H. Schmitt and J. Thomassen (eds), *Political Representation and Legitimacy in the European Union*, Oxford: Oxford University Press.

Wessels, B. (2005) 'Roles and orientations of Members of Parliament in the EU context: Congruence or difference? Europeanisation or not?', *Journal of Legislative Studies*, 11: 446–65.

Wood, D.M. and Yoon, J.-B. (1998) 'Role orientations of junior MPs: A test of Searing's categories with emphasis on constituency activities', *Journal of Legislative Studies*, 4: 51–71.

Woshinsky, O.H. (1973) *The French Deputy*, Lexington: D.C. Heath.

Zittel, T. and Gschwend, T. (2008) 'Individualized campaigns in mixed-member systems. Candidates in the German federal elections 2005', *West European Politics*, 31: 978–1003.

3 The emergence and transformation of representative roles

Heinrich Best and Lars Vogel

This contribution starts from the assumption that representative roles are constituent, formative and relatively stable elements of the political order, linking cognitions and norms to positions occupied by MPs in the arena of political competition and the organizational hierarchies of parliaments and parties (Merton 1957; Linton 1945; Searing 1991; Searing 1994). Roles will be considered here as systems of boundary conditions to which the actors who play such roles are supposed to conform, and as the corresponding rights that these boundaries confer. Being both structured and structuring elements of systems of social interaction (Parsons 1951), roles define areas of obligations and constraints that correspond to areas of conditional autonomy.

Special emphasis will be given to MPs' own orientations or perceptions of the part they are supposed to play in the political game, i.e. to their inner definitions of what someone in their position should think and do. Following the lines of Levinson and other protagonists of interactionist role theory, representative roles are seen here as a matter of limited choice, in which legislators "select, create and synthesize certain forms of adaptation rather than others" (Levinson 1959: 175). These adaptive choices are not completely free, but constrained and directed by "structurally given demands [...] associated with a given social position" (Levinson 1959:172). It takes a considerable effort to make these choices, to adopt legislative roles and to display them to others. These choices should, therefore, result in a fairly stable attachment of individual MPs to their representative roles, thereby creating a relatively constant environment for communication among legislators, and between legislators and their extra-parliamentarian role partners. MPs' attachment to their representative roles will be reinforced by positive feedback from the aggregate role structure that emerges in the parliamentary environment as a result of MPs' adaptive individual choices. We also suggest that MPs' self-definitions of legislative roles are directed by previous socializing experiences as well as by the political affiliations of MPs, i.e. by their social and political backgrounds that shaped their initial cognitions and norms as political beings.

The taking and making of representative roles will not, however, lead to role persistency. *Collective* changes of MPs' role perceptions may result from a change of the rules of the game, i.e. from a fundamental change in the political or societal context of action that urges them to redefine the boundary conditions in their transactions with relevant actors in their environment. *Individual* changes of role perceptions will result from the horizontal and vertical movements of MPs within the grid of positions provided by the polity, assuming that different role expectations are linked to different positions. Role taking and role gradation will therefore be considered as dependent variables, dependent on legislators' previous and actual positions in the social and institutional order of parliaments, in their affiliated parties, and in society at large. In particular, we will examine whether and in which way role changes can be attributed to movements in the system of positions provided by the organisational grid of parties and parliaments (see Figure 3.1). By taking the formative conditions – particularly the temporality of representative role taking, role definition and role gradation – into consideration we will address a subject largely neglected in extant political research.[1] Conations attached to role definitions and other aspects of roles as independent variables will not be addressed in this contribution.

How to measure representatives' roles

The focus of our study on generic aspects of legislative roles calls for a complex research design that takes the contextuality and temporality of processes of role definition, role taking and role gradation into consideration. These conceptual requirements are met by the German Parliamentarians' Survey (GPS: Best 2009; Best *et al.* 2007; Best and Vogel 2011), which was carried out in three waves: the first in 2003/2004, the second in 2007 and a third wave was accomplished in 2010.[2] The GPS targeted the members of the German Bundestag, of State Parliaments (ten in the first wave and 13 in the second) and the German members of

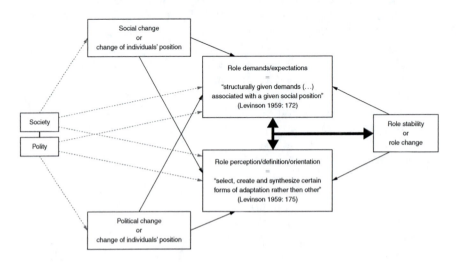

Figure 3.1 A basic model of representative role definition and role change.

the European Parliament.Overall sample coverage was 56.0 per cent in the 2003/2004 wave and 56.4 per cent in the 2007 wave. In total across both waves, 2,177 interviews with 1,703 active parliamentarians were conducted by Computer Assisted Telephone Interviewing. In addition, 794 former MPs were interviewed, bringing the total number of interviewees to 2,497. Of these, and of special interest for the present chapter, 478 MPs participated in both waves of the study as active MPs. These panelists will allow us to investigate the stability of legislative roles, and to examine why and in which ways they change.[3] However, the full 2003/2004 sample of active MPs ($n=954$) will be used as the basis for our study into the determinants of legislative role definitions and taken as the starting point for an inquiry into the dynamics of legislative role taking and role gradation. The GPS questionnaire covers a broad spectrum of social and political background variables, information about pre- and post-recruitment political careers, legislative behaviour, political attitudes and – last, but not least – MPs' role perceptions and evaluations of their own and their colleagues' work as representatives. Questions about MPs' role perceptions focus on role requirements (What qualities and qualifications have secured my candidacy and election?), role primacies (What are my principal goals as a policy maker?) and role conceptions or focus (Who are the significant others whose role expectations I have to fulfil?).

These dimensions or facets of representative roles were specified and operationalized as follows:

- "Role primacy", i.e. the precedence of one legislative role over another, is measured by an item related to the MPs' policy objectives and value concerns that determine their legislative decision-making. We called this item the "Trilemma of Policy Priorities". The interview question was worded as follows:

  > *"Balancing the budget of the state, enhancing economic growth and reducing social inequality are all important political goals. If you would have to assess these goals, what would be your priority: the reduction of inequality (31 per cent), the balancing of the state budget (23 per cent), or economic growth (47 per cent)?"*[4]

  These policy priorities can be translated into primacies of the representative role, in that we can distinguish between "procreators of wealth" who put economic growth first, "champions of equality" who opt for social equality and associated redistributive policies and "defenders of stability" who chose balancing the budget as their policy priority.
- The second dimension of representative roles investigated in our study refers to legislative role requirements. We asked MPs to give the reasons they felt underpinned their first nomination as a parliamentary candidate. The following four non-exclusive options were to be assessed by the respondents:

"*I have been nominated because...*

a   *...I represent the concerns of special social groups (72 per cent);*

b   *...of the appreciation for my personality (91 per cent);*

c   *...of my services for my party or the organizations affiliated to it (34 per cent);*

d   *...of my special skills and my knowledge as an expert (62 per cent).*"

These four options can also be translated into long established role typologies, in particular into the dichotomy between "trustees" and "delegates". Here the appreciation of MPs' personality, and the recognition of their special skills and knowledge as an expert, relates to the "trustee" model of Burkean origin, whilst representation of concerns of special social groups, and because of services rendered to parties or affiliated organisations refer to the "delegate" model.

• The third dimension of representatives' role definitions relates to their "conception" or "focus". The interview question was:

"*Do you consider yourself primarily as a representative of your party (10 per cent), of the people who voted for you (13 per cent), of your electoral district (25 per cent), or as a representative of the whole country (52 per cent)?*"

This question provides information about the institutional level of representative orientation. If one compares the answer category "representative of the whole country" to the other three options, the dichotomy between the "trustee" and "delegate"-models is seen again, whereby those MPs who chose to be "representatives of the whole country" can be considered as trustees *pur et dur*, whilst respondents who chose one of the other categories of answer can be considered to see themselves as delegates of one of various limited constituencies. In the undertaken analyses as part of this study the answer categories "people who voted for you" and "your electoral district" were collapsed into one category "constituency".

A short overview of the aggregate results for questions related to MPs' role perceptions shows that in the 2003/2004 wave of the GPS, German MPs attributed their nomination more to their qualities than to their qualifications; that a majority favoured a universalistic concept of representation by presenting themselves as representatives of the whole country, and that "procreator of wealth" was their favoured choice when confronted with the "Trilemma of Policy Priorities". There was also an obvious reluctance to designate party as a significant part of their role set, because only one in ten of the MPs considered him- or herself to be a representative of the selectorate rather than of the electorate, and only one in three claimed to owe their nomination to former services to the party. Although some answer patterns were skewed, it is still important to investigate for the considerable overall variance in MPs' role perceptions.[5]

Does social and political background matter? Determinants of legislative role perceptions

In a first step of our analyses of the dynamics of role taking and role gradation we investigated MPs' dispositions and assessments underlying the process of legislative role taking. The assumption is that these dispositions and assessments are shaped by previous experiences and influences, which are in turn linked to MPs' locus in the structures of society and polity. Theoretical arguments for establishing a link between the social and political backgrounds of MPs and their normative and cognitive orientations can be found in socialisation and cleavage theories (Putnam 1976: 92–102; Best 2007: 393–401). For these analyses we have included a set of "acknowledged" social and political background characteristics used in earlier studies (Edinger and Searing 1967; Schleth 1971; Bourdieu 1990), such as family occupational background (i.e. social origin), educational level, sex, age, region of residence and income of respondents. Income was measured according to the threshold criterion of whether MPs' remuneration parliamentary allowances exceed or fall short of their income prior to becoming an MP. Social origin was classified according to a three-class scheme, whereby fathers' occupations were classified "lower class" if they required no or only a basic formal qualification and entailed no authority over other persons. "Party" was included as the pivotal political background variable to control for the effects of political socialisation and party loyalty on representatives' role orientations. "Tenure", i.e. the time elapsed since their first entering parliament, was introduced as a control variable indicating how long MPs had been in office and thus how long they had been exposed to the impact of post-recruitment socialisation.

Region was classified according to the criterion whether in 1989, i.e. the year the Berlin Wall fell, the MP was living in the GDR or in West Germany. The different age of systems of representative democracy in "old" and "new" Europe, different political experiences and different social backgrounds of legislators in both regions should result in different role expectations and role perceptions in the legislative arena. Research opportunities provided by German reunification are particularly rich and valuable in this respect: Here we find the unique situation of political personnel with a biographical background in a communist political and social system sharing a unified institutional setting with the descendants of an "old" capitalist democracy. It is obvious, therefore, that a German-based study on the impact of social origin on legislative role definitions must include regional differentiation of actual past experience.

In the following, three dimensions and ten facets of representative role structures will be investigated. In particular we are interested in determining the extent to which and in what ways the social and political backgrounds of MPs are related to their role requirements, role primacies and role conceptions. Altogether ten models, one for each "facet" of the role structure, were tested by logistical regression analysis using Maximum–Likelihood–Estimation to predict a dichotomous dependent variable (in the given case: the agreement to an item

Table 3.1 Determinants of representative role perceptions (synopsis)

	Role primacy			Role requirement				Role conception			Sum of sig.
	Growth	Equality	Stability	Embodiment	Personality	Services	Expertise	Party	Constituency	Polity	
Age	*	n.s.	*	n.s.	*	n.s.	***	n.s.	n.s.	n.s.	4
Sex	n.s.	n.s.	n.s.	**	n.s.	n.s.	n.s.	n.s.	n.s.	n.s.	1
Region	***	**	n.s.	*	*	n.s.	n.s.	n.s.	n.s.	n.s.	4
Income	n.s.	n.s.	n.s.	n.s.	n.s.	*	n.s.	*	n.s.	n.s.	2
Social origin	n.s.	n.s.	n.s.	n.s.	n.s.	n.s.	n.s.	n.s.	n.s.	n.s.	0
Party	***	***	**	***	n.s.	n.s.	***	**	**	n.s.	7
Education	n.s.	n.s.	n.s.	**	n.s.	n.s.	*	n.s.	**	*	4
Tenure	**	n.s.	*	n.s.	n.s.	n.s.	***	*	n.s.	*	5
Model	***	***	***	***	n.s.	n.s.	***	***	***	**	8

Notes
Significance levels: *** sig. <0.001; ** sig. <0.01; * sig. <0.05; n.s. =not significant.

or an answer category related to the representative role) on the basis of a set of independent variables of any measurement level. As eight independent variables (age, sex, region, income, social origin, party, education and tenure) will be used in all ten models, whilst the dependent variables will be exchanged, a line-by-line, i.e. a background-variable-by-background-variable comparison, will be pursued.

Results of the logistical regression model show that not one independent variable is significant in all ten models. The most successful predictor is "party",

Table 3.2 Determinants explaining policy priorities of parliamentary representation: role primacy

Independent variables	Policy priorities		
	Enhanced economic growth [exp(B)]	Reducing social inequality [exp(B)]	Balanced budget of the state [exp(B)]
Age (main effect)[1]	*		*
36 to 55	1.20	1.75	0.56
Over 55	0.74	1.64	0.97
Sex (0 = male; 1 = female)	0.79	1.34	1.03
Regional background (0 = West; 1 = East)	1.93***	0.47**	0.80
Income level[2] (Allowance higher than former salary)	0.94	1.17	0.95
Father's occupational status[3]			
Middle class	1.15	0.83	1.00
Upper class	1.20	1.06	0.78
Parliamentary group (main effect)[4]	***	***	**
SPD	0.19***	18.97***	1.02
FDP	1.07	(0.00)	1.22
PDS	0.05***	157.63***	0.16**
B90/Greens	0.09***	13.26***	2.41*
Others	0.14**	44.96***	0.37
Education[5]	1.02	1.04	0.99
Tenure	1.20**	0.95	0.85*
Intercept	1.33	0.02***	0.92
Model Chi[2]	212.31***	340.13***	52.74***
Prediction success (%)	73.3	79.4	76.6
Nagelkerke R^2	0.31	0.49	0.10
Number of observ. (n)	805	805	805

Notes
Significance levels: *** sig.<0.001; ** sig.<0.01; * sig.<0.05.
1 Reference category: age under 36.
2 Question in the survey: My allowance as a parliamentarian is greater than my former salary was, even taking all expenditure into account. (Possible answers: "fully agree", "agree", "disagree" and "completely disagree"; fully agree and agree merged.)
3 Reference group: lower class.
4 Reference group: CDU.
5 Ordinal categories: basic education, intermediate education, academic degree.

Table 3.3 Determinants explaining reasons of first candidacy: role requirements

Independent variables	I was nominated because...			
	...I embody particular interests [exp(B)]	...of my personality [exp(B)]	...in appreciation of my services [exp(B)]	...of my expertise [exp(B)]
Age (main effect)[1]		*		***
36 to 55	1.47	4.20**	0.54	2.95**
Over 55	1.82	2.96*	0.57	4.70***
Sex (0 = male; 1 = female)	1.82**	0.95	0.88	1.04
Regional background (0 = West; 1 = East)	1.43*	0.54*	0.76	0.84
Income level[2] (Allowance higher than former salary)	0.99	0.90	1.26*	0.94
Father's occupational status[3]				
Middle class	1.24	1.05	0.87	1.02
Upper class	1.05	0.58	0.99	1.29
Parliamentary group (main effect)[4]	***			***
SPD	0.90	0.69	1.21	0.77
FDP	0.33**	1.67	0.96	1.91
PDS	3.10**	0.88	0.84	3.10***
B90/Greens	2.99*	0.79	1.05	1.66
Others	0.22*	<0.01	0.56	2.69
Education[5]	0.59**	1.53	0.92	1.47*
Tenure	1.00	0.89	0.91	0.81***
Intercept	4.60*	3.37	1.00	0.28*
Model Chi²	75.52***	22.00	19.65	68.34***
Prediction success (%)	72.2	91.7	66.2	65.1
Nagelkerke R²	0.13	0.06	0.03	0.11
Number of observ. (n)	821	815	811	820

Notes

Significance levels: *** sig. <0.001; ** sig. <0.01; * sig. <0.05.

1 Reference category: age under 36.

2 Question in the survey: My allowance as a parliamentarian is greater than my former salary was, even taking all expenditure into account. (Possible answers: "fully agree", "agree", "disagree" and "completely disagree"; fully agree and agree merged.)

3 Reference group: lower class.

4 Reference group: CDU.

5 Ordinal categories: basic education, intermediate education, academic degree.

which scores significantly in seven models. There is, however, no significant overall impact of "party" or an impact of any single party affiliation on the appreciation of respondents' personality or their services for their parties as criteria for first nomination, or on the choice of "the whole country" as reference level for their representative role-conception. Two models ("Services" and "Personality") are not significant at all. By and large, however, social and political origins have an impact on representatives' role definitions, and it is the effect of post-recruitment socialisation, gratifications and loyalties related to their party affiliations that scores most often.

Table 3.4 Determinants explaining the focus of parliamentary representation: role conception

Independent variables	Focus of parliamentary representation		
	Party [exp(B)]	Constituency [exp(B)]	Polity [exp(B)]
Age (main effect)[1]			
36 to 55	0.62	0.90	1.31
Over 55	0.70	0.67	1.65
Sex (0 = male; 1 = female)	1.40	1.11	0.81
Regional background (0 = West; 1 = East)	0.73	0.91	1.22
Income level[2] (Allowance higher than former salary)	1.51*	0.99	0.90
Father's occupational status[3]			
Middle class	1.33	0.79	1.12
Upper class	1.33	0.90	1.02
Parliamentary group (main effect)[4]	**	**	
SPD	2.44*	0.83	0.96
FDP	1.77	0.25**	2.91**
PDS	3.41**	0.83	0.82
B90/Greens	5.88***	0.31**	1.27
Others	9.74**	0.36	0.79
Education[5]	1.65	0.62**	1.40*
Tenure	0.78*	0.95	1.13*
Intercept	0.01***	4.51**	0.27*
Model Chi[2]	44.28***	40.91***	35.12**
Prediction success (%)	90.7	66.8	58.1
Nagelkerke R[2]	0.12	0.07	0.06
Number of observ. (n)	751	751	751

Notes

Significance levels: *** sig.<0.001; ** sig.<0.01; * sig.<0.05.

1 Reference category: age under 36.

2 Question in the survey: My allowance as a parliamentarian is greater than my former salary was, even taking all expenditure into account. (Possible answers: "fully agree", "agree", "disagree" and "completely disagree"; fully agree and agree merged.)

3 Reference group: lower class.

4 Reference group: CDU.

5 Ordinal categories: basic education, intermediate education, academic degree.

Variations of legislative role perceptions between single parties show a chiasmus with regards to role primacy. While MPs from parties of the left and centre–left (SPD, PDS, Greens) tend to perceive themselves as champions of equality, MPs from parties of right and the centre–right (CDU/CSU, FDP) see themselves primarily as procreators of growth. With regard to budget policies, however, we observe a polarity within the left, with MPs of the Green party putting a strong emphasis on budget stability, whilst very few MPs of the PDS consider this issue as a policy priority. An antagonism between sustainability (of the state budget) and an expansive use of resources (to reduce social inequality) seems to be the basis of this cleavage. A similarly complex pattern of differentiation between parties appears where the focus of parliamentary representation is concerned: MPs of parties of the left and the centre–left have a significantly increased propensity to designate party as their focus of representation (although even here the overall inclination to choose this focus is rather low). Members of the FDP and the Greens have a significantly reduced disposition to present themselves as representatives of limited constituencies, while MPs of the FDP show a clear preference for the trustee concept of parliamentary representation by presenting themselves overwhelmingly as representatives of the whole polity. With regard to role requirements, there is a distinct differentiation between MPs of the smaller parties, when it comes to the embodiment of particular interests: MPs of the Green party and the PDS emphasise a commonality of interest between voters and those elected as a constituent requirement of their representative role, while MPs of the FDP negate this concept. In general, we see a high significance of party in the processes of representative role definition and role taking. The position of parties in the arena of political competition, the normative and cognitive bases of party programmes, and parties' strategies in mobilising their electorates, all shape MPs' representative role definitions. Although MPs hesitate to present themselves as creatures of their parties, party affiliation leaves characteristic marks in their self-definitions as representatives.

In comparison, social origin, which is the master variable of so many elite studies, has no significant effect at all. How open recruitment is to the elite level might be symbolically and substantially important for the legitimacy and structural stability of a social system. However, the role definitions and policy preferences of representatives are not affected by having a working-class or an upper-class family background. Representatives choose their policy priorities and representative role orientations independently of their social origin. A working-class family background does not transform them into "champions for equality" or into the embodiment of working-class interests.

Gender, another dominating variable in social background studies, is found to have a significant effect only once: female representatives agree significantly more often than their male counterparts that they have been nominated because they "embody the concerns of special social groups". It is plausible to assume that this self-perception reflects, at least in part, the effect of gender quotas and affirmative action.

Income has a significant effect on choosing "services for the party" as a reason for nomination and on selecting "party" as the main focus of MPs' representative role. In the first-mentioned model, income is the only significant predictor although the model itself is not significant. In both models, representatives who earn more as MPs than they did in their previous occupations show a greater degree of "partyness" in their role definitions than the control group. This result can be plausibly interpreted by assuming that MPs who gain financially from their political career tend to perceive themselves as employed by their party. They claim to owe their position as MP to services they have rendered to their employers and thereby devote their loyalty to them.

Age, education and tenure are all related to the accumulation of knowledge and experience during the life-course and careers of representatives. The inconsistency of results and the varying explanatory status of these three indicators show, however, that they are based on different aspects of the fields of experience of representatives. In only one model do all three indicators have significant effects: the claim to have been nominated because of particular skills and expertise increases with the age and level of education of MPs, whilst it decreases with length of tenure. We assume that this reversal amongst tenured representatives results from a growing realism with regard to the prerequisites of their parliamentary careers. It might also be the case that tenure becomes a career-asset in itself, replacing the expertise and skills acquired outside parliament. Education has significant effects in two other models: the better educated MPs are, the lower the tendency to describe themselves as the embodiment of special interests or to choose limited constituencies as their focus for representation, and the more they tend to refer to themselves as representatives of the whole country. A high level of education is obviously an asset that encourages MPs to identify with universalistic or "trustee" concepts of representation.

Whilst education has no significant effect on role primacies, the variables "age" and "tenure" reveal a pattern of inverse effects on the choice of "economic growth" and "balancing the state budget" as policy priorities: after controlling for all other independent variables, MPs' inclination to choose economic growth as their policy priority decreases with age, whilst their preference for a balanced state budget increases. With regard to tenure, in contrast, we see an inverse relationship with incumbents who prefer economic growth and reject the importance of a balanced state budget. These contradictory results are difficult to interpret. We favour the somewhat pessimistic explanation that, in terms of career prospects, "procreators of wealth" stand a better chance of political survival than "guardians of budget stability", whilst older MPs are more cautious about the risks of a growing state debt and less optimistic about the sustainability of economic growth for the length of their prospected career.

This review of findings from ten regression models concludes with results related to the predictor "region", which represents the systems' histories – communist–dictatorial versus capitalist–democratic – on representative role perceptions. No significant effects were found with regard to role conceptions. Concerning representative role requirements, however, significantly fewer East than West German representatives claim to owe their first nomination to an appreciation of their personality. On the other hand, significantly more East German MPs claim that they were nominated because they embody the concerns of special groups (although significance is borderline in this model). This pattern of answers suggests that East German MPs tend to favour the "delegate" over the "trustee" model of representation. It also seems that the egalitarian *habitus* that is widespread in post-communist East Germany reduces the readiness to display "individualistic" personality factors as representative role requirements, whilst it encourages MPs to refer to "collectivistic" mechanisms of symbolic interest representation via the "embodiment" of group concerns. The egalitarian *habitus* does not, however, transform East German MPs per se into "champions of equality". From other analyses based on the GPS dataset, it can be shown that the large proportion of East German MPs favouring a reduction of inequality as their policy priority is owed to the large number of post-communists in East German state parliaments. After controlling for "party" we see a strong positive effect of an East German regional background on enhancing economic growth and a negative effect on reducing social inequality.

The review of logistic regression models has shown that our adaptation of Lewis Edinger's classical question: "Does MPs' social background matter for the moulding of representative roles?" (Edinger and Searing 1967) can be answered with a conditional "yes". Again, after controlling for "party", at least one social background variable had a significant effect in each of the ten models tested. On the other hand, we have seen that standard indicators of social background analysis like "social origin", "sex" or "income", have little or no impact when it comes to representative role definitions. These results confirm earlier findings that show social background variables have only marginal influence on purposive roles in the US Congress (Davidson 1969: 108), and on the representational focus and style of MPs in national parliaments throughout Europe (Kielhorn 2001: 203). Given these findings, we have to be sceptical about expectations that changes of recruitment patterns towards a more proportional representation according to class or gender will lead to different policies in our parliaments. MPs are "trustees" with regard to their electorates and "delegates" with regard to their selectorates, i.e. their party. "Education", "age" and "region" had a more consistent impact on representatives' role definitions. We have, however, also seen paradoxical patterns related to these indicators, such as the simultaneous display of an egalitarian *habitus* and a distance towards egalitarian policies amongst East German MPs, or the tendency to support budget stability as a policy priority by older MPs, and the tendency to drop it by tenured MPs. In general we see a relationship of equivalence between background variables and representative role definitions. This can be well demonstrated by "gender" and "income", which score only in those models where these variables indicate a functional significance of related background characteristics in legislative recruitment and careers. Social and political background characteristics help to disclose the logic of legislative recruitment and behaviour and therefore improve our understanding of the dynamics and mechanisms shaping representatives' role definitions and self-perceptions.

Legislative roles: stability and change

The assumption that representative role perceptions constitute a relatively stable link between the positions of actors in the political space and their behavioural dispositions does not imply invariability or even stability of the representative roles taken by or allocated to individual legislators (challenging this view, Price 1985: 169). It suggests only that individuals' change in role perception results from movements in the positional grid of the polity.

Although the basis for the assumption that roles are linked to positions in the society and polity can be traced back to the beginnings of sociological role theory (Linton 1945; Merton 1957), it is nevertheless still prominent in more recent debates. For example, Searing (1991: 1253) conceptualized "position roles" as determined by the formal and informal rules a holder of a leading position in parliament has to follow. Strøm (1997: 156) referred to this concept as one of two "polar points on a continuum of [institutional] constraint", whereas "preference roles" located on the other pole are not constrained by institutions.

Institutionalist hypotheses refer primarily to positional roles but conceive role orientations as not being *determined* by their positions: According to the tradition of symbolic interactionism, holders of positions possess a leeway of interpretation, because roles are defined in mutual processes of adjustment between the role expectations of others who are relevant for the position holder and the role orientations of the latter (Biddle 1986: 71; Turner 1998: 21). The outcome of this process depends on the assets and the positions of the persons involved, as well as on the structural conditions of the interaction.

Role conflict, i.e. different and contradictory demands towards the holder of a position or a person holding simultaneously more than one position with different role expectations, is supposed to be another source for an expansion of the interpretational leeway of position holders (Biddle 1986: 82; Wahlke *et al.* 1962: 15; van Sell *et al.* 1981). As roles are linked to positions, positional change results in shifting role orientations, but intervening variables like other positions held, adjustment processes and different demands articulated by others can obscure this relation.

The institutionalist hypothesis postulates that the strongest effects of positional change on roles are related to formal positions defined by the structure of organizations, whereas a much weaker effect is expected on change in role primacies. Wahlke *et al.* had already developed the concept of role primacy when they analysed "purposive roles" (Wahlke *et al.* 1962: 14); later, Searing used the term "preference roles" to describe roles that are not determined by formal positions but by the "career goals and emotional incentives" of the MPs (Searing 1991: 1253). More recently, Strøm (1997: 158) conceived roles as strategies of behaviour that are seen as the means with which to acquire individual goals. We understand role primacies as responses to the question of what MPs want to achieve in parliament. However, we extended the scope of goals beyond individual career goals to encompass political aims in general. In this respect, role primacy is also related to the social and political positions of the MPs, albeit less to their positions in formal organisations than to the positions of their parties in the arena of political competition. Nonetheless, role primacies are not completely independent of formal positions. For instance, different role primacies may be controversial within a party, but MPs who occupy leading party positions will be under much more pressure to represent the role primacies prevalent in their parties.

According to the socialisation hypothesis, role change occurs after entering parliament in a process of post recruitment socialisation, whereby newcomers who enter parliament for the first time adapt to the prevalent role orientations, if they had previously held different orientations (Asher 1973; Bell and Price 1975). The socialisation hypothesis also relies partly on the institutionalist hypothesis, because MPs who are elected for the first time change their positions after entering parliament by their transformation from ordinary citizens to legislators. Since newcomers are neither in a position – nor possess the competencies – to reinterpret role expectations, they are likely to adapt their role orientations to the dominant role expectations in their respective parliament or political party. The empirical evidence gathered gives evidence for parliamentary socialisation in different areas. For example, Fenno (1962; 1973) has shown the tendency for elder members in a committee of the US House of Representatives to pressure newly elected MPs to adjust to established practices. Davidson revealed that members of the US Congress shift from "outsiders to insiders" with tenure, meaning that they focus increasingly on issues debated in parliament instead of treating their mandate as a means to pursue particularistic local and regional interests (Davidson 1969: 72). While those studies focused mainly on role conceptions, Mughan et al. suggested that post-recruitment socialisation also affects role primacy. For the British House of Commons, they found a tendency towards more conservative opinions on several policy areas with increasing tenure (Mughan et al. 1997: 100; Scully 2005: 54). Much of recent research is concerned with the European Parliament (EP) and the question whether MEPs tend to understand themselves as representatives of European interests and whether they are endorsing pro-European policies with increasing tenure in the EP. However the empirical evidence gathered shows only marginal or even no signs of MEPs becoming more "Europeanized" during their parliamentary career at the European level (Franklin and Scarrow 1999: 57; Scully 2005: 54, 133). In contrast to the EP the works of Patzelt show a tendency among MPs in the German Bundestag to become trustees and – in accordance to Davidson – to focus their work on parliament instead of spending time in the constituency as an effect of post-recruitment socialisation (Patzelt 1997: 72).

The party-rigidity hypothesis assumes that the amount of change in role orientations differs between types of parties. Parties compete for votes whereby they address different parts of the electorate. In particular, parties with a sharp ideological profile and/or a clearly demarcated electorate – typically one-issue parties – are expected to represent foremost the interests of their supporting social or political groups. In contrast, catch-all parties tend to present a rather fuzzy profile to their heterogeneous electorates in order to address the interests of as many

Table 3.5 Changes of focus of legislative roles, 2003/2004–2007 (panel data)

		2003/2004 survey				
		Party	*Constituency*	*Polity*	*Total*	
					n	*%*
2007 survey	Party	11	9	18	38	9.0 (11.0)
	Constituency	10	92	42	144	34.0 (39.5)
	Polity	17	63	161	241	57.0 (49.4)
	Total *n*	38	164	221	423	100.0
	%	9.0	38.8	52.2	100.0	
		(9.8)	(37.8)	(52.4)		

Notes
All values that are not explicitly labeled as percentages are absolute number of cases.
Percentages in brackets: values for total survey population (n: 2003/2004 = 868, 2007 = 815).

voters as possible. These different positions in the electoral competition result in different degrees of freedom in shaping their representative roles. Whereas MPs of catch-all parties need to respond to varying and multiple preferences in the electorate, MPs of small and ideological parties should adhere to the well-defined goals and interests of their party repute. MPs of catch-all parties should therefore not only display a higher degree of heterogeneity, but also demonstrate more flexibility in their role definitions compared to ideology-driven single-issue parties.

With regard to change of role perceptions, in the following section we will discuss the overall amount of change, the direction of change, and the factors involved in causing change. Analyses of individual changes in role perception will be restricted to role primacy and role conception or focus. Role requirements, i.e. the reasons MPs give as to why they were originally nominated by their party as candidates for election, will not be discussed, because these reasons are logically invariant.[6]

Stability on aggregate level and volatility on individual level

A first look at *aggregate results* for the whole 2003/2004 and 2007 samples (the 2007 sample was adjusted to the 2003/04 sample design) shows a remarkable stability with regard to conception or focus of the representative role (Table 3.5). Aggregate answer patterns vary between both waves within a maximum range of only three percentage points. Conforming to our assumptions, the order and relative weight of elements of representative role perception remains unchanged. However, a dramatically different picture is revealed by a cross-sectional analysis of role primacies (Table 3.6). Economic growth, which was ranked first and was by far the dominant policy priority in the 2003/2004 survey wave, is ranked third and last in the 2007 wave, being replaced by the reduction of social inequality as top policy priority. Control of budget deficits comes second in the 2007 wave with a slight gain of five percentage points against those seen in 2003/2004. Since

November 2007, massive shifts, which anticipated the dramatic change in the agenda of the German public debate with the economic upturn between 2006 and 2008, seem to indicate that policy priorities might be not stable components of representative roles but circumstantial responses to actual political challenges. These aggregate results are remarkably well reproduced when we focus on the panel of respondents who participated in both waves of the GPS: here we find the same high stability of totals with regard to the focus of representative roles versus high levels of change of policy priorities with a strong trend towards egalitarian policies.

However, these results could be well used as a textbook example for possible fallacies resulting from the cross-sectional analyses of aggregate data. If we make full use of the longitudinal design of our study and look at the volatility between panel waves, we see a surprisingly high amount of change in the focus of roles at the *individual level*, which is even slightly higher than the individual change of role primacies: *38 per cent of individual MPs have changed focus, 35 per cent have changed primacy, and 62 per cent of MPs have changed their perception in one or both of these aspects of their representational role within a period of four years.* Some elements of role definitions are particularly unstable: 70 per cent of MPs who had chosen "party" as the focus of their representational role in the 2003/2004 survey made a different choice – predominantly "polity" – in the 2007 wave. Because exactly the same number of MPs switched to "party" in 2007, the total remains unchanged and misleadingly suggests stability of role conceptions at the aggregate level. Of the MPs who participated in both panel waves, 53 per cent abandoned economic growth, which they had given as top policy objective in the first panel wave. In the 2007 wave, most of them opt for a balanced budget, which in turn provided the main source category for MPs switching to social equality as their top priority in 2007.

Obviously the "migration" of MPs through the cells of the mobility tables follows certain patterns and exposes the susceptibilities of some groups to

Table 3.6 Changes of primacy of legislative roles, 2003/2004–2007 (panel data)

		2003/04 survey				
		Equality	Growth	Stability	Total	
					n	%
2007 survey	Equality	141	29	24	194	44.4 (46.7)
	Growth	9	88	11	108	24.7 (26.3)
	Stability	10	69	56	153	30.9 (27)
	Total n	160	186	91	437	100.0
	%	36.6	42.5	20.8	100	
		(30.8)	(46.8)	(22.5)		

Notes
All values that are not explicitly labeled as percentages are absolute number of cases.
Percentages in brackets: values for total survey population (n: 2003/2004 = 926, 2007 = 851).

change their policy priorities in certain directions. This is especially distinct in the case of MPs from the SPD, who turn massively to social equality as their top priority, and MPs from the FDP and the CDU/CSU, who tend to switch from economic growth to budget stability. This pattern of change suggests an underlying ideological cleavage between Social Democrats and non-socialist parties, which becomes virulent after the German economy turns from stagnation to moderate economic growth: Whilst many social democratic MPs switch their policy priorities to redistribution – i.e. increasing state intervention – many MPs from non-socialist parties switch to austerity – i.e. withdrawal of the state from the economy and society. Change of policy priorities should not, therefore, be interpreted as an indication of anomy or opportunism of MPs, but of the presence of deeper layers of normative orientations and cognitive concepts that resurface when room for political manoeuvre widens. It should be mentioned here that the 2007 parliamentarians' survey was conducted *before* the SPD had begun to distance itself from the policies of welfare state cuts of the Schröder government and before the Party of the Left (Linkspartei/Die Linke) had started its triumphant progress in West German state elections. With regard to the focus of legislative roles, we see – unlike in our observations concerning role primacies – no significant impact of party as a context of change of role conceptions. Changes in the focus of legislative roles occur frequently, but they are undirected at party level, as well as at the level of the total population of panelists. A shift of 20 MPs, approximating 5 per cent of the total population, from constituency to polity is too small to constitute a trend. One final party-related observation, however, concerns both dimensions of legislative role perceptions: The PDS shows by far the highest volatility of role focus (50 per cent) and by far the highest stability of role primacy (85 per cent) of all parties. This finding challenges the assumption that changes of legislative role perceptions are indistinguishably linked to MPs' movements in the institutional grid of the polity and supports clearly the party-rigidity thesis for policy priorities (Table 3.7).

The institutionalist hypothesis (i.e. change in legislative role perceptions is linked to movements between positions in the polity) was tested together with the socialisation hypothesis (i.e. legislative roles crystallize in a process of

Table 3.7 Susceptibility to change of role perceptions: comparison between parties (percentages having changed role perceptions, 2003/2004–2007, panel data only)

| | Parties | | | | | |
	CDU/CSU	SPD	FDP	PDS	Greens	All parties
Change of focus	36.4% (n = 151)	37.0% (n = 146)	22.7% (n = 22)	50.0% (n = 74)	26.7% (n = 30)	37.6% (n = 423)
Change of principality	39.7% (n = 156)	41.3% (n = 160)	36.8% (n = 19)	14.9% (n = 74)	21.4% (n = 28)	34.8% (n = 437)

Table 3.8 Determinants of change of legislative role orientations

Independent variables	Change in role orientations	
	...in focus [exp(B)]	...in primacies [exp(B)]
Change in leading party positions[a]	1.07	1.25
Change in local/regional offices[a]	0.93	1.23
Change in leading positions in parliament[a]	0.93	1.38
Newcomer[b]	1.60*	0.68(*)
Parliamentary party group (main effect)[c]	(*)	**
SPD	1.06	1.03
FDP	0.51	0.87
PDS	1.77*	0.25***
B90/Greens	0.69	0.43(*)
Intercept	0.47**	0.61*
Model Chi^2	14.04(*)	29.03***
Prediction success (%)	63.4	65.9
Nagelkerke R^2	0.04	0.09
Number of observ. (*n*)	423	437

Notes
Significance levels: *** sig.<0.001; ** sig.<0.01; * sig.<0.05; (*) sig.<0.10.
a 0 = no change; 1 = change.
b 0 = tenured MP; 1 = newcomer.
c Reference Group: CDU.

post-recruitment socialisation (Davidson 1969; Franklin and Scarrow 1999) and the party-rigidity hypothesis (high organisational and ideological rigidity of parties enforces stability of legislative role perceptions) by a multiple logistical regression model. Institutional mobility was conceptualised using three indicators measuring positional change (mostly related to career mobility) at party level, parliamentary or governmental level, and local or regional level. The socialisation thesis was tested by introducing newcomer-status as an independent variable and the party-rigidity thesis was conceptionalized by treating parliamentary party affiliation (using CDU/CSU MPs as contrast group) as a generic variable. Changes in the focus or primacy of legislative role perceptions were used as dependent variables, which resulted in two logistical regression models for both dimensions of legislative role perceptions.

In Table 3.8, the results of logistical regression analyses show that (career) mobility had no impact on the amount of change of role perceptions in either model. The institutionalist hypothesis can, therefore, be refuted provisionally with regard to changes of the primacy and conception of legislative roles. This has far-reaching implications, because redefinitions of representative roles can hardly be interpreted as part of an ordered process of role gradation if their occurrence is unrelated to mobility between positions in the polity. What we see in our data looks rather like role discontinuity. The socialisation hypothesis is confirmed with regard to focus of representative roles: newcomers show a significantly higher inclination to readjust their role conceptions than tenured

MPs. With regard to readjustments of role primacies, newcomer-status has no significant effect. This difference between both models is plausible, given the fact that policy priorities are moving targets that might be changed circumstantially. Party has a highly significant overall effect on changes of role primacy, indicating that some parties leave more leeway to choose between policy priorities than others. Odds-ratios indicate that MPs of large catch-all parties, such as the SPD, are more volatile in this respect than MPs of smaller parties. The PDS stands out with a highly significant effect. Here MPs define themselves overwhelmingly as 'champions of equality' and tend to adhere to this self-definition over time. A further significant effect for the PDS – although no significant overall effect for party – is also found in the model with change of role conception as dependent variable. Here, PDS MPs are extremely volatile, changing the focus of their representative role frequently during the four-year period between both waves of the GPS. It seems that MPs of the PDS have difficulty finding a focus for their legislative role in the institutional setting of representative democracy, but are very sure about their principal goals as policy-makers. In general we consider the party-rigidity thesis as being confirmed.

Directions of role change

However, the overall fit of both models is weak, and the chi-square of the model with change of focus as dependent variable fails even to attain significance. At this point, the overall findings indicate that – besides clues resulting from previous analyses – the causes of definition and redefinition of legislative roles remain largely unaccounted for. A simple addition of all possible positional movements may, however, be inappropriate for testing the institutionalist hypothesis, while differentiating between directions of change – e.g. into or out of those positions – may reveal a closer relationship. Another reason why it might be premature to refute the institutionalist hypothesis is based on a simple consideration of the process of role taking and role making: role orientations need to be learned. This learning can be conceptualized as a matching process between role orientations of the role taker and the role expectations of significant others (Turner 1979; Turner 1990). The outcome of this process is more contingent than determined, and depends on the assets and positions of the persons involved, as well as on the structural conditions of the interaction. It is obvious that this process needs time before change can be observed. Thus the lack of evidence for an impact of positional change may be overcome by a more intricate measurement of the temporality aspect of positional movements. The following logistical regression model of legislative role taking is, therefore, based on the assumption that positional movements do not lead immediately to change in role orientations but need time to become effective.

While the former models examined change in various facets of representative roles, the forthcoming logistic regression is restricted to an explanation of why some MPs move their focus of representation to representing the whole polity. Role primacy is not examined any further since it seems to be determined primarily by the position of an MPs' party in the cleavage structure and the competition for votes, and is therefore largely unrelated to formal positions in the polity. Neither is the party rigidity-thesis tested, because it refers not to the direction but to the amount of change, which is considered to be diminished by high organizational or ideological rigidity. Therefore, the outcome variable indicates whether a change towards representing the whole polity has occurred between 2003/2004 and 2007 or not, and the population is narrowed to include only those MPs, who claimed in 2003 to represent their party, their voters, or their electoral district. Out of those 201 MPs, 40 per cent had changed between the first and second wave towards representing the whole polity, whereas the remaining 60 per cent either retained their original focus or changed their focus between voters, electoral district and party. Thus, the predominant direction of change is the movement towards representing the whole polity, which makes it the most interesting movement.

Table 3.9 shows the results for some determinants of change. The positional movements not only show whether a position was entered or vacated since 2003, they also indicate whether an MP had occupied a position continuously since 2003. The reference categories comprise always those MPs who neither in 2003 nor in 2007 occupied one of the aforementioned positions. Beside these positional movements, tenure and newcomer-status are included to control for the socialisation hypothesis. Loss of an individual MPs' electoral district is introduced since the mode of election – representing a single-member district (SMD) or having entered parliament via a party list – is assumed to be an important predictor for the choice of MPS' representational focus (see Zittel, Chapter 6 this volume: 108). Hence the loss of ones' own electoral district may lead to readjusting the focus of representation towards the whole polity.

Before the results are presented, we have to draw attention to the fact that the overall number of cases is comparatively low and that some predictors display a heavily skewed distribution (e.g. the amount of MPs who lost their district is just 9 per cent of all 201 MPs under consideration). Therefore we are cautious about refuting results that are insignificant on the conventional levels of 5 and 1 per cent, while on the other hand significant effects indicate highly influential predictors.

The interpretation starts with the most important indicator for the socialisation hypothesis: newcomer-status. Being neophyte in parliament generally increases the probability of change – as shown in the former model – but has no significant influence on the particular change towards representing the whole polity. Furthermore, tenure does not altogether increase the probability of a move towards representing the whole polity. It can be shown, however, that longer serving MPs share this focus more often if we use bivariate data analysis. This contradictory result is explained by other determinants in the model, especially leading positions in parliament and within the MPs' parliamentary party group (PPG). Since MPs who have served more terms are more likely to assume leading positions in parliament, the effect of tenure is explained by the occupation of these positions during a political career. We can demonstrate that tenure – but not newcomer-status – acquires significant influence by excluding

Table 3.9 Logistic regression for change towards representing the whole country (exp(B))

Reference	Indicator	Exp(b)
Tenured MP	Newcomer	2.1
	Tenure (in terms)	1.3
No leading parliamentary position in 2003 and 2007	Continuous in …	2.8[(*)]
	Change in …	1.0
	Exit out …	4.3[*]
No leading PPG position in 2003 and 2007	Continuous in …	1.8
	Change in …	1.1
	Exit out …	2.5
No leading party position at lower levels in 2003 and 2007	Continuous in …	0.8
	Change in …	0.5
	Exit out …	1.5
No local/regional public offices in 2003 and 2007	Continuous in …	0.8
	Change in …	1.5
	Exit out …	0.7
No leading party position at higher levels in 2003 and 2007	Continuous in …	0.3[*]
	Change in …	2.0
	Exit out …	0.4[(*)]
Elected in SMD[1] in 2003 and 2007	Lost SMD	3.4[*]
	Won SMD	0.6
	Not elected in SMD both times	1.4
Nagelkerkes R^2		18.1
Model Chi^2		29.7 (*)
n		201

Notes
Significance levels: *** sig.<0.001; ** sig.<0.01; * sig.<0.05; (*) sig.<0.10.
1 Single-member district.

such positions from the model. Thus, at least for this type of role change, the institutionalist hypothesis and the socialisation hypothesis seem to be inter-locked: socialisation within parliament occurs by and through a career encom-passing different positions.

If we compare the impact of different formal positions, those leading offices in parliament that are not leading positions within the MPs' own PPGs,[7] appear to be closely connected to certain role expectations. Initially, legislators who enter such a position are no more likely to rearrange their focus of representation than their colleagues who are (still) not in such a position. But MPs who occu-pied such a position continuously since at least 2003, or who have left such a position, show an increased probability of adopting a universalistic concept of their representative role, i.e. of defining themselves as representatives of the whole polity. This result reveals a kind of inertia in the role orientations attached to these formal positions and their potential to shape role orientations. MPs just entering parliamentary positions do no adapt immediately to the universalistic role concept, but the longer they hold such a position, the more likely adaptation occurs. The same inertia is responsible for a lag between leaving a formal position and abandoning the associated role orientation. An MP who occupied such a position for a while and who has changed focus towards the whole polity during this time keeps this focus even when resigning from office. This effect is estimated by the increased probability of change towards the whole country among those who have left a leading parliamentary position.

The close link between the mentioned positional movements and the change in focus of representation reflects the clearly articulated expectations that the holders of leading parliamentary offices in Germany that are not leading offices of the PPGs will carry out their office impartially, meaning that holders of those positions should not represent any special constituency – neither their party, nor their voters, nor their electoral district – but the whole country. These expectations are not only legally formalized in the internal rules of procedure[8] but they may also be secured by public scrutiny, since the political opposition will accuse them immediately of any violations against impartiality.

However, a pattern of delayed role adaptation pointing towards the universal focus of representation could also be observed in leading PPG offices.[9] Although the effect is not significant, the direction of the effect is counter-intuitive: leading positions within MPs' own PPGs incline them towards representing the whole polity instead of turning them into representatives of their own party.

The fact that even PPG leaders who may have been seen as representatives of their party in parliament move in the direction of a universalistic concept of representation points toward post-recruitment socialisation in leading offices in parliament. We attribute this impact to the status of parliament as the main representative institution that focuses on the whole polity by dealing daily with issues primarily concerning the whole polity. Universalistic perspectives and general policy choices are required by leading office-holders, whereas backbenchers are supposedly entangled by the demands of particularistic interest representation.

Furthermore, the claim to represent the whole polity focuses not on a singular interest group of the polity but on a range of different, mostly contradictory, often implicit and unarticulated interests. In order to represent the whole polity, MPs are compelled to integrate these different interests and to form them into a coherent political programme representing a maximum of the eligible population. In everyday routines of parliamentary work, the same process of universalistic integration has to be achieved in leading offices in parliament and PPG, although it is not the whole polity but only the MPs' PPG or a committee that has to be integrated. Thus, holding leading office in parliament tends to boost a universalistic self-definition of an MPs' role, because universalism is a normative standard attached to leading positions in parliament.

This explanation is supported by the fact that no trend towards universalistic orientations could be found attached to leading political positions outside of parliament – as is demonstrated by the odds for holding offices in the party organisation or offices in regional or local self-administration. It seems that the level of the institutional contexts in which the leading position is allocated interacts with general expectations towards leading positions. Whereas there is a much higher expectation for a holder of a leading office in parliament to represent the whole polity than for a backbencher, a holder of a leading political position outside parliament is expected to represent his or her institutional affiliation to a party organization or a self-administrative body much more than a member of these institutions who holds no leading position. Leading public and party positions at regional and local level especially seem to increase the sensibility of issues related to these levels and hence inhibit a reorientation towards the whole polity. Only those MPs who recently acquired local public office, or who left a party office at local level, show a stronger inclination to define themselves as representatives of the whole country. Tenure in these offices, therefore, reduces the probability that an MP will shift orientation towards the whole polity and increases the tendency for holding limited foci of representation. While results for offices and positions at lower levels are not statistically significant, incumbents of high-level offices in party organisations show a significantly reduced inclination to define themselves as representatives of the whole polity.

It seems that the higher the position in a given organisation or representative body, the more explicit will be the demand on the focus of the representative role in these contexts: A holder of a leading position in parliament is supposed to represent the whole polity, a party leader has to represent the interest of the party, and occupants of public offices at the regional or local level have to focus on interests at these levels. Thus the level of the institutional context interacts with the position held by individual MPs within these contexts, and both affect their role focus. These observations reveal an obvious source for role conflicts. A large number of MPs who are simultaneously incumbents of higher party positions and leading offices in parliament are thereby confronted with contradictory role expectations.

In a final step of the analysis, the effect of being elected in a single-member district (SMD) as compared to winning a seat via a party list is examined. Earlier studies led us to expect that different modes of election will be associated with different foci of representation. Former results from the GPS also suggest that MPs who entered parliament by winning an SMD are more likely to claim that they represent their own districts, because the focus of their electoral campaigning is shifted towards the electoral district (Pekkanen *et al.* 2006; Zittel and Gschwend 2008). Since the German electoral system is mixed, both types of MPs can be found in almost all parliaments included in our study, resulting in half of the deputies having been elected in SMDs and the other half having been elected via party lists. A preliminary cross-tabulation using the full sample of the GPS shows that one-third of those MPs who acquired their mandate by winning an SMD claim to represent their constituency, while this share amounts to less than 18 per cent of those who entered parliament on the party ticket. We assume therefore, that losing a seat in an SMD and reentering parliament through a party list will lead to a reorientation of parliamentary role perceptions towards a more universalistic focus of representation. We can indeed observe that the small number of MPs in the first wave (2003/2004) who had been elected in an SMD, and subsequently lost their constituency and thus entered parliament via the party list, have a significantly increased likelihood of changing their focus towards the whole polity. In contrast to the change between formal positions mentioned above, this leads to an immediate shift in the focus of representation. Here we have a clue regarding differences in the pace of adaptation between roles related to formalised positions and to roles that are related to informal positions, with occupants of the latter adapting faster. The reason for this may be that the role expectations directed towards MPs elected in SMDs are more obvious and clear than the expectations attached to leading parliamentary positions, since the position of the former is closely related to a well-defined constituency: the electoral district. However, the universalistic focus of representation refers to a heterogeneous and rather abstract constituency, and it needs more time to learn how to integrate conflicting interests in order to represent the whole country.

Conclusion

Our study into self-definitions of the requirements, foci and primacies of representative roles has revealed some of the structuring principles and dynamics shaping processes of legislative role making and role taking. We have shown that legislators choose between varied sets of elements constituting their role perceptions, although there was a strong tendency to favour a universalistic focus of their legislative role and to emphasise personal qualities as role requirements. The choice of role primacies showed a clear preference for presenting oneself as "procreator of wealth" in the first wave of the GPS.

Self-definitions of legislative roles were shaped mainly by representatives' political background, i.e. their party affiliation. There was, however, no significant overall effect of party on the choice of the two modal elements of legislative role perceptions, i.e. "appreciation of respondents' personality" as role requirement and "whole country" as focus of the legislative role. We interpret this result as an indication of a party-transcending integrative function of two dominant modalities of representative roles. Social origin, i.e. family occupational background, had no significant impact on any of the role perceptions considered in our models. This finding indicates that legislative role taking is part of a process of secondary political socialisation that overrides deeper layers of representatives' social identities. The effect of "age" and "tenure" in some models supports this view. However, the impact of other social background variables, such as gender and region of origin, shows that the positioning of MPs in the overall social structure may have an impact on self-definitions of legislative roles if it is functionally linked to legislative recruitment through quota systems or legal procedures of candidate selection.

A longitudinal analysis showed that legislative roles are relatively ephemerous (self-)concepts: Within a period of four years, 62 per cent of the panel members had changed the focus and/or the primacy of their legislative role. In a first step of analysis, we also observed that these changes were unrelated to the number of movements between positions in different layers and sectors of the political system. These initial findings indicated that changes of legislative roles could be at least partially explained by a process of post-recruitment socialisation, which means that changes of role definitions are transitory phenomena. We could also show that changes of role definitions are both limited and directed by party affiliations, meaning that some parties provide their legislators with clearer guidelines than others with regard to the desired focus or primacy of their legislative role. This also suggests that all parties, even if they allow their MPs some freedom in defining their legislative roles, have "favoured" sets of legislative role definitions limiting MPs' freedom of choice. Beside these general conditions, the more intricate analysis showed that the conceptualisation of role change has to consider three intervening variables: time, role conflicts and the type of positions taken in an MPs' positional career.

While the first models were based on a simple count of movements between formal positions, the second model accounted additionally for sequence and timing. This approach revealed a time lag between the acquisition of a (new) position and the associated role change, which explains the poor fit of the first models. The conception of positional change, as used here, considers a "socialisation lag" by allowing for the time-demanding process of mutual adjustments between role actors and their respective role partners. We could also show that these adjustments were structured by formal regulations and stable conditions of the political competition that constrained the scope of outcomes in this process.

Career mobility into leading positions in parliament and higher levels of party hierarchies seems to result in conflicting role expectations, which weakens the effects of positional change. We found evidence that MPs who are faced with contradicting demands after changing positions do not immediately adjust their role orientations to their new status. Diverging role orientations may have weakened the effects of career mobility, because MPs who are faced with contradicting demands after changing positions do not immediately switch their role orientations. Further research should take into account the effects of office-accumulation by analysing sets instead of single positions. These position sets can vary in the coherence of associated role orientations, whereby positional mobility, which increases the homogeneity of the role set, raises the likeliness of role change.

Analyses of the direction of role change have shown that role expectations concerning the focus of representation are more explicit towards the holders of leading offices compared to ordinary MPs, and that they vary with the hierarchical level. The fact that occupants of hierarchically superior offices are significantly limited in their role definitions challenges the interactionistic concept of role making as a bargaining process with a considerable degree of freedom. One would expect that holders of leading offices should typically dispose of assets that allow them to adopt idiosyncratic role orientations resulting in a weaker correlation between positional movements and role change. However, in the case of electoral offices, these assets are granted by selectorates and electorates. The wish for (re-)election seems to impel office-holders to conform to role expectations that are articulated by the (s)electorates attached to the respective electoral office. Considering this mechanism, it becomes plausible that holders of leading offices tend to accumulate different positions because a heterogeneous role set allows them to adopt multiple role orientations (Merton 1957). Representatives who hold simultaneously positions with different or even conflicting role definitions can exploit this situation by increasing the degrees of freedom in their role play.

Our study into the emergence and transformation of representative roles has revealed that role definitions are ephemerous and that role attachments are fluid. There is obviously a wide leeway for actors in the parliamentary arena and their role partners to shape and reshape representative roles in their interactions. However, the freedom to do so is limited. We have shown that the movements of MPs between positions in the polity and the cumulation of positions in the course of their political careers shaped their role definitions in specific ways. Career mobility was the causal antecedent of role change because we found a clear sequence and a "socialization lag" between the former and the latter. In these processes parties are significant in shaping MPs' role definitions and especially important when it comes to acquiring role primacies. Empirical evidence supported therefore the institutionalist, party rigidity and the socialization hypothesis. We could also show that a dynamic view of representative roles adds significantly to their understanding.

Our general conclusion is that representative roles are crucial elements in the interactions between actors in the core arena of representative democracy and in their communications with various audiences. They set normative standards and provide cognitive guidelines that increase the predictability of outcomes in interactions by promoting the concerted behaviour of role partners. The integrative impact of representative roles on the polity as a whole is further enhanced by a widespread and party-transcending tendency towards a universalistic role focus of representation and an individualistic attribution of role requirements to the personal qualities of respondents.

Notes

1 The statement of Hibbing that "internal congressional careers are virtually terra incognita" (Hibbing 1991: 407) can still be expanded to a longitudinal analysis of change in roles, attitudes or the (reported) behaviour of MPs. The few attempts into this territory are restricted to comparisons between cohorts of MPs, between MPs of different legislative terms (Saalfeld 1997), or MPs of different tenure (Andeweg 1997; Scully 2005; Davidson 1969), or use of retrospective questions (Müller and Steininger 2001). Only few studies use panel data (Badura and Reese 1976; Asher 1973; Bell and Price 1975). Most of the mentioned studies focus on processes of institutional socialization in parliament or try to explain aggregate changes by referring to varying political circumstances. Therefore, the combination of panel-data analysis with the approach of explaining change in role orientations by positional movements breaks new ground.

2 The GPS (Best 2009; Best *et al.* 2007; Best and Vogel 2011) is directed by Heinrich Best (University of Jena) and funded by the German Science Foundation in the context of the Collaborative Research Centre "Social Developments following Systemic Change" (SFB 580).

3 Compared to the main sample the panel is unbiased concerning the main variables referred to in the study.

4 Throughout, percentages in brackets refer to the share of respondents agreeing in the 2003/2004 wave of the German Parliamentarians survey. The order of answer categories was changed at random between interviews.

5 Distributions of the role facets differ in varying degree between the three parliamentary levels. These differences are to a large extent the effect of varying group composition between state, federal and European level of parliamentary representation. Therefore, and because we are primarily interested in the *general* mechanisms which link role perceptions to MPs' positions in society and polity we will not take into consideration these level differences.

6 Possible *empirical* variations are not further investigated for reasons of limited space.

7 These positions comprise chairman of the committee, speaker and co-speaker of the house.

8 See *pars pro toto* the informal rules concerning the office of the speaker of the house of the German Bundestag (GOBT §7, 1).

9 These positions comprise the office of the chair, member of the board or manager of the parliamentary party group and member of the executive branch.

References

Andeweg, R.B. (1997) "Role specialisation or role switching", in W.C. Müller and T. Saalfeld (eds.) *Members of Parliament in Western Europe: Roles and Behaviour*, London: Frank Cass.

Asher, H. B. (1973) "The learning of legislative norms", *American Political Science Review*, 67: 499–513.

Badura, B. and Reese, J. (1976) *Jungparlamentarier in Bonn – Ihre Sozialisation im Deutschen Bundestag*, (= problemata, 55), Stuttgart/Bad Cannstatt: Fromann-Holzboog.

Bell, C.G. and Price, C.M. (1975) *The First Term: A Study in Legislative Socialization*, Beverly Hills, CA: Sage.

Best, H. (2007) "Cleavage representation in European parliamentary history", in M. Cotta and H. Best (eds.) *Democratic Representation in Europe*, Oxford: Oxford University Press.

Best, Heinrich (2009): "Associated rivals: Antagonism and cooperation in the German political elite", in: *Comparative Sociology*, 8(3), 428.

Best, Heinrich and Vogel, Lars (2011): Politische Eliten im vereinten Deutschland. Strukturen – Einstellungen – Handlungsbedingungen, in: Lorenz, Astrid (Ed.): *Ostdeutschland und die Sozialwissenschaften. Bilanz und Perspektiven 20 Jahre nach der Wiedervereinigung*, Berlin: Barbara Budrich, p. 122f.

Best, Heinrich, Edinger, Michael, Schmitt, Karl and Vogel, Lars (2007): Zweite Deutsche Abgeordnetenbefragung. Ausgewählte Ergebnisse. Available online in English: http://www.sfb580.uni-jena.de/typo3/index.php?id=287 (accessed November 2011).

Biddle, B.J. (1986) "Recent developments in role theory", *Annual Review of Sociology*, 12: 67–92.

Bourdieu, P. (1990) *The Logic of Practice*, Cambridge: Polity Press.

Davidson, R.H. (1969) *The Role of the Congressman*, New York: Pegasus.

Edinger, L. and Searing, D. (1967) "Social background in elite analysis: A methodological inquiry", *American Political Science Review*, 61: 428–45.

Fenno, R. (1962) "The House Appropriations Committee as a political system", *American Political Science Review*, 56(2): 310–24.

Fenno, R. (1973) *Congressmen in Committees*, Boston, MA: Little, Brown, and Company.

Franklin, M.N. and Scarrow, S.E. (1999) "Making Europeans? The socializing power of the European Parliament", in R. Katz and B. Wessels (eds.) *The European Parliament, the National Parliaments and the European Integration*, Oxford: Oxford University Press.

GOBT, German Bundestag (ed.) "Duties of the President". Rules of Procedure of the German Bundestag. Available online at http://www.bundestag.de/htdocs_e/documents/legal/index.html (accessed 11 November 2010): §7, 1.

Hibbing, J. (1991) "Contours of the modern congressional career", *American Political Science Review*, 85: 405–28.

Kielhorn, A. (2001) "Rollenorientierungen von Abgeordneten in Europa: Eine empirische Analyse von Bestimmungsgründen und Konsequenzen der Repräsentationsrolle von Parlamentariern in elf EU-Ländern", Berlin (Diss.). Available online at http://webdoc.sub.gwdg.de/ebook/diss/2003/fu-berlin/2002/103/indexe.html (accessed 4 April 2009).

Levinson, D.J. (1959) "Role, personality, and social structure in the organizational setting", *Journal of Abnormal and Social Psychology*, 58: 170–80.

Linton, R. (1945) *The Cultural Background of Personality*, New York: Appleton-Century.

Merton, R.K. (1957) "The role-set: Problems in sociological theory", *British Journal of Sociology*, 8: 106–20.

Mughan, A., Box-Steffensmeier, J. and Scully, R. (1997) "Mapping legislative socialization", *European Journal of Political Research*, 33: 93–106.

Müller, W.C. and Steininger, B. (2001) "Veränderungen der Abgeordnetentätigkeit", in: W.C. Müller, J. Marcelo, B. Steininger, M. Dolezal, W.Philipp and S. Preisl-Westphal (eds.) *Die österreichischen Abgeordneten*, Wien: Schriftenreihedes Zentrums für angewandte PolitikforschungBd. 23.

Parsons, T. (1951) *The Social System*, Glencoe, IL: Free Press.

Patzelt, W.J. (1997) "German MPs and their roles", in W.C. Müller and T. Saalfeld (eds.) *Members of Parliament in Western Europe: Roles and Behaviour*, London: Frank Cass.

Pekkanen, R., Nyblade, B., Krauss, E. (2006) "Electoral incentives in mixed-member-systems: Party, posts and zombie politicians in Japan", *American Political Science Review*, 100: 183–93.

Price, K.C. (1985) "Instability in representational role orientation in a state legislature", *Western Political Quarterly*, 38: 162–71.

Putnam, R.D. (1976) *The Comparative Studies of Political Elites*, Englewood Cliff, NJ: Prentice Hall.

Saalfeld, T. (1997) "Professionalisation of parliamentary roles in Germany: An aggregate-level analysis 1949–94", in W.C. Müller and T. Saalfeld (eds.) *Members of Parliament in Western Europe: Roles and Behaviour*, London: Frank Cass.

Schleth, U. (1971) "Once again: Does it pay to study social background in elite analysis?", *Sozialwissenschaftliches Jahrbuch für Politik*, 2: 99–118.

Scully, R. (2005) *Becoming Europeans? Attitudes, Behaviour, and Socialization in the European Parliament*, Oxford: Oxford University Press.

Searing, D.D. (1991) "Roles, rules and rationality in the new institutionalism", *American Political Science Review*, 85, 1: 239–60.

Searing, D.D. (1994) *Westminster's World: Understanding Political Roles*, Cambridge, MA: Harvard University Press.

Strøm, K. (1997) "Rules, reasons and routines: Legislative roles in Parliamentary democracies", in W.C. Müller and T. Saalfeld (eds.) *Members of Parliament in Western Europe: Roles and Behaviour*, London: Frank Cass.

Turner, R.H. (1979) "Strategy for developing an integrated role-theory", *Humboldt Journal of Social Relations*, 7: 123–39.

Turner, R.H. (1990) "Role change", *Annual Review of Sociology*, 16: 87–110.

Turner, R.H. (1998; 1st edn 1962) "Role-taking: Process versus conformity", in A. Rose (ed.) *Human Behavior and Social Processes*, Boston: Houghton Mifflin.

Van Sell, M., Brief, A.P., Schuler, R.S. (1981) "Role conflict and role ambiguity: Integration of the literature and directions for future research", *Human Relations*, 34: 43–71.

Wahlke, J.C., Eulau, H., Buchanan, W. and Fergusson, L.C. (1962) *The Legislative System: Explorations in Legislative Behaviour*, New York: John Wiley and Sons.

Zittel, T. and Gschwend, T. (2008) "Individualised constituency campaigns in mixed-member electoral systems: Candidates in the 2005 German elections", *West European Politics*, 31: 879–1003.

4 The consequences of representatives' role orientations

Attitudes, behaviour, perceptions

Rudy B. Andeweg

> The value of role analysis for most political scientists lies in its potential for improving explanation and prediction of legislative behavior. As yet, this is a potential that remains largely unrealized in practice.
>
> (Jewell 1970: 484)

The concept of roles can be seen as the application of a particular institution's 'logic of appropriateness' (March and Olsen 1989) to the level of individual 'inmates' of that institution: a role orientation is an individual's perception of what is generally expected of her as a holder of her current institutional position. Although roles can have an impact on other variables than an individual's behaviour, for example by attributing meaning to (making sense of) an institution, the primary reason for studying role orientations is that they are supposed to affect behaviour. This is no different in the study of legislative roles. As the pioneers in this field, Wahlke and associates, put it:

> It is important to emphasize the normative aspect of the concept in order that the role of legislator not be confused with the office, or position, of legislator. [...] the concept postulates that legislators are aware of the norms constituting the role and consciously adapt their behavior to them in some fashion.
>
> (Wahlke *et al.* 1962: 8–9)

Thus, 'role theory helps us predict certain general types of response by legislators, given certain stimuli' (Wahlke *et al.* 1962: 20). The purpose of this chapter is to ascertain the extent to which representative roles do indeed help us explain the beliefs, attitudes, and especially the behaviour of MPs in their relationship with the electorate.

Representatives' roles: defining the independent variable

The study of representational roles has been dominated for half of a century by the typology of 'representational style' designed by Eulau and Wahlke (1959).

Following Edmund Burke's famous distinction between representatives as delegates, acting on the instructions of the voters in their constituency, and representatives as trustees, following their own judgment as to what would be in the best interest of the nation as a whole, they defined the role of the representative in terms of focus and style. The focus of representation concerns the proper object of representation (district, nation, or some other interest), and the style of representation refers to the degree of freedom that a representative should observe vis-à-vis the focus of representation (instructed delegate or free agent). It is this concept of 'style' that has become the standard reference for students of representational roles. Eulau and Wahlke saw the two role orientations as the poles of a dimension, and recognized that the role orientations may overlap, allowing representatives to take on the role of 'trustee' or the role of 'delegate' depending on the circumstances. This in-between role orientation was labeled 'politico'. Later, the authors embedded representational roles within a more comprehensive repertoire of legislative roles (pressure-group roles, subject-matter-expert roles, etc.) (Wahlke *et al.* 1962: 14), but it is the trustee–politico–delegate typology that hugely influenced research on legislative roles, also in more recent years (e.g. Converse and Pierce 1986; Katz 1997; Müller and Saalfeld 1997; Judge 1999; Mendez-Lago and Martinez 2002). This persistence is remarkable, given its well-known weaknesses, both theoretically (e.g. Rehfeld 2009), and empirically. Here we focus on the latter.

First, the roles of delegates and trustees are operationalised as a relationship between an individual MP and a geographical constituency, without reference to the existence of cohesive and disciplined political parties (Thomassen 1994). To be fair, Eulau and Wahlke did mention parties, even though parties mattered less in the context of US politics than in Europe, at least at the time of their studies. However, they were not consistent in their treatment of parties. At first they viewed them as a potential focus of representation (Eulau and Wahlke 1959: 745). In this perspective, MPs are either representatives of their constituency or representatives of their party, but not both. Later they identified a 'party role' as a 'purposive role', not as one of the representational roles. In this way, parties influence the norms and expectations with regard to several aspects of legislative behavior, but not with regard to political representation. In their study of political representation in France, Converse and Pierce attempted to solve the problem by transforming the dimension from delegate to trustee into a triangle with the loyal partisan as a third role type (Converse and Pierce 1986: 664–96). In fact, this comes close to Eulau and Wahlke's original solution of treating party as a focus of representation: according to Converse and Pierce the loyal partisan is merely a variety of the delegate role, with the party rather than the constituency as focus. None of these solutions allows for strong parties to structure the way in which MPs interact with their voters.

Second, the distinction between delegates who put instructions from the represented above their own judgment, and trustees, who follow their own judgment rather than that of their constituents, is part of a normative debate, known as the 'mandate–independence controversy'. That debate has not been a fruitful one:

by its very nature, representation implies that the representative cannot be identi-fied completely with the demands of the represented, and neither can the repre-sentative be completely divorced from those demands: at both ends of the dimension from mandate to independence representation ceases to exist, or: 'insofar as the mandate–independence controversy contains a conceptual dispute based on the meaning of representation, both sides are right' (Pitkin 1967: 154). Translated to Eulau and Wahlke's empirical typology, this means that the pure types do not exist:

> if 0.00 means a representative's legislative record which is purely and unyieldingly Burkean, totally without regard for expressed district wishes, and 1.00 reflects a legislative record laid down at every step in response to perceived district instructions, we should be surprised if many political rep-resentatives in legislative bodies could be created much outside the limits of a narrower range, such as .30 to .70, or even .35 to .65.
>
> (Converse and Pierce 1986: 497)

Thus, all representatives can be classified as politicos, for whom 'it depends' whether priority is given to the voters' views or to the MP's own judgment. In the Netherlands at least, this indeterminate role orientation seems to be in the ascendancy.

From Table 4.1 it is clear that the Burkean trustee is gradually losing ground in the Dutch parliament, from 71 per cent in 1972 to 40 per cent in 2001 with a modest recovery to 49 per cent in 2006. The category of politicos has benefited more from this decline than the delegates. By 2001 four out of ten Dutch MPs answered that 'it depends' whether representatives should follow their party's voters or their own opinions in case these two conflict, followed by a decrease to a still sizeable third in 2006. Regardless of what this rise of the politico implies about the validity of the typology, it bodes ill for its explanatory power as it is hard to hypothesize what behaviour can be predicted from the answer 'it depends'.

For these reasons, it may be useful to study not just the behavioural conse-quences of the Eulau–Wahlke typology, but to include an alternative set of rep-resentational role orientations in the analysis. For this we turn to Esaiasson and Holmberg (1996). They contrast the studies of representation originating in the US with its relatively weak political parties, with representation in political

Table 4.1 The Eulau–Wahlke typology of representational style in the Dutch Parliament (%)

	1972	1979	1990	2001	2006
Delegates ('follow party voters')	7	7	10	21	19
Politicos ('it depends')	22	29	34	40	32
Trustees ('follow own judgment')	71	64	56	40	49
Totals	*100*	*100*	*100*	*100*	*100*
N	141	129	130	129	104

systems that are dominated by strong parties. There, they argue, the Responsible Party Model is more pertinent. This model also originated in the US (APSA, 1950), but more as a proposal for political reform than as a description of the reality of representation in the US. In the Responsible Party Model, various parties put clearly distinct election manifestos to the voters; at elections voters opt for the party with the manifesto that they agree with most; depending on the proportion of the vote received, parties receive a mandate for implementing the policies in their manifesto in the following parliamentary term. For Esaiasson and Holmberg, the essential difference is not so much the existence of strong parties in itself, but the consequence. With strong parties, MPs do not seek to aggregate the exogenous preferences of their constituents ('representation run from below'), but they seek a mandate from their constituents for the preferences of their party ('representation run from above'):

> A run-from-below representational model stresses the positive connections between the policy preferences of citizens and the actions taken by their government. This view of how democracy functions [...] emphasizes gov-ernmental responsiveness. [...] The key characteristics of a democratic system, according to elitist run-from-above representational models, are accountability and leadership.
>
> (Esaiasson and Holmberg 1996: 5)

Esaiasson and Holmberg do not present a typology of representational roles – they actually revert to Eulau and Wahlke's typology for that purpose – but their two types of representation can easily be translated into two distinct role orienta-tions that MPs may embrace.[1]

Whatever its theoretical merits, for this typology of role orientations too, the proof of the pudding is in the eating. In this chapter we shall compare the behav-ioural consequences of both typologies.

The consequences: defining the dependent variable

Although the emphasis in the study of representational roles lies more on their occurrence and their causes than on their consequences, there has been some research into their impact on legislative behaviour, primarily in the 1970s. Need-less to say, these studies used the Eulau–Wahlke typology as the independent vari-able. Most of these studies have employed the ultimate legislative behaviour, roll-call voting, as the dependent variable. The oldest of these studies, by Sorauf (1963), found only small differences between role orientations, and those differ-ences were contrary to what would be expected: Pennsylvania legislators with a trustee orientation (inclined to put their own judgment above anything else) toed the party line more consistently than legislators with a delegate orientation (inclined to put their voters' preferences above anything else). Also counter-intuitively, Friesema and Hedlund (1974) reported that delegates are not more likely to vote according to their perceptions of their constituents' view than are trustees. In the same vein, Gross (1978) found that the correlation between perceived constituency opinion and roll-call voting in the US Congress was exactly as strong for trustees as it was for delegates, and that the path from constituency opinion to roll-call voting ran slightly more often through the perception of constituency opinion for trustees than for delegates. On the other hand, Kuklinski *et al.* assert that the roll-call votes by delegates were slightly more representative of constituency prefer-ences than those by trustees provided that the issue at stake was a salient one (Kuklinski and Elling 1977), or that constituents provide consistent cues regarding district preferences (McCrone and Kuklinski 1979). All we can say on the basis of the literature is that the evidence is inconclusive and that the correlations are rather weak. As Searing put it: 'Definitely disappointing' (Searing 1994: 12).

However, linking parliamentary roles to roll-call votes is probably too tall an order. First, both delegates and trustees have to vote on a host of issues: too many for a trustee to develop her own considered opinion about each and every-one of these issues (and thus forcing her to rely on outside cues), and including many on which a delegate's constituency does not hold strong views (forcing him to either develop his own opinion or to look elsewhere for cues). The result is that the distinction between a delegate's and a trustee's roll-call votes is blurred (Jewell 1970). Second, all studies mentioned above rely on data collected in the US, with its unique separation of powers and weakly developed parlia-mentary parties. In parliamentary systems, in which the government's survival is at stake in every parliamentary vote, and where political parties tend to be cohe-sive and disciplined, roll-call votes are even less promising aspects of an indi-vidual MP's behaviour to relate to his or her role orientation.

Hence, this study will look at the impact of parliamentary roles on behaviour other than parliamentary votes. As such, it adds to previous studies that have, for example, analysed representatives' efforts to find out what their voters' prefer-ences are. Both Hedlund and Friesema (1972), and Erikson *et al.* (1975) observed that trustees gave more accurate assessments of constituency opinion than delegates did. Gross (1978), found only minimal differences between trus-tees and delegates in the importance attached to consulting individuals and groups in the district, but a clearer difference when it comes to their efforts to find out district opinion. On the other hand, in one of the few studies done in Europe (i.e. on MEPs), Katz (1997) reports that delegates ('agents' in his termi-nology) report receiving more mail, and contacting ordinary citizens and groups more frequently, than do trustees, but the correlations are generally weak. Although the conclusion that these results 'seem to be very damaging to those who argue that a legislator's behaviour is systematically influenced by his repre-sentative style' (Gross 1978: 369) may be too strong, it is worrying that the impact of representational roles is less evident not only for roll-call voting, but also for forms of behaviour that are tied more directly to political representation.

Political representation is about the relationship between elected representa-tives and the electorate or citizenry. In this study I shall therefore look at MPs' attitudes about citizens, at MPs' interactions with citizens and social groups, as well as their activity on behalf of these citizens and social groups, and at MPs' perceptions of the political preferences of citizens. I do not pretend that this is an exhaustive list of representational attitudes, behaviour, and cognitions, but it provides a useful sample to assess the explanatory power of the two typologies of representational roles. Both role typologies used in this study contain a more elitist role orientation (trustee, representation-from-above) and a more populist role orientation (delegate, representation-from-below). The general expectation driving the analysis in this chapter is that, in comparison with MPs with a more populist role orientation, relatively elitist MPs have more negative attitudes about ordinary citizens, invest less in contacts with citizens and social groups, are less active in approaching the government on behalf of citizens and groups, and have less accurate perceptions of what their voters want.

Data

We shall make use of the Dutch Parliamentary Studies (DPS), in which (nearly all) members of the Dutch Second Chamber of Parliament have been interviewed in 1968, 1972, 1979, 1990, 2001, and 2006. Both open and closed questions have been used in these oral interviews. In 2001 and 2006, all interviews have been recorded so that we can also use the full answers or comments of the MPs to closed questions. The average response rate was 85 per cent of the 150 MPs. In this paper we concentrate on the two most recent studies as they allow us to compare the two typologies of representational role orientations.

The Eulau–Wahlke role orientations were measured by the question:

- Supposing that an MP thinks that most of his party's voters have an opinion on a particular issue that is different from his own, what should he do? Should his parliamentary vote be in accordance with the opinion of his party's voters, or in accordance with his own opinion?

Note that this question wording deviates from the question that is usually employed to tap these role orientations: no mention is made of a constituency for the simple reason that for all practical purposes geographical districts have no importance in the Dutch electoral system. Instead, the question refers to the people who voted for the MP's party. The distribution of MPs has already been presented in Table 4.1.

The role orientations based on the Esaiasson–Holmberg modes of representation were measured by the question:

- In their relationship with their voters, politicians may emphasize different aspects. Which of these aspects do you think is most important? (a) translating the political views of citizens into policy as accurately as possible; (b) seeking support from the voters for the political views of their own party.

This question was asked only in the 2001 and 2006 studies. The distribution of MPs is presented in Table 4.2.

Table 4.2 Esaiasson–Holmberg role orientations in the Dutch parliament (%)

Most important direction of representation:

	2001	2006
From below	33	34
From above	67	66
N	126	102

Other than the distribution of the Eulau–Wahlke role orientations, the distribution of Esaiasson–Holmberg role orientations remained stable over the five-year period between the two studies despite considerable political upheaval in Dutch politics (the rise of populist parties, the murders of politician Pim Fortuyn and film-maker Theo van Gogh, considerable electoral volatility and cabinet instability). The two typologies are different, but not entirely unrelated: MPs who can be classified as trustees are slightly more inclined than delegates to see representation from above as more important, especially in 2006 (Cramer's V is 0.146 but insignificant in 2001, and 0.246 with $p = 0.022$ in 2006).

Turning to the dependent variables in this study, we have selected political cynicism to measure the MPs' attitudes about citizens. Political cynicism about politicians on the part of the voters has attracted considerable interest from political scientists. However, political cynicism of politicians about citizens has rarely been studied. The recent Dutch Parliamentary Studies include three questions that may serve as indicators of this type of cynicism among representatives:

- Would you please indicate whether you agree strongly, agree, neither agree nor disagree, disagree, or disagree strongly with the following propositions:

    a   Most citizens pay more attention to their own interests than to the general interest.

    b   Although they should know better, most citizens demand too much of politicians.

    c   Many who vote for my party do not have clear policy preferences.

For MPs' interactions with citizens and social groups, we used a question, only asked in the 2001 study, about the frequency of contacts:

- In your function as a member of parliament, in the past year, how often have you had contact with:

    a   Individual citizens
    b   Regional organizations
    c   Youth organizations
    d   Elderly organizations
    e   Trade unions
    f   Employers' organizations

g   Women's organizations
h   Farmers' organizations
i   Minority organizations
j   Religious organizations?

MPs were asked whether they had such contacts hardly ever/never, several times a year, several times a month, or several times a week. I recoded these nominal categories into annual frequencies of 0, 1, 12, and 52 respectively, which makes it possible to calculate an average frequency per group of MPs sharing the same role orientation. Note that the resulting figures underestimate the real frequency of such contacts: 'hardly ever/never' may be more than 0, and several times a week is more than 52. Also note, however, that it is self-reported frequency of contacts that is measured, not the interactions themselves. This opens up the possibility of MPs giving socially desirable answers, and what they consider socially desirable may depend on their role orientation. Although this possibility cannot be dismissed entirely, the risk of contamination seems small, as the relevant questions were not adjacent in the questionnaire.

Much later in the interview (also in 2001), MPs were asked about the frequency of interactions with government officials on behalf of citizens and social groups:

- How often in the last year have you yourself had contact with ministers or civil servants with respect to:

    a   the problems of individual voters who have turned to you for help
    b   views which you personally feel are important
    c   the views of your own party
    d   the interests of your own region
    e   the views and interests of young people
    f   the views and interests of the elderly
    g   the views and interests of employees
    h   the views and interests of trade and industry
    i   the views and interests of women
    j   the views and interests of farmers
    k   the views and interests of cultural minorities
    l   the views and interests of certain religious groups?

Note that the list of views and interests that are represented in contacts with the government corresponds with the list of contacts with citizens and social groups, with two additions: an MP's personal views and an MP's party's views. The answering categories were also similar, and recoded similarly to permit the calculation of (underestimated) average frequencies of contacts.

The two questions on frequency of contact were not included in the questionnaire for the 2006 study. However, both in 2001 and in 2006 MPs were asked about their time investment, broken down into several types of activities:

- How much time do you spend a week on average on your parliamentary work (not counting the recess period)?

- And how can this time be broken down? Could you indicate on this form
how many hours you spend on average a week on each of the activities
mentioned in it (not counting the recess period)?

    ...

    e   Activities within the party
    f   Contacts with individual citizens
    g   Maintaining contact with social organizations.

For our purposes the number of hours spent on intra-parliamentary activities
(preparing for and attending committee meetings, etc.) is not relevant.

Finally, to assess the accuracy of MPs' perceptions of the political preferences of their party's voters', left–right position was selected as an overall indicator of political preference. In the Netherlands, the left–right scale is widely
used, but it is not given the same interpretation by everyone. Some religious
respondents still see it as meaning 'secular versus religious', rather than as 'state
interventionist versus market oriented'. In our analysis this disadvantage is miti-
gated somewhat by using the scale only to compare MPs' perceptions and
voters' positions within the same party. In the Parliamentary Studies of 2001 and
of 2006, MPs were asked:

- It is often said of political views that they are left-wing or right-wing. On
this card you can see a line that runs from far left to far right.
    Where would you place the voters of your party?

We compare these results with the actual self-placement of these parties' voters on
the left–right scale in the nearest Dutch Parliamentary Election Studies (DPES), in
2002 and 2006. In 2006 exactly the same (11-point) scale was used in both the Parliamentary Study and the Election Study, and the interviews with MPs were held
only weeks before the voter survey went into the field. The comparison between the
2001 interviews with MPs and the 2002 Election Study is complicated by the longer
time lag (nearly a year), but also by the fact that the DPES employed an 11-point
scale (1–11), and the DPS used a seven-point scale (1–7). We converted the
11-point scale into a seven-point scale to make the mean positions comparable.[2]

Cynicism about citizens

The role orientation of a delegate is premised on the idea that voters have exogenous preferences that are well worth being translated into public policy, whereas
the idea of a trustee orientation is that voters either have no clear opinions or pay
insufficient attention to the general interest. Similarly, we expect MPs who value
representation from below to have a less cynical attitude vis-à-vis their voters
than MPs who attach more importance to representation from above. In order to
give an overview, Table 4.3 only shows the percentages of MPs who agree or
completely agree with the cynical statements (and does not show the percentages
who completely disagree, disagree, and who neither agree nor disagree).

With the exception of the statement about over-demanding citizens in the 2001 study, we see predominantly cynical reactions to the propositions about self-interested and over-demanding citizens, whereas there is widespread agreement among MPs that their voters do have clear policy preferences. However, from this table it would seem that our expectations with regard to the effects of role orientations are not borne out. Only one statement in one year shows a significant association with the Eulau–Wahlke typology: 'voters have no clear preferences' in 2001 (Chi-squared$=9.71$ with 4 df, n$=129$, $p=0.046$), and that association is in the expected direction. As the Dutch Parliamentary Studies aimed to interview the entire population of MPs, and not a random sample, tests of statistical significance may be deemed inappropriate, and any difference in percentages may be considered real. The fact remains, however, that the differences tend to be small, especially in the 2006 study. Moreover, the differences between role types are mostly contrary to what was expected. In general, politicos tend to be least cynical about voters, and delegates are most cynical. Delegates are most inclined to see citizens as self-interested, over-demanding, and (with the 2001 exception just mentioned) lacking clear preferences. In the meantime, the alternative Esaiasson–Holmberg role typology does not seem to fare better. There are no significant associations with the cynical propositions, the differences are small, and also in a direction opposite from what were expected: MPs who believe representation from below to be most important are more cynical than MPs who attach more importance to representation from above.

It could be argued that the expectation that MPs with more elitist role orientations will exhibit most cynicism about voters is naïve. After all, trustees need not engage in interactions with their voters at all, and representatives-from-above only try to sell their party's policies to the voters and need not try to find out what the policy preferences of these voters are. As a result, they need not encounter the self-interest, the inflated demands, or the lack of clear preferences that may frustrate those MPs who do engage with their voters: the delegates and the representatives-from-below. From this alternative perspective, both role typologies live up to the expectations, with the only complaint being that the inter-role differences in cynicism tend to be small.

Table 4.3 MPs' cynicism by role orientation (% (completely) agree)

		Delegate	Politico	Trustee	From below	From above	All MPs
Citizens are only	2001	63	45	45	57	46	49
self-interested	2006	75	64	74	82	70	72
Citizens are over-	2001	48	24	33	33	31	31
demanding	2006	65	55	61	68	58	61
Voters have no clear	2001	4	2	10	10	4	5
preferences	2006	10	6	4	6	5	6

Contacting civil society

As mentioned above, the behaviours of representatives (other than roll-call voting) that have been studied most often are the efforts they put into finding out what the preferences of their constituents are. The expectation is that delegates display a higher frequency of such contacts than do politicos or trustees, and that bottom-up representatives likewise have higher contacting frequencies than top-down representatives. Please recall that the average annual frequencies reported in Table 4.4 are underestimations.

From Table 4.4 it is clear that MPs have by far the most frequent contacts with individual citizens, with regional organizations at a respectable distance in second place. This is interesting in itself given the fact that the Dutch electoral system is based on a single 150-member district (Dutch MPs do not have a territorial constituency), and constituency work, surgeries, etc. are unknown in the Netherlands (Cf. Thomassen and Andeweg 2004).

A simple analysis of variance shows no significant F-coefficients for the associations between the Eulau–Wahlke typology and the interactions with citizens and various social groups. The differences between the role orientations are small, but surprisingly delegates show lower average contacting frequencies than politicos and trustees (these latter two role orientations show no consistent differences). The alternative typology based on Esaiasson and Holmberg fares better: an analysis of variance produces significant F-coefficients for most contacts (the exceptions being contacts with individual citizens, trade unions, and employers' associations), ranging from 3.8 for contacts with religious organizations to 11.9 for regional organizations. Leaving statistical significance aside, all differences are as expected: MPs who attach more importance to translating the views of the citizens into policy than to seeking citizen support for their party's views have consistently higher contacting frequencies: an average 48 contacts with citizens per year compared to 42 for representatives from above, 19 contacts with regional organizations against 9, etc.

Table 4.4 Average annual frequency of contact with civil society per year by role orientation (2001)

	Delegate	Politico	Trustee	From below	From above	All MPs
Individual citizens	42.4	45.5	44.9	48.1	42.2	44.4
Regional orgs	9.3	14.1	11.7	19.4	8.8	12.2
Youth orgs	2.5	5.3	4.9	7.7	3.2	4.6
Elderly orgs	1.8	3.1	3.5	5.2	1.6	2.9
Trade unions	3.4	7.1	4.3	5.5	4.5	5.3
Employers orgs	3.9	7.2	4.4	5.3	5.3	5.5
Women's orgs	1.8	2.2	2.4	4.4	1.2	2.1
Farmers orgs	2.1	1.3	3.2	4.4	1.3	2.2
Minority orgs	3.5	3.6	4.2	6.1	2.6	3.7
Religious orgs	0.4	1.6	3.1	3.9	1.3	2.0

Turning to the frequency of interactions with government officials in order to represent particular views or interests, we expect that delegates have such contacts on behalf of civil society more frequently than trustees, while the latter have more frequent contacts to advocate their personal preferences. The same expectation applies to bottom-up representatives versus top-down representatives. MPs with this latter role orientation (seeking a mandate for the views of their party) are also expected to contact ministers or civil servants more frequently representing their party's views.

As shown in Table 4.5, contacts with ministers and their departments are considerably less frequent than those with civil society, and the inclusion of such contacts on behalf of party or personal preferences relegates contacts on behalf of the problems of individual citizens to third place. As expected, delegates have contacts on behalf of individual citizens more often than trustees, whereas trustees more often have contacts about their personal views (the only significant F-coefficient in Table 4.5!), but other than that the pattern is inconsistent. The distinction between representation from below and representation from above does not produce any significant associations with interactions with government officials, indicating that the differences between role orientations tend to be small, but the pattern of contacting frequencies is much more consistent with top-down representatives displaying higher frequencies only when their own party's or their personal views were concerned.

Information on contacts with or on behalf of civil society is lacking for 2006. Fortunately, the results are confirmed by the MPs' allocation of time to various activities for which we have information for 2006 as well. MPs report average working weeks of 65 hours (in 2001) and 64 hours (in 2006). They were asked how many of these hours were devoted to a number of activities inside parliament (committee work, plenary sessions, parliamentary party meetings, etc.), but also activities outside the parliament: activities within their political party,

Table 4.5 Average annual frequency of contact per year with ministers or civil servants regarding ... by role orientation (2001)

Views/interests of	Delegate	Politico	Trustee	From below	From above	All MPs
MP him-/herself	7.1	3.9	9.4	4.0	7.6	6.5
MP's party	9.9	8.4	9.8	8.9	9.0	9.4
Individual citizens	6.2	1.8	4.0	3.9	3.5	3.5
Region	1.2	0.6	2.5	2.6	1.2	1.6
Youth	1.5	0.6	1.5	2.2	0.7	1.1
Elderly	0.9	0.5	1.4	1.8	0.7	1.0
Employees	3.0	0.9	1.8	1.8	1.8	1.7
Trade and industry	3.4	0.9	1.4	2.4	1.5	1.7
Women	1.7	0.6	1.7	2.0	1.0	1.2
Farmers	5.5	1.3	1.8	3.8	2.0	2.4
Minorities	3.3	0.8	1.5	2.5	1.2	1.5
Religious groups	0.7	0.1	1.2	1.5	0.3	0.7

contacts with individual citizens, and contacts with social organizations. We expect delegates to spend more time on contacts with citizens and social organizations than politicos and trustees, whereas the hours allocated to party activities should not show important differences. Representatives giving priority to representation from above may spend more time on party activities than bottom-up representatives, whereas the latter give more hours to individual citizens and social organizations.

The results for the Eulau–Wahlke typology are mixed, as shown in Table 4.6. In both years, delegates allocate more hours to citizens than do trustees or politicos, but the latter two invest more time in contacts with social organizations. An analysis of variance reveals no significant F-coefficients. As with the data on contacting frequencies, however, the results for the distinction between representation from above and from below are unequivocal: top-down representatives spend more time in their party while bottom-up representatives allocate more time to citizens and social organizations. However, the evidence for behavioural consequences of the role typology lies primarily in the consistency of the pattern: the differences are relatively small, in particular in 2006, and an analysis of variance shows a significant F-coefficient only for contacting individual citizens in 2001 ($F = 7.2, p = 0.009$).

Knowing what their voters want

As mentioned above, some older US studies looked into the relationship between role orientation and correctly gauging the preferences of constituents. Just like these studies, I expect delegates to give more accurate assessments than politicos or trustees. I also expect bottom-up representatives to perceive voter opinion more accurately than top-down representatives. If representation is to serve the transformation of exogenous voter preferences into public policy, the voter preferences have to be perceived accurately by MPs. Our test is not very demanding: we do not demand that MPs accurately perceive their voters' preferences on a particular policy's details, but we merely expect them to know what general direction their party's voters prefer in public policy, as measured on a left–right dimension.

Table 4.6 Average time investment in representational activities (hours per week) by role orientation

		Delegate	Politico	Trustee	From below	From above	All MPs
Activities within own party	2001	6.3	6.1	8.9	5.9	7.6	7.2
	2006	6.9	6.4	7.5	6.5	7.1	7.0
Contacts with individual citizens	2001	6.6	5.7	5.9	7.7	5.4	6.0
	2006	9.8	9.2	7.9	9.2	8.4	8.6
Contacts with social organizations	2001	6.5	7.4	7.5	8.4	6.7	7.3
	2006	6.3	8.0	8.0	9.0	7.4	7.7

The figures presented in Table 4.7 refer only to the three largest parties, the christian democrat CDA, the social democrat PvdA, and the conservative liberal VVD, as these are the only parties for which we have more than one MP in each cell. Because of the breakdown of the table both by party and by role orientation, the number of MPs involved in each cell is small. The figures represent the average misperception of their own voters' average position by MPs with a particular role orientation in a particular party. A 'plus' sign indicates that the MPs perceive their voters to be more right-wing than they actually are, and a 'minus' sign indicates the opposite, but the number following the sign is all that matters in terms of perception accuracy. The bottom row gives the average misperception across parties, regardless of the direction of the misperception. In general, MPs think that their voters are more right-wing than they are (with CDA in 2006 and VVD in 2001 as exceptions), but it is more striking how accurate MPs are about their voters' average position: in 2001 the biggest misperception was 0.43 on a seven-point scale; in 2006 it was 0.63 on an 11-point scale.

In 2001 the average delegate was marginally more accurate than the average politico or trustee, but this is primarily due to the difference between conservative–liberal delegates and trustees/politicos. In 2006 delegates are as accurate as trustees, with politicos least accurate, and this year only Christian Democrat delegates are clearly more accurate. In view of their greater efforts in contacts with and on behalf of citizens (see the preceding section of this chapter), it is surprising to note that MPs who see translating the views of citizens into policy as most important misperceive their voters' wishes to a greater extent than MPs who find seeking citizen support for their party's views most important. Only bottom-up representatives from CDA in 2001 have more accurate perceptions than their top-down colleagues. The difference is clearest in 2006, when the average top-down representative misperceived his or her party's voters by a negligible amount (0.04 point on an 11-point scale) while the average bottom-up representative was 0.41 points off the mark. A potential explanation for this paradoxical finding would be that the misperceptions by representatives-from-below are actually caused by their greater effort to contact individuals and social groups: inevitably they meet a biased sample of citizens, as those with a grievance, and

Table 4.7 MPs' misperception of their party's voters on a left–right scale by role orientation

		Delegate	Politico	Trustee	From below	From above
CDA	2001	+0.11	+0.22	+0.09	+0.08	+0.22
	2006	−0.13	−0.63	−0.17	−0.38	−0.02
PvdA	2001	+0.17	+0.01	+0.21	+0.31	+0.02
	2006	+0.15	+0.59	+0.14	+0.46	−0.03
VVD	2001	+0.27	−0.43	−0.53	−0.26	−0.22
	2006	+0.11	−0.22	+0.11	+0.36	+0.11
Average	2001	0.18	0.21	0.2	0.19	0.12
	2006	0.14	0.56	0.14	0.41	0.04

with sufficient skills and resources, are more likely to seek out MPs. Top-down representatives on the other hand, probably base their perceptions more on secondary sources such as opinion polls, which are presumably less biased.

Discussion

The older American studies failed to establish the existence of a clear impact of parliamentary roles on parliamentary behaviour. We sought to remedy that situation by looking at other behaviour than roll-call voting (cynicism about voters, interactions with and on behalf of voters, and accuracy of perceptions of voter preferences), in another political system (a parliamentary system with strong political parties), and by including another typology of representational roles in the analysis besides the Eulau–Wahlke typology (i.e. Esaiasson and Holmberg's distinction between representation run from below and representation run from above). This study confirms the impression from the earlier studies that the Eulau–Wahlke typology does not seem to have a clear and consistent impact on MPs attitudes and behaviour, at least not in the hypothesized direction. The fact that delegates tend to be more cynical about their voters than trustees, may still be discounted if one accepts that they have become more cynical because of their initial idealized view of citizens. But the fact that delegates have less frequent contact with individual citizens and with many social organizations runs counter to expectations. The evidence with regard to contacting the government on behalf of citizens and social groups, and on time investment in contacting citizens and social organizations is mixed: in some years or with respect to some social groups, delegates conform to the expectations, in other cases they do not. Delegates are about as accurate as trustees are in their perception of their voters' position on a left–right scale.

However, this should not be interpreted as meaning that moving beyond roll-call analysis and looking at other behaviours and beliefs is no improvement. The problem appears to lie with the Eulau–Wahlke role orientations rather than with the operationalisation of the dependent variable, because the alternative role typology does produce more consequences, in particular with regard to actual behaviour: bottom-up representatives consistently have more frequent contacts with individual citizens and with organizations representing civil society, they spend more time on these contacts, and they have more frequent contacts with ministers or their officials to discuss the problems of individual citizens. MPs who value representation from above have more frequent contacts with the government to discuss their personal views or those of their party, and they spend more time on party activities. This expected behavioural consequence may even help explain two consequences that were not expected initially: representatives from below see citizens as more self-interested, over-demanding and lacking clear political preferences than representatives from above, and they are more prone to misperceive the political position of their party's voters than representatives from above. The more frequent interactions with a necessarily biased sample of citizens may well produce both the higher levels of cynicism and misperception among representatives from below.

The fact that the bottom-up/top-down distinction performed better than the delegate/trustee distinction, in particular when it comes to explaining actual behaviour, makes clear that it is premature to discard the utility of parliamentary roles as explanatory variables altogether. However, the fact that the differences between MPs with different role orientations tend to be relatively small also makes clear that there is still considerable room for improvement. I suggest two alternative ways forward, one with regard to the operationalization of parliamentary roles, and one with regard to the way we analyse their impact on MPs' behaviour and beliefs.

First, Searing argues for a radically different approach to parliamentary roles in order to improve their explanatory power. The role orientations that have been used as the independent variables in this and in previous studies are deduced from theory; they are 'constructs that existed in the minds of many social scientists rather than in the minds of many of the politicians we studied' (Searing 1994: 13). Instead, he advocates a more inductive approach: 'by directing our concepts and measures toward roles as politicians themselves conceive of them, we will be in the best possible position to explain the behaviour that is inherent in such roles' (Searing 1994: 14). This quote illustrates one of the risks of this inductive approach: if a particular behaviour is 'inherent' in a particular role orientation, can we still see the role as the determinant of the behaviour, or are we involved in circular reasoning, with roles induced from behaviour used to explain that same behaviour? This would certainly increase the explanatory power of our roles, but the analysis would rest on a fallacy quite similar to that of rational choice theorists who rely on 'revealed preferences' to show how consistent the strategies chosen by political actors are with their preferences.

A second way forward is to stop equating MPs with a specific role. I have argued elsewhere that it is a gross oversimplification to classify MPs on the basis of a single role orientation, just as odd as classifying great actors as either 'Hamlets', 'Uncle Vanyas' or 'Algy Moncrieffs' (Andeweg 1997). In that sense, the growing proportion of Dutch MPs who answer that 'it depends' when asked about their representational style probably have it right: roles come with institutional positions, but institutions are not monolithic. In different situations, or with regard to different types of issues, different aspects of an institution become relevant, and different role orientations become salient. In the field of executive–legislative relations, for example, Dutch MPs primarily play the role of loyal party soldier, but in the context of a parliamentary inquiry that partisan role seems to be considerably less relevant. Unfortunately, no data is yet available on possible switching between representative roles, but that possibility has always been recognized in the literature. Wahlke *et al.* warned that 'even logically contradictory role orientations may be held without the experience of conflict. The legislator may take roles seriatim, one role in one connection but not in another, without any feeling that a problem of consistency is involved' (Wahlke *et al.* 1962: 384), and Miller and Stokes suggested that 'No single generalised configuration of attitudes and perceptions links Representative with constituency but several distinct patterns, and which of them is invoked depends very much on the issue involved' (Miller and Stokes 1963: 56). This part of early representational role theory has generally been ignored in empirical studies.

The sometimes inconsistent patterns that we found in our Dutch data may be the result of MPs being 'framed' differently (for example by the policy issue they were just working on just before the interview) when answering our questions. The 2006 Dutch Parliamentary Study contains interviews with 24 MPs who had also been interviewed in the 2001 Parliamentary Study. Of these 24 MPs, 11 (46 per cent) gave identical answers to the question we used to operationalize the Eulau–Wahlke role typology. None of the MPs who switched roles in this five-year period exchanged a trustee role for a delegate role or vice versa: all transformations involved the in-between role of the politico. The Esaiasson–Holmberg typology does not contain an intermediate category. Here the number of MPs have gave the same answer in 2001 and in 2006 is higher: 15 (63 per cent), but it is interesting to note that half of the role-switchers could not or would not choose between the two role orientations in one of the studies. These patterns seem to tell us that the answers to our questions about representational roles are not without reliability (given both the substantial number of consistent answers and the very low numbers of clearly contradictory answers), but that for many MPs the context of the two interviews was sufficiently different to make them hesitate in at least one of the interviews.

The study of role switching and its impact on parliamentary behaviour will not be easy as it involves measuring an MP's role orientations in different contexts (different issues, different settings (committee meetings, parliamentary party meetings, constituency work, etc.), and at different times), necessitating more than a simple single interview. But it may very well provide the key to solving the current weaknesses in linking parliamentary roles to behaviour, for example allowing an MP to be a 'representative from below' in constituency work, or when dealing with petitions, but a 'representative from above' when planning party strategy, or sitting on the Committee on Foreign Affairs. This more realistic approach will relate context-specific roles to behaviour in that same context, rather than assuming that one role fits all contexts.

Notes

1 Elsewhere I have argued that Esaiasson and Holmberg's contribution is to emphasize the direction of the interactions between voters and representatives (bottom-up or top-down), but that their model does not distinguish between an ex-ante mandate and ex-post accountability. For that reason I have amended their model to also distinguish between prospective and retrospective interactions (See Andeweg 2003; Andeweg and Thomassen 2005). However, the behavioural data needed to test for the impact of this ex-ante/ex-post dimension is not available. For that reason I confine myself in this chapter to the from-above/from-below dimension.

2 This was done by using the formula: $y = a + bx$ where 1 must equal 1 and 11 must equal 7, hence $0.4 + 0.6x$ (see Irwin and Thomassen 1975: 417–18, fn 10).

References

Andeweg, R.B. (1997) 'Role specialisation or role switching? Dutch MPs between electorate and executive', *Journal of Legislative Studies*, 3: 110–27.

Andeweg, R.B. (2003) 'Beyond Representativeness? Trends in political representation',
European Review, 11: 147–61.

Andeweg, R.B. and Thomassen, J.J.A. (2005) 'Modes of representation: Toward a new
typology', *Legislative Studies Quarterly*, 30: 507–28.

APSA (1950) *Toward a More Responsible Two-Party System*, Washington, D.C.: American Political Science Association.

Converse, Ph.E. and Pierce, R. (1986) *Political Representation in France*, Cambridge, MA:
Belknap.

Erikson, R.S., Luttbeg, N.R. and Holloway, W.V. (1975) 'Knowing one's district: How legislators predict referendum voting', *American Journal of Political Science*, 19: 231–46.

Esaiasson, P. and Holmberg, S. (1996) *Representation from Above: Members of Parliament and Representative Democracy in Sweden*, Aldershot: Dartmouth.

Eulau, H. and Wahlke, J.C. (1959) 'The role of the representative: Some empirical observations on the theory of Edmund Burke', *American Political Science Review*, 53: 742–56.

Friesema, H.P. and Hedlund, R.D. (1974) 'The reality of representational roles' in N.R.
Luttbeg (ed.), *Public Opinion and Public Policy*, Homewood Ill.: Dorsey Press,
pp. 413–17.

Gross, D.A. (1978), 'Representative styles and legislative behavior', *Western Political
Quarterly*, 31: 359–71.

Hedlund, R.D. and Friesema, H.P. (1972) 'Representatives' perceptions of constituency
opinion', *Journal of Politics*, 34: 730–52.

Irwin, G.A. and Thomassen, J.J.A. (1975) 'Issue-consensus in a multi-party system:
voters and leaders in the Netherlands', *Acta Politica*, 10: 389–420.

Jewell, M.E. (1970) 'Attitudinal determinants of legislative behavior: the utility of role
analysis, in A. Kornberg and L.D. Musolf, *Legislatures in Developmental Perspective*,
Durham, NC: Duke University Press.

Judge, D. (1999) *Representation: Theory and Practice in Britain*, London: Routledge.

Katz, R.S. (1997) 'Representational roles', *European Journal of Political Research*, 32:
211–26.

Kuklinski, J.H. with Elling, R.C. (1977) 'Representational role, constituency opinion, and
legislative roll-call behavior', *American Journal of Political Science*, 21: 135–47.

March, J.G. and Olsen, J.P. (1989) *Rediscovering Institutions*, New York: Free Press.

McCrone, D.J. and Kuklinski, J.H. (1979) 'The delegate theory of representation', *American Journal of Political Science*, 23: 278–300.

Mendez-Lago, M. and Martinez, A. (2002), 'Political representation in Spain: an empirical
analysis of the perception of citizens and MPs', *Journal of Legislative Studies*, 8: 63–90.

Miller, W.E. and Stokes D.E. (1963) 'Constituency influence in Congress', *American
Political Science Review*, 57: 45–56.

Müller, W.C. and Saalfeld, Th. (eds.) (1997) *Members of Parliament in Western Europe:
Roles and Behaviour*, London: Frank Cass.

Pitkin, H.F. (1967) *The Concept of Political Representation*, Berkeley: University of
California Press.

Rehfeld, A. (2009) 'Representation rethought: on trustees, delegates, and gyroscopes in
the study of political representation and democracy', *American Political Science
Review*, 103: 214–30.

Searing, D.D. (1994) *Westminster's World: Understanding Political Roles*, Cambridge, MA: Harvard University Press.

Sorauf, F. (1963) *Parties and Representation*, New York: Atherton.

Thomassen, J.J.A. (1994) 'Empirical research into political representation: failing democracy or failing models' in M.K. Jennings and Th.E. Mann (eds.) *Elections at Home and Abroad*, Ann Arbor: University of Michigan Press.

Thomassen, J.J.A. and Andeweg R.B. (2004) 'Beyond collective representation; individual members of parliament and interest representation in the Netherlands', *Journal of Legislative Studies*, 10: 47–69.

Wahlke, J., Eulau, H., Buchanan, W. and Ferguson, L.C. (1962) *The Legislative System*, New York: Wiley.

5 Roles as strategies

Towards a logic of legislative behavior

Kaare Strøm

Introduction

In any large-scale community, roles help make social life bearable. Roles are regularized patterns of behavior that individuals display in different social circumstances, most typically in common and repeated activities on which others depend. Roles simplify our lives and reduce our uncertainty about effective and appropriate behavior. They similarly help others develop plausible expectations about the ways in which we are likely to behave. And for these reasons, they may reduce social uncertainty, transaction costs, embarrassment, and conflict. Roles exist in politics as they do in innumerable other aspects of social life.

Roles are important to those that engage in them (the subjects) as well as to those who observe and interact with these role-players (their audiences). While subjects and audiences may often perceive particular roles in similar ways, there is no guarantee that they will always and invariably do so. Generally, subjects perceive more nuances in the roles they play than are visible to their audiences, and they may also typically see themselves as having more discretion or individuality in their behavior. So, for example, legislators may see many different roles acted out by their peers in politics, whereas ordinary citizens are more likely to see all politicians as playing the same game.

Political roles are an obvious and venerable topic of scholarly research in political science. The scholarly analysis of political roles has examined both their subjective side, focusing on how roles are understood by those who play them, and their objective side, emphasizing how the same roles are perceived by their audiences. One of the recurrent debates in either of these literatures has to do with the extent to which political roles, as played and observed, are generated and driven by the values and perceptions of their subjects, by the constraints imposed by social institutions, or by needs and efficiencies ultimately grounded in different social functions. Thus, there is a psychological, an institutional, and a functional side to role analysis.

In representative democracies, what elected politicians do is what the voters have to live with. Therefore, the study of elite behavior has a venerable tradition in political science. Much of this scholarship has examined the regular patterns of behavior of members of parliament, since they are at the same time sufficiently

powerful to be interesting and sufficiently numerous to permit sensible generalizations. The object of such studies has been defined in terms of the roles of parliamentarians. "The noun role," Donald Searing (1994: 1) claims in his magisterial
study of Westminster's World, "is a word that we cannot do without." And yet the
scholarly focus on legislative roles, Searing observes, has for some time been in
decline. "Articles continue to be produced on the topic, but they aren't much discussed. There aren't any major research projects under way on political roles. Nor
are there signs of significant innovation in theory and method."

In his analysis of British parliamentarians, Searing defines roles as "particular
patterns of interrelated goals, attitudes, and behaviors that are characteristic of
people in particular positions." Searing distinguishes between position roles and
preferences roles, between roles driven primarily by rules and reasons, respectively. In identifying the latter roles in particular, he relies on a wealth of interviews with British politicians. Searing's paradox, and the scope, ambition, and
innovative character of his work make it a natural starting point for a discussion
of the roles of parliamentarians not just in Britain, but in representative democracies in general. The purpose of this chapter is to suggest that position and preference roles can all be nested within a common framework. Building on a
number of Searing's insights, I suggest that parliamentary roles in general can be
fruitfully understood within a neo-institutional rational choice framework.
Indeed, this research tradition is perfectly conducive to a marriage of "rules" and
"reasons," and its parsimony and deductive rigor make it the most plausible
vehicle for such a theoretical project. In brief, institutions are the "rules" than
constrain "reason," but such constraints can be more or less binding. Position
roles (fully institutionally determined strategies) and preference roles (institutionally unconstrained strategies) are the polar points on a continuum of constraint. Most real-world legislative roles lie somewhere in-between these
extremes.

What, then, are legislative, or parliamentary, roles? How do they shape political behavior? In what ways are parliamentary roles themselves a function of the
institutional rules that govern parliamentary life? To what extent can a simple
conception of legislators' goals and parliamentary institutions help us understand
and predict differences in legislative behavior across parliamentary democracies? These are the questions to which this chapter is devoted. In addressing
them, I shall draw on evidence primarily from European parliamentary democracies, but also from the United States Congress and other legislative settings. My
discussion builds on a previous article published in the *Journal of Legislative
Studies* (Strøm 1997). For present purposes, however, I have revised some of my
analytical claims, updated the discussion, and recast those parts of my argument
that applied most specifically to the scholarly debate of the 1990s.

Parliamentary roles as strategies

The study of legislative roles in parliamentary democracies has proceeded from
a number of different perspectives. The scholarly literature thus variously

associates roles with tasks, functions, behaviors, or motivations. Role-governed behavior is in turn described in positive or normative ways. Searing thus distinguishes between structural, interactional, and motivational approaches. The first of these focuses on norms related to institutional functions, the second on individual negotiation and learning in specific settings, and the third on the purposes, goals, and incentives of politicians. Searing favors the third of these, the motivational approach, in large part because it seeks to capture the conceptions parliamentarians have of their own activities. In other words, it privileges the subjective aspect of political roles.

The motivational approach thus sets great store by the relationship between the behaviors that define roles and the motivations that underlie them. In fact, Searing defines these motivations, or preferences, as part of the roles themselves. I agree with Searing that in order to understand the roles of parliamentarians, we must pay attention to their preferences. However, I wish to draw a distinction between preferences and roles. Roles are routines, regular patterns of behavior. Although such routines may be shaped by cultural expectations, they are most likely to flow from reasoned and deliberate pursuits in which parliamentarians engage. Legislative roles can thus be viewed as behavioral strategies driven by the goals of politicians, yet roles are not identical with preferences or fully determined by them. Instead they are conditioned also by the institutional settings in which parliamentarians operate. The institutional features that matter most are those of the legislature itself, but also those of their national and local parties, as well as the electoral process. Parliamentary roles, therefore, are routinized strategies, driven by reasons (preferences), and constrained by rules.

By invoking the concept of strategy, I suggest the parliamentary role analysis can fruitfully be conducted under the broad umbrella of the most rigorous and parsimonious of motivational approaches: the rational choice tradition. This approach distinguishes clearly between preferences and strategies. Preferences are the exogenously given "tastes" that actors such as parliamentarians have over the outcomes that affect their political fortunes, such as nominations, elections, appointments, and policy decisions. But while the goals of politicians surely influence the patterned behavior they display, these goals do not in themselves constitute such roles. Instead, it is more meaningful to think of roles as strategies, or game plans. Strategies are endogenous prescriptions as to how actors (here: parliamentarians) may most successfully and efficiently act to maximize the likelihood of whatever outcomes they favor. Thus conceived, strategies are akin to the common definition of roles: they take the form of consistently patterned political behavior. Yet, strategies only make sense when we understand the preferences that drive them, as well as the institutions or structures that shape them.

Strategies have to prescribe specific forms of behavior under the control of the actors in question. For parliamentarians, strategic choices typically have to do with their commitment of scarce resources such as their time, money, and other assets. Role differentiations characterize various ways in which parliamentarians can allocate such scarce resources. These different patterns of resource allocation reflect differences in the efforts parliamentarians put into the pursuit of their various goals. Some members spend a lot of their time trying to get rese-lected by their parties, others engage mainly in activities designed to boost their general election prospects, and yet others put their efforts into work that is likely to earn them promotions within their parties or within parliament.

The strategies of parliamentarians are thus prescriptions, or game plans, that help these politicians choose how to employ their scarce resources. Legislative strategies are not directly observable, but instead we infer them from the pat-terned behavior that parliamentarians display. What sorts of behavior, then, can we use to identify different parliamentary strategies? I have suggested that par-liamentarians' strategies prescribe their commitment of their most important scarce resources. But where can these resources be put to use, and for what pur-poses? To answer these questions, we need to think systematically about the scarce resources that parliamentarians have at their disposal and about how insti-tutions affect their use.

Empirical role analysis has indeed often focused on legislators' use of their scarce and consequential political resources, such as their voting power, time, attention, media access, or money. The ultimate resource within the parliamentary arena is the representatives' voting power, which they can use to promote causes that favor their constituency, their party, some social group to which they have ties, or their personal vision of the common good. Parliamentarians can also influence the parliamentary decision making process in other ways, by sponsoring, amend-ing, or filibustering bills, by participating in legislative investigations or audits, by asking questions of ministers, etc. All such activities take time, and some may also require policy expertise, which it is often costly to acquire. There are plenty of competing demands on a legislator's time and attention. One set of such competing demands emanates from his electoral constituency, in which there will often be vir-tually insatiable demands for attention to individual case work and district projects. Local or national interest groups will present yet another set of demands. Last, but certainly not least, the parliamentary and extra-parliamentary party leadership will expect the member's loyalty and diligent service in a variety of arenas, including perhaps campaign efforts for other candidates, service on committees or in offices that have little or negative electoral payoff, and the like. The choices that parlia-mentarians make between these competing demands on their resources constitute their political strategies.

These strategies will be driven by the legislators' goals but also conditioned by the institutions in which they operate. Institutions affect roles in part by defining the range of behaviors available to members of parliament. Institutions do so by enabling and constraining behavior, that is to say, by making such forms of behav-ior feasible and others infeasible, and by shaping the incentives that different legis-lators face. Parliamentary roles, I would suggest, can best be understood as consistent strategies induced by the members' pursuit of their political objectives, constrained by the institutional environment in which they operate. When a parlia-mentarian chooses to focus her energies on constituent casework, for example, we first seek to explain that behavior with reference to her goals and the constraints that political institutions place on her behavior and opportunities. The critical challenge is therefore to identify the most important objectives of parliamentarians and then the institutions that most significantly impinge on the ability of these legislators to achieve their objectives. It is to these tasks that I now turn.

Legislators' preferences

The motivations of legislators have been a focal point of a rapidly growing literature on legislative organization and behavior. This literature has transformed scholarship on the United States Congress and contributed to a shift that Searing observes, from sociological role analysis to rational choice incentive-based explanations of legislative behavior. The single work most responsible for this revolution is David Mayhew's (1974) book *Congress: The Electoral Connection*. Although Mayhew did not formalize his argument or put it in game-theoretic terms, it profoundly influenced scholars in the rational choice tradition, which was only beginning to hit its stride in the 1970s. Mayhew argues that much can be understood about the behavior of United States Congressmen if one assumes that they are "single-minded seekers of reelection" (Mayhew 1974: 5). The pursuit of reelection, he argues, "underlies everything else, as indeed it should if we are to expect that the relations between politicians and public will be one of accountability" (Mayhew 1974: 16–17).

Mayhew's stark stylization proved both catchy and enormously influential. Nonetheless, other scholars have added to its characterization of politicians' objectives and abandoned some of its simplicity. Joseph Schlesinger (1991) added some nuance to the electoral motivation. Much in the vein of Mayhew, he argued that political ambition is the key to understanding candidate behavior and even to political parties as organizations. Political ambition, however, can take several different forms: discrete, static, and progressive. Discrete ambition is the desire for a particular office for a single term. Static ambition consists in the pursuit of the same office for multiple terms. Finally, progressive ambition is where an individual aspires to some office more powerful or important than the one that he or she now holds. This is where one political office becomes a stepping-stone for another and more desirable one.

Thus, Mayhew's archetypical congressman holds only one of three possible forms of political ambition, as Schlesinger portrays it, namely the static one. Politicians with discrete ambition do not fit Mayhew's description of the single-minded seeker of reelection. Nor do those with progressive ambition. But there may be good reasons why members of the US House of Representatives so commonly display static ambition. It may be because the next election is never far away and because for many of them, the risks of running for higher office (displaying progressive ambition) are prohibitive. The two-year terms of US representatives focus their attention admirably on the next election. Moreover, the two-year terms means that there is hardly ever a time when these representatives can run for higher office without at the same time vacating their House seats. Most parliaments, in contrast, are elected for terms of four or five years, rather than the two-year term faced by member of the US House of Representatives. And in the Westminster system, there is no necessary conflict between running for reelection and progressive ambition.

Even as a characterization of American legislators, Mayhew's thesis has hardly gone uncontested. Among Mayhew's own contemporaries, Richard Fenno (1973, 1978) argued that members of Congress have multiple objectives, which may often conflict. Some of these goals, however, are more fundamental than others: reelection, influence within the House, and good public policy. Fenno adds to these external career considerations and private gain, which he treats peripherally or not at all. Gary Cox and Mathew McCubbins (1993) and John H. Aldrich (1995) expand on Fenno's second motivation in particular. But although they reject Mayhew's stylized claim that members of Congress are single-minded in their quest for reelection, Cox and McCubbins (1993: 109), for example, "do believe that it is an important component of their motivation."

Although all these works are studies of legislators in the American presidential systems, they hold important lessons for the study of parliamentary ambitions and roles as well. Building on these analyses, I argue that parliamentarians have four distinct types of goals related to their legislative service. The four parliamentary goals, or the components of the parliamentary utility function, are: (1) reselection (renomination), (2) reelection, (3) party office, and (4) legislative office. (In addition, legislators may of course have other goals that pertain to their lives outside of parliament, as Fenno suggests.) By party office, I mean such positions as party leader, whip, member of the parliamentary party leadership or steering committee, or front bench status – in other words such forms of privilege that are entirely under the control of the party itself. By legislative office, I mean positions to which a member must be elected by parliament as a whole, or by some cross-partisan subset of the legislature, such as speaker/president, committee chair, member of the parliamentary steering group, etc. In pure two-party systems, the distinction between party and legislative office may in practice be of no consequence, if the majority party controls access to all-important legislative offices. In multiparty parliamentary democracies, on the other hand, the allocation of legislative offices is typically at the hands of some coalition of parties.

Clearly, several of these objectives are mainly instrumental: they are means to an end. Thus, politicians wish to be nominated and elected because of the benefits that flow from holding office rather than because of the pure joy of winning or simply seeing their names in print. That is to say that legislative objectives are often hierarchically ordered. The attainment of one goal may be a precondition for any or all of the others. For example, in most legislatures, party renomination is critical to the attainment of any other goal. If you do not receive your party's nod for the ballot, you cannot be elected, and if not elected, you obviously cannot enjoy any of the benefits of parliamentary membership. Election is thus necessary for any further goal attainment in parliament. The iron-clad necessity of election in democratic legislatures (other than the odd assemblies such as the House of Lords) makes the "single-minded pursuit of reelection" the primary instrumental goal of legislators. Typically, party office is also more or less of a prerequisite for legislative office, although the necessity here is less strict. Some members become legislative leaders (e.g. presiding officers) without achieving any high position in their respective parties.

There is a fairly clear hierarchy of legislator objectives. The first goal, which is typically critical to any further ambition, is to gain ballot access, most commonly by receiving one's party's nomination. Once nomination has been secured, election is the next concern. Both of these are critical to any further goal achievement. Once elected, parliamentarians may to some extent be able to choose between party and legislative career objectives. To the extent that these are interrelated, partisan office is more likely to be a precondition for advancement in legislative office, rather than vice versa. Yet, the hierarchy between the latter two objectives is less strict in some multiparty democracies than it is in the Westminster model.

Institutions help determine what discretion parliamentarians have in choosing their roles based on these objectives, as such rules may strictly constrain the viable ways in which parliamentarians can husband their scarce resources, or leave them with greater choice and discretion. The most important institutional constraints are in turn driven by the two masters that legislators serve: their voters and their parties, respectively. Parliamentarians serve as "common agents" of these two democratic "principals" (Strøm *et al.* 2003), and it is their accountability to these masters, and the latter's respective demands, that most decisively constrain these legislators' pursuit of their political goals.

The freedom with which parliamentarians may choose their legislative roles depends on the demands of these accountability relationships. The more tightly constrained parliamentarians are by the demands of their parties or voters, the less freedom they have to choose what Searing calls preference roles. And the tighter the constraints, the more we should expect to see parliamentary role playing determined by constitutional principles and party rules and statutes.

The political institutions that most powerfully enable and constrain parliamentarians are those that regulate their attainment of ballot access, reelection, party office, and legislative office. The first two of these objectives are conditioned in large part by the electoral system, which embodies the legislators' accountability to their constitutional principals, the voters. Yet, of course political parties also keenly seek to control the selection and election of parliamentary candidates. The third and fourth objectives are most directly governed by party rules and legislative procedure, which in turn in large part reflect the interests of the parliamentary parties. Let us now consider how the demands of voters and parties constrain the roles of politicians in the pursuit of each of their four goals.

Candidate selection

Candidate selection (or nomination) is the first official step on the way to parliament, and the first hurdle that incumbent members have to face. There are typically a large number of regulations on the selection of legislative candidates by the relevant political parties. Some such regulations are embedded in national legislation, although relatively few countries (including, however, the United States and Germany) go very far in regulating the candidate selection process through ordinary legislation. More commonly, regulations are imposed by the parties themselves, which means that they may differ between different parties in the same political system, or even between different electoral districts in the same party.

The candidate selection process may be more or less centralized. In some parties, such as the Liberal Democratic Party in Japan or the conservative parties in France, the national executive committee is a decisive player. More commonly, the process is decentralized to the individual constituencies. Some parties, especially those with a civil-libertarian bent, practice intraparty primary elections, but in far more parties local party officers and/or officials are effectively in charge. Under multi-tier electoral systems, different procedures may be in place at different tiers. Finally, some "corporative" parties allow selected interest groups (e.g. labor unions, farmers' groups, or women's groups) an institutionalized role in the candidate selection process.

The importance of the selection process varies with the electoral system. In single-member district systems, of course, candidate selection is typically critical to electoral success. It is true that in recent US Senate elections, two incumbents denied renomination by their respective parties (Democrat Joseph Lieberman in 2006 and Republican Lisa Murkowski in 2010) have nevertheless won reelection by running as the candidate of a minor party (Lieberman) or even through a write-in campaign (Murkowski). Yet, such stories remain the exception rather than the rule, as reselection by your party is close to a necessary condition for reelection. The same is by and large true in closed-list proportional representation (PR) systems, in which nomination at the top of a major party list can virtually guarantee election and thus remove practically all risk from the general election. Under open-list proportional representation, and under the single transferable or non-transferable vote, on the other hand, candidate selection is far less likely to guarantee success. Under these systems, parties nominate multiple candidates in each district, and the success of each candidate depends on the preferences of the ordinary voters. Thus, party nomination is typically necessary for electoral success, but often by no means sufficient. Moreover, in political systems that allow independents or write-in candidates easy access to the ballot, party reselection may not even be necessary even though it is virtually everywhere at least helpful.

Yet, reselection efforts may not be a very salient concern for the legislator to begin with. Strategies aimed at reselection only make sense when the party's endorsement is scarce or contested. Yet, in most systems and parties, the deck is stacked in favor of incumbents interested in reelection. This is true in general of British parties, where strategies focused on reselection rarely seem to dominate legislator behavior. Indeed, none of the many parliamentary roles described by Searing describes a parliamentarian whose main concern is reselection. In systems where ballot access is easy, we would expect a similar lack of concern.

Closed-list PR systems with competitive selection processes should tend to experience a great deal more partisan constraint on role identification. Here, selection is critical and the specific placement a candidate gets on the list is likely to be decisive. It is therefore interesting to see that in his comparative analysis of Nordic parliamentarians, Peter Esaiasson (2000: 59) reports that MPs in Sweden and Norway, the two Nordic countries whose electoral systems most approximate closed-list PR, are much more likely to define themselves as agents of their respective parties than their opposite numbers in Finland, which has a much more open form of candidate preference voting.

How is the pursuit of reselection likely to influence legislative strategies or roles? The motivation can find expression in a variety of behaviors, depending on the locus and rules of the candidate selection process. If the national executive committee were decisive, then we would expect behavior designed to please the central party leadership (such as legislative obedience and diligence). If the more common pattern of local control obtains, then reselection-minded legislators should aim to please their local constituents and specifically the often narrow set of party selectors more than the ordinary constituency voter. Local activists would tend to be the decisive constituency, and issue-oriented local efforts (rather than, for example, "random" casework for constituents) the most plausible key.

Election

As noted in an earlier section, the electoral motivation forms the basis of the most famous and powerful explanations of the behavior of politicians. The fact that democratic societies fill most important political offices directly or indirectly through elections obviously supports such understandings of the political process. Getting elected is crucial, indeed strictly necessary, for members of almost all significant legislative chambers. Yet, there may be scenarios under which parliamentarians' behavior is not at all or not significantly constrained by the electoral connection. That is where (1) legislators cannot realistically aspire to be reelected, or (2) candidate selection is virtually tantamount to election. In the former case, reelection is impossible. In the latter, it is more or less assured once the member has been reselected. In neither case would we expect the reelection motive to dominate legislative behavior.

Both situations could occur for a number of reasons having to do with the electoral system. If legislators cannot hope to be reelected, it is most commonly because the constitution or other binding regulations prohibit their reelection. Although formal term limits are uncommon in parliamentary democracies, they do exist in many presidential regimes. In American state legislatures, rather strict term limits have become quite common. In a number of Latin American countries, they are even stricter. The Costa Rican and Mexican constitutions, for example, permit no reelection for any member of the national legislature. Where such restrictions apply, it is obviously senseless for members to worry about reelection (at least in the short term), and we expect their behavior to be driven by all sorts of other considerations. Where reelection is restricted in parliament-ary democracies, however, it is typically due to informal party rules rather than constitutional prohibitions.

The opposite situation is where politicians, once selected, have little or no reason to worry about the general election. This is most likely to be the case for high-ranking candidates of major parties in closed-list PR systems. In Norway, for example, the first-ranking candidates (or even number two or three) of either the Labor Party or the Conservatives in large districts like Oslo do not have to give a lot of attention to their personal reelection prospects. Naturally, these are list positions that party leaders such as prime ministerial candidates often occupy. For those who wish to escape electoral competition, the next best thing is to be the candidate of the favored party in uncompetitive single-member dis-tricts. Once selected, Democratic candidates for inner-city congressional dis-tricts in the United States typically have little to worry about in the general election. The same could be said for British Labour candidates in major indus-trial cities, as well as for Conservative candidates in the southeastern English countryside. As a consequence, such candidates should be free to devise legis-lative strategies not significantly constrained by their electoral accountability to the voters.

Most parliamentarians, however, are not so lucky. Competitive single-member districts and systems that permit intraparty preference voting are likely to exhibit particularly high levels of electoral constraint. In such systems, the fate of each legislator depends not only on the general support of his (or her) party (which he may be able to affect only marginally), but also on his own per-sonal standing with the voters. The effects of the popularity of co-partisans vary widely between such systems. Under the single, non-transferable vote, long used in Japanese elections, members are in no way helped by votes for other candi-dates from their own party. In fact, if one's own vote is held constant, increased support for a fellow partisan is as likely to hurt as to help. Under the same condi-tions in a single transferable vote system (such as Ireland), on the other hand, increased support for co-partisans is more likely to help than hurt, as long as candidate preferences are positively constrained by party.

But electoral formula is not the only factor that determines the constraining power of elections on legislative strategies. Members' concern for reelection is also likely to show cyclical fluctuations, which may be dramatic. Legislators elected for long and fixed terms (such as US senators) can have the luxury of a respite from the pressures of campaigning in the first part of their terms. Simi-larly, members of legislatures where the power of parliamentary dissolution is restricted can at least feel a little more insulated than where a prime minister or president (perhaps from an unfriendly party) may freely choose to dissolve par-liament at any time.

In their perennial (or nearly so) struggle for reelection, members develop a number of strategies designed to improve the popular standings of their parties and, in particular, themselves. The literature on political campaigns is replete with descriptions of the former and more general phenomenon. The latter topic has been examined mainly in the growing literature on the personal vote. In their analysis of personal voting in Britain and the United States, Cain, Ferejohn, and Fiorina (1987) distinguish between personal contacts, casework, project assistance, mail solicitations, and "surgeries." The more electorally constrained the member, and the more his or her fortunes depend on a personal vote, the more diligently we should expect that person's resource commitments to conform to these patterns. Searing identifies two types of "constituency members" among the backbenchers in the House of Commons: "welfare officers" and "local promoters." It is roles such as these that we should expect to see among members with particularly competitive electoral constituencies.

Party office

Most members of parliaments have to give serious attention to their prospects for reselection and reelection. For many, or at least for good parts of the tenure of many, the pursuit of these objectives stretches their time and resources to their limits. Although most might in principle wish to rise above the ranks of backbenchers, few in practice have the opportunities to do so without jeopardizing their political survival. But although few are actually chosen, many may condition their parliamentary behavior on the aspiration to rise above the rank of backbencher, either through party or parliamentary office.

The degree to which such aspirations affect legislative strategies and thus roles depends upon opportunities as well as on constraints. And the institutions that in turn shape the opportunity structures are themselves in part parliamentary ones and in part those that pertain to other political offices, particularly those likely to be valued above a backbench position in parliament. Whereas candidate selection and election processes are not necessarily any different in parliamentary systems than in presidential ones, the incentive structure defined by the structure of party and legislative office opportunities clearly diverge from those of non-parliamentary regimes.

A defining characteristic of parliamentarism is that the cabinet "emerges from" parliament itself. In the classical Westminster tradition, this implies not only cabinet accountability to parliament, but also that cabinet members are drawn from the ranks of the legislature (and continue to serve there). In this sense, the cabinet is a true subset of the legislative branch of government, and the relationship between the two branches one of internal delegation. This constitutional arrangement has obvious incentive effects for parliamentarians with progressive ambition, as virtually all the objects of their desire may be under the control of their respective party leaders. In presidential regimes, progressive ambition is by definition incompatible with continued service in the same legislative body. In order to serve in higher political office, members have to look beyond the confines of their chamber and ultimately to give up their seats there. In parliamentary systems, on the other hand, higher (particularly cabinet) office is achieved through a career in parliament, and there is no sense in which politicians have to choose between two discrete career paths.

Party office, such as one's party parliamentary leader, deputy leader, whip, or a member of its parliamentary executive (steering) committee, is one of the two types of ambition that members of parliament might harbor beyond reelection. As mentioned above, we can at least analytically distinguish this kind of ambition from legislative office ambition, although in practice the same party leaders may control both sets of offices. Party office objectives are most likely to be associated with progressive ambition in Schlesinger's classical sense. Parliamentarians who aspire to party leadership positions in parliament are also likely to harbor explicit or implicit ambitions of becoming cabinet-level leaders within their respective parties. This is particularly likely in systems where cabinet members are either required or permitted to hold simultaneous membership in parliament, and where a large share of cabinet members are in fact recruited directly from parliament. The United Kingdom, Ireland, Belgium, and Italy are examples. Indeed, particularly in unitary Westminster systems, the cabinet is by far the most attractive avenue for upward political mobility.

Party office in parliament is normally filled by election among the party's members in parliament. Often, however, these selections are subject to formal or informal approval by the party leadership, particularly perhaps in governing parties. For cabinet office, of course, the approval of the party leadership is even more crucial and in fact usually decisive. Parliamentarians who aspire to party office therefore have two constituencies they have to please: their peers and the party leadership. Ways to please the party leadership include loyalty, diligence, versatility, and a willingness to take on arduous and unrewarding tasks for the good of the party. The same behaviors may in general also be good ways to build favors among one's fellow partisans, although unswerving loyalty to the party hierarchy may find more favor among the party's leaders than among the backbenchers, who might instead prefer mutual deference, mutual support in campaigns and committee work, or the like.

A successful aspirant to party office must therefore be willing to devote time and energy to party objectives, even if that means neglecting one's local constituency or supporting causes that have little local support. This strategy may or may not involve the acquisition of policy expertise, which can at least be useful for credit claiming purposes. A politician who has such ambitions and who can afford to take such risks vis-à-vis his or her constituency, is likely to fall into the category of backbenchers that Searing calls ministerial aspirants, or perhaps that of policy advocates. Clearly, this is a potentially treacherous pursuit for MPs whose constituency preferences differ sharply from those of the party leadership, or who for other reasons face stiff competition for reselection or reelection.

Legislative office

Legislative office, which is the final source of the benefits that drive parliamentary behavior, refers to all those positions in parliament that are involved in the execution of important legislative responsibilities and which are predominantly non-partisan or cross-partisan in nature. Legislative organization is, according to

Krehbiel (1991: 2), "the allocation of resources and assignment of parliamentary rights to individual legislators or groups of legislators." In the great majority of modern legislatures, members are elected equal. All members, regardless of, say, the pluralities by which they gained election or the number of voters they represent, have the same parliamentary rights and privileges. With rare exceptions, voting rules in legislatures are egalitarian and "undifferentiated," and each legislator's vote counts as much as that of any other. One person, one vote. Yet, in reality there are all kinds of differences between members. Such differences take two general forms: hierarchy (vertical differentiation) and specialization (functional or horizontal differentiation).

These forms of differentiation define legislative organization. Parliamentary organization (the distribution of rights and powers assigned to parliamentarians individually and collectively) and procedures (decision-making rules within parliament) define a large part of the repertoire of member strategies. For example, parliamentary standing committees may or may not be an important arena for activities aimed at reelection or partisan advancement in parliament. Whether or not they do, will depend on the specific composition, powers, and procedures of the committees. For example, if committees engage in highly visible and publicized hearings or investigations, they may be important arenas in which reelection and perhaps reselection goals can be pursued. If, on the other hand, committees meet behind closed doors, but have substantial powers to initiate or amend bills, then they may be important arenas for the pursuit of party or legislative office, but less useful campaign fora. If neither of the above is true (as with standing committees in the British House of Commons), then committees are unlikely to be of much strategic importance for members seeking to please their parties or constituencies.

Legislative organization can be shaped wholly or in part by the interests of the political parties that control the assembly. In Westminster systems, there is little room in legislative organization for rules or procedures that are likely to hamper the dominant parties. In the US system, in contrast, there are more legislative procedures that sometimes stand in the way of party interests. Of course, most parliamentary offices are directly or indirectly filled through partisan selection processes. Yet the "inter-party mode" is not the only aspect of parliamentary politics. Building on King (1976), Andeweg and Nijzink (1995) identify both the "non-party mode" and the "cross-party mode" as important facets of legislative politics in European parliamentary democracies. These facets of parliamentary politics are reflected in such symbolic issues as seating arrangements, where in Norway and Sweden, members are seated by district, regardless of partisan affiliations. More importantly, specialized parliamentary committees sometimes constitute fora in which members may advance relatively independently of their fortunes within their own party hierarchies. Indeed, for some politicians, a parliamentary committee career may be a very attractive alternative to cabinet aspirations. Andeweg and Nijzink also point out the plethora of intra-parliamentary caucuses, such as for regional, gender, or language groups, that exists within many parliaments.

Even more importantly, internal affairs committees and boards of presiding officers sometimes offer opportunities for legislative office that may compete with more partisan career paths. According to Jenny and Müller's (1995) informative survey of presiding officers in European parliaments, such offices vary considerably both in partisanship and in power. Powerful and partisan presiding officers, such as the Speaker of the United States House of Representatives, are by no means the only or even the most common type of presiding officer. In fact, among the European countries surveyed by Jenny and Müller (1995), only Greece has a president who is both very powerful and highly partisan. In many other parliamentary democracies, MPs may become speaker (presiding officer) without having achieved any high position in their respective parties. This pattern is most typical of Westminster-style parliaments, but similar cases can be found in Belgium, Iceland, and Switzerland as well.

The institutions that most decisively affect members' pursuit of such legislative office are those that regulate the selection, powers, and accountabilities of presiding officers and other relevant internal officers of parliament. Since these rules are manifold and complex, it is difficult to generalize about their specific effects. Yet, I expect to see parliamentarians increase their efforts toward legislative office as (1) their reselection opportunities improve, (2) their reelection opportunities improve, (3) the attractiveness of legislative, as opposed to partisan, office increases, and (4) their opportunities for partisan office decrease. In other words, strategies aimed at legislative office should be particularly common among MPs with relatively secure seats and limited frontbench prospects, and in parliaments where legislative offices are comparatively desirable.

The strategies of those who seek legislative office are most akin to the roles Searing lumps into his category of "parliament men." Of all his backbench roles, this is the most diverse category, with the largest set of subtypes. The general role of parliament man is also a fair description of frontbencher Charles Seymour's ultimate career choice in Jeffrey Archer's (1984) novel *First Among Equals*. As Searing puts it, the parliament man is "a role that is neither widely recognized nor well defined." This is primarily because there are so few parliament men. To Searing, this scarcity "seems strange, for this role was common and indeed dominant during earlier eras."

But should this paucity be such a surprise? Applying the argument I have developed above, the incidence of parliament men should decline as reselection and reelection get more competitive, and as the attraction of legislative office declines relative to that of partisan office. Putting the issue in such comparatively static terms, we may in fact recognize a plausible description of the evolution of the British House of Commons over the past century and a half. What has happened is precisely that the conditions that favor parliament men (or, strategies aimed at the pursuit of legislative office) have become less and less prevalent. Indeed, today's British House of Commons, with its high levels of partisanship, is precisely one that we would expect not to be very conducive to legislative office pursuits.

Conclusion

In order to understand representative democracy, we need to develop analytical tools by which we can make sense of the behavior of the elected representatives of the people. The concept of roles is one such tool that has been prominently employed in studies of legislative institutions. Role analysis promises to give us simple and applicable tools with which we could describe and explain legislative behavior. Yet, in contemporary political science role analysis has fallen somewhat out of favor. This is, I believe, at least in part because role analysis has not always been quite clear about what it can do or about its own limitations. The concept itself has seemed to subsume individual beliefs, common expectations, actual behaviors, and even institutional functions, without clear demarcations or causal stipulations between these different components.

In this chapter I have suggested that parliamentary role analysis can be cast as a study of the strategies of legislators for the commitment of scarce resources. These strategies are likely to be conditioned by the relative scarcity of various institutionally generated "goods" that parliamentarians seek. These goods include reselection, reelection, party office, and legislative office. Ultimately, then, the incidence of different parliamentary roles should bear a powerful and predictable relationship to the supply of such political benefits. Yet, their accountabilities to voters and to their respective parties often constrain the behavior of legislators sufficiently that it can drive what we observe as their role behaviors. For example, there are many institutional circumstances in which we would definitely not expect members of parliament to be single-minded in their pursuit of reelection.

Much of the diversity of parliamentary lives, I have argued, is subject to relatively simple explanation. We can gain important insights by portraying legislators as if they were purely instrumental in their pursuits of different benefits that legislative institutions afford them. To some, this argument may seem both cynical and restrictive. I do not want to argue that altruism and other non-self-interested motivations play no role in determining the behavior of parliamentarians. Clearly, my aim has been to simplify reality, and the motivations of legislators are more complex than what any simple scheme can capture. Yet, many legislators cannot afford to indulge their less self-interested motivations. Doing so might lead to a shorter and less gratifying political career than they might otherwise enjoy. And the powerful ways in which political institutions thus constrain the strategies of elected representatives may be one of the more general and comprehensible features of democratic politics.

References

Aldrich, J. H. (1995) *Why Parties?* Chicago: University of Chicago Press.
Andeweg, Rudy B. and Nijzink, L. (1995) "Beyond the two-body image: Relations between ministers and MPs," in H. Döring (ed.) *Parliaments and Majority Rule in Western Europe*, New York: St. Martin's Press.
Archer, J. (1984) *First Among Equals*. London: Hodder and Stoughton.

Cain, B., Ferejohn, J. and Fiorina, M. (1987) *The Personal Vote: Constituency Service and Electoral Independence*, Cambridge, MA: Harvard University Press.

Cox, G. C. and McCubbins, M. D. (1993) *Legislative Leviathan: Party Government in the House*, Berkeley: University of California Press.

Esaiasson, P. (2000) "How Members of Parliament define their task," in P. Esaiasson and K. Heidar (eds.), *Beyond Westminster and Congress: The Nordic Experience*, Columbus: Ohio State University Press.

Fenno, R. F. (1973) *Congressmen in Committees*, Boston: Little, Brown.

Fenno, R. F. (1978) *Home Style: House Members in Their Districts*, Boston: Little, Brown.

Jenny, M. and Müller, W. C. (1995) "Presidents of Parliament: Neutral chairmen or assets of the majority," in H. Döring (ed.) *Parliaments and Majority Rule in Western Europe*, New York: St. Martin's Press.

King, A. (1976) "Modes of executive–legislative relations: Great Britain, France and West Germany," *Legislative Studies Quarterly*, 1: 11–36.

Krehbiel, K. (1991) *Information and Legislative Organization*, Ann Arbor, MI: University of Michigan Press.

Mayhew, D. R. (1974) *Congress: The Electoral Connection*, New Haven, CT: Yale University Press.

Schlesinger, J. A. (1991) *Political Parties and the Winning of Office*, Ann Arbor, MI: University of Michigan Press.

Searing, D. D. (1994) *Westminster's World: Understanding Political Roles*, Cambridge, MA: Harvard University Press.

Searing, D. D. (1997) "Rules, reasons, and routines: Legislative roles in parliamentary democracies," *Journal of Legislative Studies*, 3: 155–74.

Strøm, K., Müller, W. C. and Bergman, T. (eds.) (2003) *Delegation and Accountability in Parliamentary Democracies*, Oxford: Oxford University Press.

6 Legislators and their representational roles

Strategic choices or habits of the heart?

Thomas Zittel

What are the sources of legislators' role orientations? The literature on this issue implies two very different answers to this question. Early role theorists perceive roles from a structural–functionalist perspective emphasizing particular socio-structural variables in explaining legislators' role orientations. More recent contributions on this issue envision roles as strategic behavior based on given interests and institutional constraints. This chapter contributes to the debate on the sources of legislators' role orientations in a twofold way. First, it contributes to our theoretical understanding in discussing both approaches to explaining legislators' roles from a micro-level perspective and in asking for particular causal mechanisms linking the contextual and behavioral levels of analysis. Second, it contributes to our empirical understanding of representational roles by testing both competing role theories for the German case drawing from the German Candidate Study 2005 (GCS).

Legislators and the types of roles they play

The concept of legislative roles came of age in the 1950s and 1960s. Among others, it was conceived as an instrument to further our empirical understandings on the relationship between citizens and their representatives in systematic ways. Thus, role theory supplements prescriptive approaches to researching the puzzle of political representation on the one hand (e.g. Pitkin 1967) and purely descriptive ones on the other.

In particular, role theory focuses on the questions of whom MPs represent in their decision-making behavior (focus of representation), and in what way they aim to represent given constituencies (style of representation). The ideal typical distinction between the delegate and trustee roles provides an early and classical answer to these questions (Wahlke *et al.* 1962). According to this typology, in their representative functions, delegates primarily focus on their electoral constituencies and perceive themselves as mouthpieces of constituency demands. In contrast, while acting as representatives, trustees are considered to primarily focus on all citizens and their long-term interests.

Subsequent empirical research on the trustee and delegate conceptions of political representation resulted in one important modification in this regard.

Empirical studies on European representative systems found little evidence for the role of the district delegate. While the notion of the district proved to be firmly rooted in the minds of American legislators (Wahlke *et al.* 1962: 281), instead, in the European context, legislators proved to be more focused on party and more likely to perceive themselves as party rather than district delegates (see e.g. Converse and Pierce 1986; Thomassen 1994). Conceptually, the party and district delegate conceptions are not distinct with regard to the style of representation; both roles fall in the "delegate category" of representation, both roles emphasize external constraints to legislators' representative behavior. However, they are distinct with regard to the focus of representation. District delegates listen primarily to voters in their district while party delegates take the party program and the voters of their party as their main points of reference.

This chapter asks about the sources of representational roles, about factors explaining differences in the dispositions of legislators to either adopt a party delegate, a district delegate, or a trustee role?[1] It contributes to the debate on this issue in a twofold way. First, it makes a theoretical contribution in discussing two competing explanatory approaches from a micro-level perspective and in identifying particular causal mechanisms linking the contextual and behavioral levels of analysis. It portrays representational roles as either flowing from learned and norm-guided behavior or from strategic considerations aimed at electoral gains and patterned by electoral incentive structures. Second, the chapter contributes in empirical ways in testing both approaches on the basis of the German case. This case allows for a quasi-experiment on the question raised. The country's mixed-member system allows varying different types of electoral incentives while holding many contextual factors constant. Furthermore, the country's system of political recruitment allows varying different experiences in political socialization while again holding many contextual factors constant.

The chapter is structured in four sections. It firstly elaborates on the two different approaches to explaining representational roles sketched above. This section aims to reconstruct both approaches from a micro-level perspective; the chapter secondly explains its case selection, specifies testable hypotheses for the German case, and introduces the data that will be used for testing the two approaches discussed; in a third step the chapter presents the findings of my empirical analysis; it closes in a fourth step with a brief discussion on the results of the analysis and on further directions for research.

Two approaches to explaining representational roles from a micro-level perspective

In general, the obvious and systematic differences between the orientations of European and American legislators have been subject to ad-hoc explanations emphasizing the macro level of politics. From this perspective, the emphasis on serving geographic districts in American politics is considered to be a consequence of presidentialism and weak political parties. In turn, the emphasis on representing national coalitions of voters in European politics is explained as being the result of parliamentarism and strong political parties. But what are the causal mechanisms mediating between the structural and behavioral levels of analysis? How persistent are these mechanisms across time? And most importantly what accounts for intra-system variance?

The purpose of explaining the orientations of legislators did not loom large in the landmark study of Wahlke *et al.* (1962) on the role concept. These authors were mainly concerned with conceptual questions surrounding legislators' orientations and with measuring them in four American state legislatures. Conceptually, Wahlke *et al.* (1962: 8) envisioned representational roles as a coherent set of norms of behavior that is considered to be of a systemic rather than of an individual nature but that nevertheless can be accessed empirically via the orientations of individual legislators. Empirically, Wahlke *et al.* (1962: 370) first highlight the prominence of the trustee role in their four American state legislatures under study; second find a significant minority of district delegates among their respondents (around 20 percent); and third observe a rather reserved attitude towards partisan orientations in their sample.

The empirical findings of Wahlke *et al.* raise the question of how to explain differences in legislators' role orientations. Their main answer can be reconstructed and summarized in the following two-step way. Wahlke *et al.* first consider the delegate role as a response to the representational function of parliaments and to the mechanism of democratic elections. The authors consider the delegate role to be a functional imperative that cannot be willfully discounted by abridging role-sets for example (Saalfeld 1997). If this is the case, then why do not all legislators in all four state legislatures under study fall into the delegate category – why are there so many trustees? The authors answer this question in a second step of their argument emphasizing district structure.

Wahlke *et al.* (1962) argue secondly that district structure determines role orientations in indirect ways (Anderson 2009: 318) by affecting the structure of district opinion. Their concrete assumption is that complex social settings increase the likelihood of representatives adopting a trustee orientation. This is because "the represented may not have the information to give intelligent instructions; the representative is unable to discover what his clienteles want; preferences remain unexpressed, structures disable legislators to understand and detect prevalent social demands" (Eulau *et al.* 1959: 750). Under the condition of less complex social structures, Wahlke *et al.* (1962) assume a greater likelihood of legislators adopting the role of a delegate. In these contexts legislators know what their constituents want, constituents are better able to express themselves, and general expectations are more likely to point into the direction of the role of a district delegate.

Wahlke *et al.* (1962: 359) supplement their structural–functionalist model with a further argument introducing party and the role of a party delegate. They argue that "partisan cultures" are likely to result in higher numbers of party delegates through "[positively affecting MPs'] orientations towards party" (Wahlke *et al.* 1962: 376). It is puzzling that Wahlke *et al.* provide little explanation on how and why "partisan cultures" could affect the role perceptions of legislators.

Clearly, in the context of structural–functional role theory, the role of party remains a mystery. At the theoretical level, this mystery can be solved in the following two ways.

First, the impact of parties on role orientations can be conceptualized in indirect ways via the process of party competition. In this process, parties propose political programs, enter into a conflict over these programs, and thus divide the public into partisans. As a result, the public will subscribe to one or the other side in this conflict and will respond on the proposed policies with respective demands (Schattschneider 1960). Thus, in the long run, party competition has important ramifications for the cognition of voters and legislators alike. It allows the represented to acquire information and to give intelligent instructions on the one hand; the representatives are able to discover what their constituents want and what the prevalent social demands are on the other. In this process, parties act as a broker between constituents and representatives, as a filter determining what legislators know and what they don't know. The partisan bias of the information legislators communicate and receive, and the need to coordinate with fellow partisans in the process of party competition provides the basis for the party delegate role. Thus, the role of a party delegate should be more common in polarized and highly competitive party systems.

This chapter emphasizes a second approach to clarifying the role of party in the context of structural–functionalist role theory. This approach emphasizes a direct link between "partisan cultures" and role orientations (Anderson 2009: 318) via the mechanism of political socialization. It presumes the existence of strong party organizational structures as outgrowths of "partisan cultures." Party organizational structures are able to act as socializing agents affecting the role orientations of legislators in most direct ways (Wahlke *et al.* 1962: 376). From this perspective, representational roles are perceived as "habits" in a Tocquevillian understanding. They are learned in the context of party organizations, and structure the beliefs of individuals in far reaching and lasting ways, independent of other experiences and independent of any strategic concern. Thus, the role of a party delegate can be understood as learned behavior that is rooted and constantly reactivated within party organizational structures.

How exactly do legislators learn the role of a party delegate within party organizational structures and what could explain differences in role perceptions? One obvious answer to this question concerns the process of organizational recruitment and the structures of party organizational careers. Individual legislators might differ in whether they held party office prior to their ascent to public office and in whether they experienced either longstanding or short lived party organizational careers. It is plausible to expect a systematic relationship between sustained party organizational careers and the likelihood of adapting a partisan role. This plausibility is based upon the assumption that longstanding partisan careers provide learning experiences at the individual level.

Longstanding party organizational careers are likely to strengthen partisan attitudes in a twofold way. First, they should function as means to reinforce legislators' ideological beliefs and policy positions and thus to increase the cohesiveness of parties (Bowler *et al.* 1999). Cohesive parties are in turn likely to support the role of a party delegate because individual MPs should see no reasons to disagree with people they simply don't disagree with. Second, party organizational careers should function as a means to socialize individuals in procedural ways. In the course of party organizational careers, individuals should learn to become team players and to play by the rules. In the process of their advancement within party organizations, individual party members should learn that they depend fellow members and that they owe their advancement to their party. This might result in an unquestioned acceptance of the role of a party delegate in the long run, maybe even despite disagreement at the levels of ideology and policy.

The recent literature on representational roles contradicts structural–functionalist theory by placing a strong emphasis on their choice-based underpinnings. Proponents of this perspective consider roles as being the results of individual motivations and interests rather than of functional imperatives and learned behavioral norms. Donald Searing's landmark study on the British case provided a crucial impulse in this regard. This author perceives roles as being partly based on individual motivations of a rather personal nature. He pictures these roles as being preference roles compared to status roles that can be derived from formal parliamentary positions and thus institutional imperatives. In the wake of new institutionalism, Searing's motivational approach to role theory was further developed by Strøm (1997) and Müller *et al.* (2001).

Müller *et al.* (2001) and Strøm (1997) emphasize the strategic nature of representational roles resulting from the interplay between given interests and institutional constraints. While they applaud Searing's focus on individual motivations, they criticize his move to equate the role concept itself with those very motivations. In turn, both authors perceive roles as behavioral strategies rather than given motivations or preferences. They emphasize the need to explain such behavioral strategies on the basis of the interplay between institutional constraints and given interests that cannot be deducted from their institutional contexts that are thus "exogenous" to these contexts. Strøm (1997: 171) argues that "much of the diversity of parliamentary lives is subject to relatively simple explanations." These "simple explanations" are assumed to be primarily rooted at the institutional level of politics. In contrast to Searing, approaches emphasizing the strategic nature of representational roles expect systematic relationships between particular institutional structures and particular role choices. However, the question remains, what particular kinds of institutions structure representational roles, how, and why?

In the context of choice-based approaches to studying representational roles, the quest for reelection and the particular structure of electoral systems are seen as concrete factors explaining role choices (Strøm 1997: 165). This corresponds to a rich literature on legislative behavior emphasizing particular hypotheses in this regard. In this literature, generally, plurality systems and open list proportional systems (preference voting systems) are considered to promote a closer relationship between representatives and geographic constituents, and thus the role of a district delegate (Cain *et al.* 1987; Carey and Shugart 1995). More particularly, students of legislative behavior suggest two explanations for these assumed relationships that are distinct with regard to the assumed causal mechanisms mediating between the electoral system level and the strategic considerations of legislators, and that are also distinct with regard to the predicted relationship.

The first mechanism concerns the visibility of legislators and the related traceability of policies and services provided to the district (Cain *et al.* 1987). In plurality systems, legislators and their services to their districts potentially are most visible and thus most beneficial in their quest for reelection. In contrast to this, in multimember districts, legislators face a severe free-rider problem. Fellow legislators can easily claim credit for any legislative action that favors the district without contributing to producing it. This provides incentives to discard the role of a district delegate and to adopt the role of a party delegate in turn. From the perspective of individual legislators, collectivist representational strategies are the only solution to this free-rider problem. Collectivist representational strategies are means to coordinate the production of constituency services and to allocate their electoral benefits in equal ways.

The second mechanism mediating between the electoral system and the behavioral level concerns intra-party competition. Carey and Shugart (1995) consider personal vote-seeking behavior, and thus a strong district focus, a reaction to the need to compete with fellow party members in the context of preference voting systems. Preference voting systems allow voters to choose between different candidates of one and the same party. From the perspective of individual candidates, this decreases the value of the party brand as a vote-winning mechanism; members of the same party need to find ways to distinguish themselves from each other to appeal to voters. Carey and Shugart (1995) furthermore argue that in preference to voting systems, increasing district magnitudes provide increasing incentives for personal vote-seeking behavior since in such contexts competition increases in fierceness.

Obviously, Carey and Shugart's model does not sit well with those theories of personal vote-seeking behavior that emphasize the visibility of legislators and the traceability of their services as core mechanisms mediating between electoral incentives and individual-level behavior. In contrast to these theories, Carey and Shugart consider plurality systems as providing few incentives for personal vote-seeking behavior, and under open list contexts these authors emphasize a positive and linear relationship between district magnitude and personal vote seeking, despite the threat of free riding.

Case selection, data, and hypotheses

The following analysis focuses on the German case for two reasons. First, in Germany, party organizational careers are of crucial importance for legislative recruitment, thus differences in length and structure could account for differences in partisan role orientations. Second, the country's mixed electoral system provides the basis for a quasi experiment. It allows varying relevant electoral incentives while holding many other contextual factors constant.

In Germany, in fact, political parties have monopolized legislative recruitment (Borchert and Golsch 1999). Parties need to select candidates for legislative offices either by nominating them for party lists or for nominal votes in one of the 299 single-seat districts. Theoretically, independent individuals are able to bypass parties at the nominal tier by collecting a specific number of signatures and thus by putting themselves on the ballot. But this remains a theoretical option without much practical relevance at the federal level (Best *et al.* 2001: 69).

Earning a candidacy to the German Bundestag presupposes long and cumbersome careers in party organizational contexts. The literature on this topic unveils crucial patterns and variables in this regard. Political careers usually start with becoming a party member. Different empirical studies find different pieces of evidence regarding the length of party membership prior to the acquisition of a mandate to the German Bundestag. Herzog (1975: 175) in his seminal study on political careers conducted in the mid-1970s found that the average (West) German legislator joined his or her party at the age of 31 (FDP), 30 (CDU) and 26 (SPD) and earned his or her first mandate to the Bundestag on average after 7.1 (CDU/CSU) and 8.9 years (FDP). This is short compared to the findings of Patzelt (1999: 252) reporting for the mid-1990s an average party membership of 18 years prior to earning a legislative mandate at the state or federal level. However, despite these differences in detail, in the German case, party membership is obviously a crucial prerequisite for earning a legislative mandate.

The timespan between joining a party and earning a legislative mandate typically includes two crucial career steps. The first step concerns an upward move within party organizational contexts by acquiring some party office at some moment in time. Patzelt (1999: 252) reports that 90 percent of his respondents held some party office at some party organizational level. The empirical findings of Herzog (1990) and Schüttemeyer and Sturm (2005) support this finding. The second career step concerns earning a mandate at the local or regional level before advancing to higher levels of electoral politics. Borchert and Golsch (1999: 126), for the German case, do not consider this second step a "must" compared to securing some kind of party office. But a successful electoral track record at the local level is nevertheless considered beneficial for further advancement. Herzog (1990: 37) reports that almost 70 percent of all legislators in the Eleventh German Bundestag in fact held a local mandate prior to their election to the Bundestag.

Most party organizational careers take off at the local level. However, this is by no means a mere gateway through which political elites pass through rapidly on their way to higher-level party offices. It rather appears to be a sustained element in most political careers for longer periods of time. Herzog (1975: 71) reports that many of his respondents kept their local party offices for an average period of ten years. Herzog (1975: 81) furthermore observed the vertical accumulation of party offices during party organizational careers. A majority of his respondents kept their local or regional offices while advancing to higher party organizational offices.

The general career patterns reported above do not rule out the existence of alternative avenues to the German Bundestag and thus the absence of political socialization via party organizational careers. According to Herzog (1975: 150), a minority of German political elites earns their way to the top through so-called crossover careers. The biographies of these individuals do not include long apprenticeships in party organizational contexts, and most of them did not take detours at lower levels before earning top positions in their parties. Approximately 10 percent of Herzog's respondents fall into this category.

The centrality of party in legislative recruitment enables party organizations to shape the role perceptions of individual party members and to function as socializing agents. Therefore, it is plausible to assume a positive relationship between the length of party membership and party office on the one hand and the likelihood of a partisan role orientation on the other. To be sure, this does not dispute the strategic basis of political careers. For example, the trend towards the vertical accumulation of party functions might reflect the highly decentralized nature of the nomination process in German politics (Schüttemeyer and Sturm 2005). To secure reelection, MPs have to gain and maintain the support of local party elites during the nomination process. It is perfectly rational and strategic in this regard. My argument focuses on the long-term effects of party organizational careers on role orientations. In the course of sustained careers in party organizational contexts, individuals are more likely to identify themselves more closely with the ideology and policy concerns of their parties, to become team players, and to accept the standards and rules governing collective decision-making in their parties. From this perspective, party organizations and party organizational careers function as independent variables explaining representational roles.

Electoral systems provide independent incentives to emphasize or downplay the role of a partisan. The German mixed-member system combines incentives for party-centered behavior flowing from PR closed-list systems with incentives for personalized behavior flowing from plurality systems. Previous research demonstrates the behavioral consequences of this system, and the existence of two subsets of MPs characterized by distinct patterns of behavior (Lancaster and Patterson 1990; Klingemann and Wessels 2001; Stratmann and Baur 2002).

German voters cast two votes associated with two different tiers of election (Kaiser 2002). They elect half of their representatives via nominal votes in single-seat districts; the other half is elected via closed party lists in multi-member districts. This latter mode of election stresses party and provides incentives for a partisan role orientation. This is because candidates run as representatives of their parties in multi-member districts without being visible and directly accountable to their voters. In contrast, legislators elected via nominal votes are directly accountable to voters in their district and thus enjoy a higher level of visibility. Thus, they should be more inclined to question partisan role orientations and to adopt a district focus.

The German electoral system is characterized by a large number of dual candidacies with approximately 80 percent of all legislators running as dual candidates (Manow 2007). Pekkanen *et al.* (2006) and Bawn and Thies (2003) argue for the predominance of the nominal mode of candidacy in cases of dual candidacies and thus emphasize contamination effects between the two tiers of election. According to this argument, any dual candidate perceives him or herself primarily as a district candidate, even if elected via the list vote. Legislators elected via party lists but running as dual candidates are considered to "shadow" the incumbent in their district (Lundberg 2006). Saalfeld (2008) argues with regard to this phenomenon, that nominally elected legislators do not possess a monopoly in constituency representation.

In this chapter I agree with the initial assumption made by the "shadowing" argument, emphasizing contamination effects between the two tiers of election. However, I disagree with the conclusions drawn assuming a systematic difference in role perceptions between "pure list legislators" on the one hand and the rest on the other. Instead, I argue that the chance to actually win a nominal vote should structure the considerations of dual candidates, and that we should see a systematic difference between those MPs who are able to win a district and those who aren't – including those who ran solely on the basis of a party list and those who ran as dual candidates but are unlikely to win their district (Zittel and Gschwend 2008). A likely future winner should be more focused on his or her district compared to a likely future loser.

The following analysis is based upon the assumption that in the German mixed system, electoral incentives to question the role of a partisan should increase with the chance to win a nominal vote independently of the actual mode of election (Zittel and Gschwend 2008). The list mode of election will not necessarily reinforce partisan orientations *if* legislators also ran in a district in the previous elections and *if* they lost by a narrow margin, which allows one to consider the district as winnable next time. In this case, I expect few differences between nominally elected legislators on the one hand and legislators elected via list votes on the other. The real distinction should be between legislators who are likely to win a district in the upcoming elections and those who are hopeless in this respect.[2]

The following empirical analysis is based on the German Candidate Study 2005 (GCS). The study is a postal survey of all 2,346 district and party-list candidates of the five parties represented in the German Bundestag in 2005: the Social Democrats (SPD), Christian Democrats (CDU/CSU), Free Democrats (FDP), Greens and the Socialist Party (Left.PDS). The majority of candidates, namely 1,050 (45 percent), pursued double candidacies, competing in a particular district as well as on a party list. Only 434 (18 percent) of all candidates solely ran in one of the 299 electoral districts and 862 (37 percent) competed only on a respective party list. The response rate of our survey with 1,032 completed questionnaires (44 percent) was more than satisfactory. Six hundred and sixty-nine district candidates and 363 party-list candidates did participate.[3]

The data set includes 220 successful candidates, meaning candidates elected to the German Bundestag in 2005.[4] This covers 36 percent of the members of the Sixteenth German Bundestag, on which the following analysis will be based. This large overlap between the GCS 2005 and the Members of the Sixteenth German Bundestag allows for the study of representational roles among German MPs on the basis of this candidate survey. It also justifies using the term "legislator" in the following to refer to the respondents of the survey, even though many of them were in fact candidates at the time they participated in the survey.

The model I will test in the proceeding analysis includes the five independent variables discussed above measuring the assumed effect of party organizational careers on representational roles. First, I will distinguish candidates according to the *length of party membership* in years. Second, I will further differentiate candidates according to their history of *party employment* in terms of years. Third, fourth, and fifth, I will distinguish candidates according to the number of years they held *party offices/functions* at the local, regional, and national levels.

To test for the effect of Germany's mixed-member electoral system, I will firstly distinguish candidates according to their *modes of election* as being nominally elected in a single-seat district (=1) or as being elected via a party-list in a multi-member district (=0). My sample is nicely balanced with 95 legislators (43.4 per cent) being elected in a nominal fashion and 124 (56.6 per cent) being elected via a party list. Second, I will differentiate candidates running in districts according to their *chances of winning* their district races in hopefuls (=1) and electorally hopeless (=0) candidates. Only seven out the 220 elected candidates in the sample did not run in a district at all. The other 213 elected candidates ran either only in a district or as double candidates in a district and on a party list. These candidates divide up in 52.5 percent (n=115) hopeful candidates, who either won the district (95) or who came close to winning and entered the Bundestag via a list mandate (20), and 47.5 percent (104) hopeless candidates who entered the Bundestag via their party list.

In the following I will test for the relative weight of electoral incentives and career patterns in explaining role orientations by running several regressions with my independent variables on two indicators that measure the importance of party and district as a focus of representation. To get at this piece of information the GCS 2005 asked the candidates to give an estimate of how important it is for them to represent the voters of their own party and the voters in their district ranging from 1 (the least important) to 5 (the most important). These items were part of a battery including other items such as "all voters in the nation," and "particular social groups." I expect candidates who perceive themselves as party delegates to place a high importance on representing voters of their own party.

In a last step of the analysis I will run a regression with my independent variables on one indicator measuring consistent priority structures only. This indicator can be perceived as a close approximation to the notion of a role concept. It distinguishes between those respondents who put a high priority on representing the voters of their parties *and* a low priority on the aim to represent their voters in the district on the one hand, and those respondents who defined their goals in the reverse consistent rank order.

To sum up, in the following analysis, I expect to find a relationship between party organizational careers and the role orientations of legislators. German legislators with a long history of party membership, a long history of party employment, and a long history of holding party offices at different organizational levels should emphasize the role of a party delegate. However, if role orientations are based upon strategic considerations rather than learned behavior, electoral incentives stemming from Germany's mixed-member electoral system should show some effect on legislators' role orientations. Compared to legislators elected via party-lists, nominally elected legislators should have an incentive to adopt the role of a district delegate; compared to legislators without any chance of winning an electoral district, legislators hopeful of carrying a district in future elections should have an incentive to adopt the role of a district delegate.

Representational roles, party organizational careers, and electoral incentives in the German Bundestag

Given Germany's reputation of being a party democracy, the role of a party delegate does not loom as large among German legislators as one would have expected. Table 6.1 demonstrates that only about one-third of our respondents rank the task of representing all voters of their parties as their top priority. A much larger portion clearly considers this goal as being of moderate importance; the mean score is 2.9. However, very few respondents perceive this aim of least importance. Party obviously does not dominate the minds of German legislators entirely but it can't be entirely discounted either.

The overall relevance of the party delegate role among German legislators can be further explored in comparison with three alternative role orientations the GCS 2005 asked for. Almost 90 percent of our respondents ranked the "representation

Table 6.1 The role orientations of legislators in the Sixteenth German Bundestag

	Representing all voters of party (n = 208)	Representing all voters in district (n = 210)	Representing all German citizens (n = 210)	Representing particular social groups (n = 202)
Most important	12	47.6	24.8	3.5
2	19.7	31	25.7	5.9
3	37.5	11	13.3	8.9
4	26	7.1	18.6	30.3
Least important	4.8	3.3	176	61.4
Mean	2.9	1.9	2.8	4.3

Note
The original (translated) question was: "There are different opinions about whom an elected member of parliament should primarily represent. What is your opinion? Please rank the following five goals from 1 (most important) to 5 (least important)".

of all of their voters in the district" as a priority (rank 1 and 2). In light of this result, the role of the district delegate appears to be more important in the German Bundestag than we intuitively would have expected. The average respondent scores 1.9 on this item. In contrast, the "representation of particular social groups" is of a relatively low priority for German legislators given the mean score of 4.3 with 61 percent of respondents rankingthis item as "least important." If judged by the mean score of 2.8, the "representation of all citizens of Germany" is of equal importance for German legislators compared to representing voters of their parties. However, there is a decisive difference between these two items with regard to their frequency distributions. The frequencies on the former item are much more polarized compared to the latter one; clearly, party runs through the minds of most respondents at moderate intensity levels.

The meaning of the district delegate role can be further investigated by looking at what exactly legislators wish to do for their district, meaning in what sense they aim to represent their district. The GCS (2005) asked respondents to rank several items related to this subject matter in terms of their importance on a scale from 1 (most important) to 5 (least important). Table 6.2 summarizes the scores for each one of these items. It demonstrates that communicating with voters in the district and helping with individual problems takes center stage in respondents' subjective understanding of the role of the district delegate. In contrast, the representation of political concerns is of a much lower importance to German legislators; the mean score for this item is 3.1. According to this finding, party and district are not necessarily competing principals but rather complementary ones. Their relative importance might vary with their functional contexts. While legislators might focus on their districts in personal and economic matters, they might be more inclined to concentrate on their parties in matters of national politics.

The previous descriptive analysis demonstrates considerable differences between individual legislators regarding their role orientations in general and

Table 6.2 Types of district responsiveness in the Sixteenth German Bundestag

	Help with individual problems (n = 213)	Take care of the economic interests of the district (n = 212)	Be accessible to voters and communicate (n = 210)	Represent political interests of voters in district (n = 208)
Most important	29.6	27.8	43.8	12
2	31	28.3	30.5	20.7
3	26.8	25.5	17.6	21.6
4	11.3	13.7	6.7	36.1
Least important	1.4	4.7	1.4	9.6
Mean	2.24	2.39	1.91	3.11

Note
The original (translated) question was: "There are different views about what an elected member of parliament should primarily do for his or her constituency. What is your opinion? Please rank the following five goals from 1 (most important) to 5 (least important)".

regarding the importance of party in particular. These differences call for an explanation that is in the center of the following analysis. In particular, this analysis asks about the role of strategic choices based on electoral incentives compared to learned behavior in the context of long and complex party organizational careers.

In the aggregate, the GCS (2005) confirms many of the findings in the empirical literature on political careers in Germany but at the micro level also highlights differences in this regard. Figure 6.1 summarizes the party organizational backgrounds of our respondents. With regard to party membership it demonstrates that all respondents were party members and that most legislators were long time party members with a mean value of 22 years. However, Figure 6.1 also demonstrates differences in this regard with extremes ranging from one year to 45 years.

With regard to offices held at all party organizational levels, Figure 6.1 demonstrates an average cumulative tenure of 18 years with extreme cases ranging from 0 years to 75 years across all levels. If we focus on the level of the positions held, the GCS (2005) stresses the importance of the local realm of party politics. A large majority of legislators (78 percent) held some function at this level while fewer served as party officials at the regional (61 percent) or national levels (29 percent). The average legislator held a local party office for 10.5 years compared to 4.8 years (regional) and 2 years (national); 25 respondents out of 220 valid cases (11 percent) did not hold any party office prior to running in the 2005 elections. Party employment is a less frequent occurrence in a German legislator's career and thus is not included in Figure 6.1. Only 8.5 percent (19 out of 220 valid cases) of our respondents were employed by their party prior to earning their mandate with employment histories ranging from 6 months to 23 years.

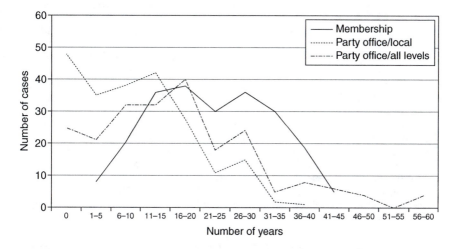

Figure 6.1 Party organizational background of legislators in the Sixteenth Bundestag.

The career patterns of German legislators reported above are interesting descriptive details in themselves. But are they able to explain the role orientations of German legislators? Table 6.3 presents the results of a regression analysis on three indicators measuring three distinct role orientations, namely the role of a district delegate, the role of a trustee, and most important in the context of this chapter, the role of a party delegate. This analysis provides a straightforward preliminary answer to my initial question. In light of its results, the role orientations of German legislators appear to be strategic choices rather than learned habits.

None of the indicators used to measure the length and the depth of party organizational careers is related in any significant way to our three dependent variables measuring the role orientations of respondents. In light of Table 6.3, it simply does not matter in the degree to which legislators subscribe to the role of a party delegate whether they held party offices for a longer or for a shorter time, whether they held party offices at the local, regional or national levels, whether they are a long time party member or freshmen in party politics, and whether they have been employed by their party or not.

Table 6.3 supports the theoretically expected relationship between the chance to win a nominal vote on the one hand and the role orientations of legislators on the other. Hopeless legislators consider the representation of the voters of their party more important compared to hopeful legislators. The results of the regressions in Table 6.3 support my assumption that the mode of election does not explain much in Germany's mixed-member system, although the relationship runs in the expected direction. Legislators elected in a single-seat district consider party less important compared to colleagues elected on the basis of party lists. However, the relationship is statistically not significant.

Table 6.3 Foci of representation and their sources in the Sixteenth German Bundestag

	Represent party (1/most thru 5/least)	Represent district (1/most thru 5/least)	Represent all citizens (1/most thru 5/least)
Mode of election (1 = district)	−0.180 (0.773)	−1.663** (0.776)	0.932 (0.779)
Chance of winning district (1 = high)	0.465* (0.272)	−1.663*** (0.291)	−0.285 (0.264)
Party membership in years	0.003 (0.019)	0.005 (0.020)	−0.022 (0.018)
Party employment in years	0.051 (0.060)	−0.032 (0.067)	0.011 (0.059)
Party office/local in years	0.005 (0.017)	−0.027 (0.019)	0.014 (0.017)
Party office/regional in years	0.017 (0.023)	0.003 (0.025)	−0.021 (0.022)
Party office/national in years	−0.020 (0.034)	−0.007 (0.037)	0.028 (0.034)
Year of birth	−0.044** (0.018)	0.047*** (0.018)	0.008 (0.017)

Source: German Candidate Study 2005.

Note
Entries are unstandardized regression coefficients, robust standard errors in parentheses; $*p<0.1$; $**p<0.05$; $***p<0.01$.

The choice-based approach to studying representational roles is further supported by the findings on the district delegate role presented in Table 6.3. On this indicator, again, we find no support for the impact of party careers on role orientations. The expected effects of electoral incentives are in turn quite visible and strong. Legislators elected in single-seat districts consider the representation of voters in their districts as more important compared to legislators elected via their party lists. Legislators' electoral prospects provide additional explanatory power in the expected way. Legislators running in single-seat districts with fair chances of winning are more likely to adopt the role of a district delegate compared to hopeless legislators not running at all in a district or running without a fair chance of winning.

The indicators used in the analyses above remain in a somehow distant relationship with the more complex concepts they mean to measure. The following final step in my analysis aims to further narrow the gap between the role constructs investigatee in this chapter and the empirical indicators used to measure them. It is based upon a regression with my independent variables on an indicator that distinguishes between two groups of MPs with consistent preference rankings regarding two foci of representation, namely party and district.

The 220 surveyed legislators include all in all 152 cases that show consistent preference patterns regarding their focus of representation. Of these 152 legislators, 29 placed a high priority (rank 1, 2, or 3) on the task of representing the voters of their parties while placing at the same time a low priority (rank 4, 5) on the task of representing voters in their districts. These representatives can be considered as pure and diehard party delegates. They stand in contrast to 123 legislators with reverse preference patterns, placing high priority on representing voters in their districts, while downplaying the representation of the voters of their party. These respondents can be considered pure and determined district delegates. Table 6.4 reports the findings of this regression analysis.

Table 6.4 Role orientations and their sources in the Sixteenth German Bundestag

	Party delegate (= 1) n = *152*
Mode of election (1 = district)	−1.121 (0.997)
Chance to win district (1 = high)	−1.452** (0.514)
Party membership in years	−0.037 (0.037)
Party employment in years	0.036 (0.099)
Party office/local in years	0.000 (0.037)
Party office/regional in years	0.012 (0.046)
Party office/national in years	−0.059 (0.084)
Year of birth	0.047* (0.029)

Source: German Candidate Study 2005.

Note

Entries are unstandardized regression coefficients, robust standard errors in parentheses; $*p<0.1$; $**p<0.05$; $***p<0.01$.

The findings reported in Table 6.4 are consistent with my previous findings, despite the more demanding dependent variable used in the analysis. Table 6.4 supports my previous argument that role orientations are strategic choices rather than learned habits. Again, neither of the measures for party organizational careers is able to explain any variance in role orientations. In contrast, Germany's electoral system and the incentives flowing from it can explain some of the observed variance. Hopeless legislators are more likely to place a high importance on the task of representing voters of their parties compared to hopeful candidates.

Conclusion and discussion

The preceding analysis provides a clear-cut answer to the research question asked in this chapter. It pictures representational roles as strategic choices rather than habits of the heart learned during a long career in party organizational contexts. The 220 German legislators included in this analysis respond to the German mixed-member electoral system in the expected strategic way. Legislators competing in single-seat districts with a fair chance of winning are more partial to the role of a district delegate compared to their colleagues. In turn, legislators unlikely to win a district are more partial to the role of a party delegate. Compared to this effect, the analysis did not produce any evidence supporting any effect of party organizational careers on representational roles.

The main finding of this chapter is particularly puzzling for students of political parties. The preceding analysis is cross-sectional in its nature; thus, the question is, whether parties never fulfilled the assumed socializing function or whether they have failed to do so in recent times. The latter ad-hoc explanation indicates a changing relationship between party organizations and their members over time and thus a changing role of parties in their function as socializing agents. This reading would somehow correspond with Katz and Mair's (1995) cartel party model, which argues for a weakening social basis of political parties and for parties about to develop into mere vehicles for political careers. However, again, another reading of my findings could question the assumed socializing function of parties altogether, emphasizing the social basis of party organizational life and the exogenous nature of representational roles.

If we subscribe to the notion of party organizational change one portion of my findings might suggest that political parties could have hit rock bottom and that they might be in a process of revitalizing themselves in their socializing function. This is because previous analyses demonstrate that young legislators are more likely to adopt the role of a party delegate, independent of the electoral incentive structure they operate under. However, this need not signal a generational effect and a brighter future for genuine partisanship. It could be based upon alternative explanations as well. Alternatively, the greater commitment of young legislators to party could signal a life-cycle effect due to greater insecurities and dependencies in a younger age. As an alternative, it could also signal the impact of professionalization, with individuals pursuing political careers at a younger age subscribing to the party delegate role for strategic reasons because they have nowhere else to go. It is beyond this analysis to further explore these alternative explanations surrounding the age effect demonstrated above.

The findings of the previous analysis carry one important ramification concerning the reform of electoral systems. The preceding analysis suggests that changes in electoral rules will have a direct effect on the significance of party in the process of representation. It suggests that changes to further personalizing electoral rules by introducing mixed-member or flexible list proportional systems could affect the role choices of legislators and thus the legislative process. While such changes might help parties to satisfy public demands for more participation and internal democracy it might also decrease their cohesiveness and thus their ability for collective legislative action (Katz 2001).

The previous analysis emphasizes the relevance of the concept of representational roles as a basis to testing crucial empirical theories of political representation. It focuses on the German case, and thus raises the issue of generalization. My strong assumption is, that it is not the exclusive prerogative of German legislators to behave rationally and to adopt representational roles in strategic ways. I would assume similar effects in any candidate-centered electoral system that allows for a personal vote.

Notes

1 The delegate and trustee conception of political representation has been subject to criticism in recent times. For example, Searing (1994, 1991) and Mueller *et al.* (2001) criticize it for being too abstract and too far removed from the empirical world. However, opponents in this debate tend to talk past each other. I consider alternative role typologies proposed by these authors as supplemental rather than contradictory to the original role types on which this analysis is based. The typologies proposed by Searing or Mueller *et al.* provide more empirical detail and explore the issue from different analytical angles, but they do not contradict the value of the delegate and trustee conception of political representation. The trustee and delegate conceptions of political representation are analytical means to research most relevant features of representative systems in light of the normative underpinnings of democratic government.

2 It is plausible to assume that representatives will calculate this estimate on the basis of a threshold rather than working on the basis of continuous increments. If the loss was narrow, in the range of up to 10 percent, the chances of winning will be considered high, and the incentives for an individualized campaign will increase with this estimate. If the margin was large in the range over 10 percent, the chance of winning will in turn be considered low with few incentives to question the habit of the role of a party delegate. This is a frequently used assumption in the literature. A 10 percent threshold to distinguish between safe and competitive districts is used, for example, by Turner (1953) or in the German case by Schmitt and Wüst (2004). The *New York Times* uses this criterion too for electoral district predictions.

3 The realized sample largely represents the population. The following provides evidence for this: in the realized sample the distribution of candidates by party does systematically deviate from a theoretically expected uniform distribution (SPD 18 percent; CDU/CSU 21 percent; FDP 20 percent; Greens 20 percent; Left.PDS 21 percent); the mean

age of the candidates in the realized sample and in the population of all candidates of these parties are identical (forty-six years); even when considering the mode of candidacy, the distribution in the realized sample (35 percent party list-only candidates; 20 percent district-only candidates) is essentially the same as in the population (37 percent party list-only candidates; 19 percent district-only candidates). The share of double candidacies in the realized sample is the same as in the population (45 percent). Moreover, the realized sample does realistically reflect the rate of incumbents to non-incumbents (7:93) compared to the one in the population (11:89).

4 The sample of 220 elected candidates largely represents the whole population of German MPs in the Sixteenth Bundestag in terms of party affiliation, sex and age. The small parties are slightly overrepresented in the sample with 13.4 percent (FDP), 10.1 (Greens) and 9.7 (PDS). The SPD is also slightly overrepresented with 37.3 percent; the CDU/CSU is underrepresented with 29.5 percent. The sample contains 64 percent male (68 percent) and 36 percent female (32 percent) MPs; 10 percent (14 percent) are born between 1932 and 1945, 57 percent (57 percent) are born between 1946 and 1960 and 33 percent (29 percent) are born in 1960 and after. The sample is more skewed with respect to the parliamentary status of the respondents. It contains 52 percent newly elected MPs compared to 24 percent in the Sixteenth Bundestag.

References

Anderson, C.J. (2009) "Nested citizens: Macropolitics and microbehavior in comparative politics," in M.I. Lichbach and A.S. Zuckerman (eds.) *Comparative Politics. Rationality, Culture, and Structure*, Cambridge: CambridgeUniversity Press.

Bawn, K. and Thies, M.F. (2003) "A comparative theory of electoral incentives," *Journal of Theoretical Politics*, 15: 5–32.

Best, H., Cromwell, V., Hausmann, C., and Rush, M. (2001) "The transformation of legislative elites. The cases of Britain and Germany in the 1860s," *Journal of Legislative Studies*, 7: 65–91.

Borchert, J. (2003) *Die Professionalisierung der Politik. Zur Notwendigkeit eines Ärgernisses*, Frankfurt am Main: Campus.

Borchert, J. and Golsch, L. (1999) "Deutschland: Von der 'Honoratiorenzunft' zur politischen Klasse," in J. Borchert (ed.) *Politik als Beruf*, Opladen: Leske and Budrich.

Bowler, S., Farrell, D., and Katz, R.S. (1999) "Party cohesion, party discipline, and parliaments," in S. Bowler, D.M. Farrell, and R.S. Katz (eds) *Party Discipline and Parliamentary Government*, Columbus, OH: Ohio University Press.

Cain, B., Ferejohn, J., and Fiorina, M. (1987) *The Personal Vote. Constituency Service and Electoral Independence*, Cambridge, MA: Harvard University Press.

Carey, J.M. and Shugart, M.S. (1995) "Incentives to cultivate a personal vote: A rank ordering of electoral formulas," *Electoral Studies*, 14: 417–39.

Converse, P.E. and Pierce, R. (1986) *Political Representation in France*, Cambridge, MA: Harvard University Press.

Eulau, H., Wahlke, J.C., Buchanan, W., and Ferguson, L.C. (1959) "The role of the representative. Some empirical observations on the theory of Edmund Burke," *American Political Science Review*, 53: 742–56.

Herzog, D. (1975) *Politische Karrieren. Selektion und Professionalisierung politischer Führungsgruppen*, Opladen: Westdeutscher Verlag.

Herzog, D. (1990) "Der moderne Berufspolitiker. Karrierebedingungen und Funktion in westlichen Demokratien," in H.-G. Wehling (ed.) *Eliten in der Bundesrepublik Deutschland*, Stuttgart: Kohlhammer.

Kaiser, A. (2002) "Gemischte Wahlsysteme. Ein Vorschlag zur typologischen Einordnung," *Zeitschrift für Politikwissenschaft*, 12: 1547–74.

Katz, R.S. (2001) "The problem of candidate selection and models of party democracy," *Party Politics*, 7: 277–96.

Katz, R.S. and Mair. P. (1995) "Changing models of party organizations and party democracy," *Party Politics*, 1: 5–28.

Klingemann, H.-D. and Wessels, B. (2001) "The political consequences of Germany's mixed-member system: Personalization at the grass root?," in M.S. Shugart and M.P. Wattenberg (eds) *Mixed-Member Electoral Systems. The Best of Both Worlds?*, Oxford: Oxford University Press.

Lancaster, T. and Patterson, D.W. (1990) "Comparative pork barrel politics: Perceptions from the West German Bundestag," *Political Studies*, 22: 458–77.

Lundberg, T.C. (2006) "Second-class representatives? Mixed-member proportional representation in Britain," *Parliamentary Affairs*, 59: 60–77.

Müller, W.C., Jenny, M., Steininger, B., Dolezal, M., Philipp, W., and Preisl-Westphal, S. (2001) *Die österreichischen Abgeordneten. Individuelle Präferenzen und politisches Verhalten*, Vienna: WUV Universitätsverlag.

Patzelt, W.J. (1999) "Parlamentarische Rekrutierung und Sozialisation. Normative Erwartungen, empirische Befunde und praktische Empfehlungen," *Zeitschrift für Politik*, 46: 243–82.

Pekkanen, R., Nyblade, B., and Krauss, E.S. (2006) "Electoral incentives in mixed member systems: Party, posts, and zombie politicians in Japan," *American Political Science Review*, 100: 183–93.

Pitkin, H.F. (1967) *The Concept of Representation*, Berkeley, CA: University of California Press.

Schattschneider, E.E. (1960) *The Semi-Sovereign People. A Realist's View of Democracy in America*, Chicago, IL: Holt, Rinehart and Winston.

Schmitt, H. and Wüst, A. (2004) "Direktkandidaten bei der Bundestagswahl 2002: Politische Agenda und Links-Rechts-Selbsteinstufung im Vergleich zu den Wählern," in F. Brettschneider, J.v. Deth and E. Roller (eds) *Bundestagswahl 2002*, Wiesbaden: VS Verlag für Sozialwissenschaften.

Schüttemeyer, S. and Sturm, R. (2005) "Der Kandidat – das (fast) unbekannte Wesen: Befunde und Überlegungen zur Aufstellung der Bewerber zum Deutschen Bundestag," *Zeitschrift für Parlamentsfragen*, 36: 539–53.

Saalfeld, T. (1997) "Parliamentary roles in Germany," in W.C. Müller and T. Saalfeld (eds) *Members of Parliament in Western Europe. Roles and Behaviour*, London: Frank Cass.

Saalfeld, T. (2008) "Germany: Stability and strategy in a mixed-member proportional system," in M. Gallagher and P. Mitchell (eds) *The Politics of Electoral Systems*, Oxford: Oxford University Press.

Searing, D. (1991) "Roles, rules, and rationality in the new institutionalism," *American Political Science Review*, 85, 1: 239–60

Searing, D. (1994) *Westminster's World: Understanding Political Roles*, Cambridge, MA: Harvard University Press.

Stratmann, T. and Baur, M. (2002) "Plurality rule, proportional representation, and the German Bundestag: How incentives to pork-barrel differ across electoral systems," *American Journal of Political Science*, 46: 506–14.

Strøm, K. (1997) "Rules, reasons and routines: Legislative roles in parliamentary democracies," in W.C. Müller and T. Saalfeld (eds) *Members of Parliament in Western Europe. Roles and Behaviour*, London: Frank Cass.

Thomassen, J. (1994) "Empirical research into political representation: Failing democracy or failing models?" in M.K. Jennings and T.E. Mann (eds) *Elections at Home and Abroad*, Ann Arbor, MI: University of Michigan Press.

Turner, J. (1953) "Primary elections as the alternative to party competition in 'safe' districts," *Journal of Politics*, 15: 197–210.

Wahlke, J.C., Eulau, H., Buchanan, W., and Ferguson, L.C. (1962) *The Legislative System. Explorations in Legislative Behavior*, New York, NY: Wiley.

Zittel, T. and Gschwend, T. (2008) "Individualized campaigns in mixed-member systems. Candidates in the German Federal Elections 2005," *West European Politics*, 31: 978–1003.

7 Party dimensions of representation in Westminster parliaments

Australia, New Zealand and the United Kingdom

Anika Gauja

Representation is a complex and multi-dimensional activity, involving public, parliamentary and party duties. In this chapter I analyse the strength of the party dimension of representation, based on a comparative analysis of parliamentarians' perceptions of, and attitudes towards their legislative roles. I examine several key elements of this dimension: whether MPs perceive themselves as independent representatives or as party partisans, and whether representing one's political party conflicts (both theoretically and in actual practice) with a duty to the parliament (the nation) and representing a geographic electorate. I also analyse the impact of party policy, the degree to which MPs engage with their constituency parties and their relationship with the parliamentary leadership as indicators of the extent to which political parties influence parliamentarians' legislative decision-making on an everyday basis. In doing so, the chapter engages with the broader question of how responsive MPs are to their political parties and the policies on which they were elected, which is an important aspect of the operation of party government in contemporary democracies.

In analysing the extent to which the legislative role perceptions of MPs are shaped by the political parties to which they belong, the study adopts a neo-institutional framework in treating parties as structures that have the capacity to socialize and direct the behaviour of political agents (the party's elected representatives). A total of seven parties are examined, representing three party types in three Westminster-style parliaments. I employ a multi-methodological research design, combining both in-depth interviews with a limited number of surveys previously undertaken in these democracies. This approach allows for a more contextual account of the complexities, strategies and processes of reasoning involved in the representative task, which may otherwise be obscured by relatively static quantitative evidence alone.

Legislative roles and political parties

With the exception of studies that examine the relationship between party allegiance and voting behaviour as measured by-roll call votes (see for example, Kam 2009; Thomassen 1994; Converse and Pierce 1986; Barnes 1977), there has been little academic analysis to date on the effects of party on parliamentary role perceptions and the style and focus of representation. Role theory has done relatively little to accommodate the complexities of party politics with the agency of individual MPs: political parties are often treated in Westminster democracies as unitary actors and the prevalence of party discipline is such that the role of individual MPs is largely insignificant. Studies of individual MPs' attitudes to representation tend to focus on instances where they have either rebelled from the party line (see for example Cowley 2005, 2002); or the vote has been one of conscience (see Judge 1999: 62–9; Pattie *et al.* 1998).

Furthermore, previous role orientation research is predominantly concerned with differences between national legislatures and electoral systems, and for the most part does not highlight variations between MPs of different political parties.[1] Of the studies that have examined the impact of party orientation on role perceptions, the results are mixed. Research on the European Parliament (Navarro 2005; Katz 1999: 72–3) and the US Congress (Page *et al.* 1984), legislatures both characterized by low levels of party discipline, has found the effect of party on role perceptions to be very weak.

However, studies undertaken in legislatures with higher levels of party cohesion suggest that party affiliation nonetheless does influence representative style, broadly along left–right dimensions with left MPs more likely to perceive of themselves as party representatives and conservative MPs as trustees. For example, in Denmark, Damgaard (1997: 84) finds that whilst centre, liberal and conservative MPs are strongly individualist, socialist MPs see themselves as party partisans. A similar pattern has been reported between social democratic, liberal and conservative groupings in Australia, the Netherlands and the UK (Cowley 2002; Rush and Giddings 2002: 11–13; Andeweg 1997: 120; Studlar and McAllister 1996). In Norway there is significant variation in role conceptions between MPs of different parties, but this case does not correspond with the simple left–right scale. Although Norwegian conservative parties adhered to the trend of containing relatively more trustee MPs amongst their ranks, the Socialist left party did not fit this image with equal numbers of trustees and delegates in its party group (Heidar 1997: 101).

Research hypotheses and methods

Are parliamentarians' attitudes to their representative roles influenced by the party to which they belong? Considering the rather disparate results of the limited research to date, do parliamentarians of leftist parties display the qualities of a party partisan to a greater extent than party MPs situated in the centre/centre right of the ideological spectrum?

To answer these questions I examine legislators' role conceptions within three different party types (social democratic, green and liberal democratic) across three parliamentary democracies (Australia, New Zealand and the UK). Seven parliamentary parties are included in the study: the Australian Democrats, the Green Party and the Labor Party (Australia), the Green Party and the Labour Party (NZ) and the Liberal Democrats and the Labour Party (UK). The ideological positions of the parties follow a similar pattern in all three democracies: the Greens occupy a political space furthest to the left of the ideological spectrum, followed by the social democrats (centre–left) and finally the liberal democratic parties (centre) (Whiteley *et al.* 2006; Marsh 2006; Miller 2005). Conservative parties were excluded from the analysis as these party types typically allow their parliamentarians a greater degree of freedom in the legislative arena, refraining from attempts to impose the party programme and removing key aspects of party socialization relevant to this study (the impact of the extra-parliamentary party organization and party policy).

Although adopted as a starting hypothesis, the utility of the left–right dimension in explaining role orientations may derive from the history and organization of these broad party groupings rather than any difference in their ideological standpoints. Parties of the left in the democracies under consideration (social democratic and green parties) have historically prioritized the supremacy of the membership and the role of the parliamentary party as delegates of a broader industrial or environmental movement. Conversely, both the Australian Democrats and Liberal Democrats evolved from existing parliamentary party groupings or were founded by MPs, and emphasize the independence of parliamentarians in their organizational ethos. Other variables that are considered here and which may provide some explanation for role orientations include the legislative status of a party – whether it is in government or opposition; variations in the method of election for any given parliament; and the age and size of the parties themselves.

As New Zealand and Australia adopted their parliamentary traditions from the UK, all three states function under the Westminster system of government and have developed from similar constitutional and legal frameworks governing the executive and representative duties of MPs. Therefore, what would otherwise be a key variable is held constant in this sample. All three democracies have traditionally had very strong two-party systems. This is still the case in the UK, which effectively functions as a unicameral legislature[2] elected by a first-past-the-post electoral system. However, significant electoral reforms undertaken throughout the 1990s saw New Zealand transform from a two-party to a multi-party system with up to eight political parties now routinely present in parliament. As a bi-cameral parliament, parties in Australia are elected under two systems: preferential voting in the lower house (House of Representatives) and by proportional representation in the upper house (Senate). Whilst the former electoral system has maintained the strong two-party character of the House of Representatives, the quota system in the Senate has otherwise allowed smaller parties (such as the Australian Democrats and the Australian Greens) to secure seats in the parliament.

The distinction between two-party and multi-party systems (facilitated by proportional representation) may influence the responsiveness of party MPs to party policy and their attitudes to representation,[3] particularly when they have been elected by virtue of a party list (as occurs in New Zealand). This would, on first examination, eliminate the tension between representing one's party or a specific electorate. However, consensus democracies also introduce an element of compromise that must be reached for parties to form coalitions and govern effectively, which in certain circumstances may produce pressure on the parliamentary party to deviate from party policy in reaching agreement on legislation.

Given the largely contradictory evidence on the effect of party on role perceptions reported by previous quantitative surveys, this study takes a different approach utilizing in-depth interviews with 34 MPs conducted by the author between 2003–2008 to analyse with greater precision and detail the individual attitudes of legislators towards their roles and duties.[4] To supplement this original evidence, I have also used previous qualitative studies of Green MPs' attitudes to representation in Australia (Vromen and Gauja 2009; Turnbull and Vromen 2006) and Labour Party MPs in the United Kingdom (Cowley 2005; 2002).

The use of interviews and qualitative analysis enables the researcher to examine 'why' MPs vote the way they do, adding insight into previous quantitative studies of 'how' MPs vote (Rasmussen 2008). They are also useful in overcoming some of the problems of administering surveys constructed according to predefined representative roles and potential influences, to which MPs may provide 'socially acceptable' answers (Katz 1999: 64). Although I explored a number of common topic areas with interviewees (for example, how they interacted with their local parties, how they weighed up legislative issues, their thoughts on party discipline), the interviews were essentially unstructured so as to appreciate the behaviour of MPs 'without imposing any a priori categorization that may limit the field of inquiry' (Dexter 2006; Fontana and Frey 2005: 706).[5]

Nonetheless, conducting interviews as the means by which to analyse MPs' attitudes to their representative roles suffers from a number of difficulties. Although it may be unintended, the interviewer inevitably shapes the discussion or narrative between the MP and himself/herself. Interaction inevitably occurs on a personal level, and may be influenced by such factors as gender, age, insider/outsider status and country of origin. For example, can we assume that the answers a parliamentarian gives to a young female researcher from a university outside the interviewee's country of origin will be the same as those given to an older male who has previous experience working in the parliament? Access to political elites is difficult without insider status, and this in turn compounds the problem of gathering a representative sample. The response rate amongst parliamentarians to political science research is notoriously low. For example, the British Representation Study conducted in 1997 obtained a sample of 78 respondents – a response rate of only 12 per cent.[6] The problem is not so acute when analysing smaller parties with limited parliamentary representation; but does present a significant barrier to researching MPs from the larger parties and conducting cross-party research. Given the representativeness of the sample, criticism could also be made of the limited potential such data yields for generalizations to be made and meaningful comparative research to be undertaken. However, the research does present an opportunity to examine the applicability of previous findings to individual cases (Rasmussen 2008: 12) and to formulate a number of inductive hypotheses that can be tested in future research.

The complexity and multi-dimensional nature of representation is such that surveys may also produce seemingly contradictory results, for example when legislators cite numerous (and inconsistent) influences upon their legislative decision-making and behaviour. Interviews can provide a way of exploring these contradictions and constructing possible explanations. The use of in-depth interview techniques, rather than simply asking focussed questions, allows a more nuanced analysis of legislative roles combining both function and description – that is, legislators' perceptions of their roles with accounts of their actual political practice.

What do surveys reveal about role perceptions in Westminster parliaments?

Before analysing the effects of *political parties* on role perceptions, it is important to note that the institutional context (the parliament) within which legislators operate is potentially a significant determinant of their legislative behaviour and attitudes to representation (Rush and Giddings 2002). To this end, the constitutional design of representative democracy in the UK, Australia and New Zealand is rooted in Burkean conceptions of the role of the parliamentarian as an independent representative, which might constitute an important influence on parliamentarians' overall view of their representative task.

Most House of Commons (UK) MPs, regardless of whether they are Labour, Liberal Democrat or Conservative members, share a common conception of their roles as 'independent' legislators. As Burnell (1980: 14) has argued, 'they see themselves as representatives very much defined by Burke: they claim the right to exercise their individual judgement, and on that basis to treat the Party's Election Manifesto and Programme as little more than advisory' (see also Norton 1997; Searing 1994). In the 1997 British Representation Study, UK MPs were asked whether they should vote with their party, regardless of conscience or the national interest.

Table 7.1 shows that only a small proportion of MPs agreed with this statement. On average, 11 per cent of respondents across the Conservatives, Labour Party and Liberal Democrats felt that they should vote with their party over their conscience, and only 7 per cent indicated that they would vote with their party

Table 7.1 UK MPs should vote with their parties over conscience and national interest (% in agreement)

	Labour	Conservative	Liberal Democrat
Party over conscience	19	10	4
Party over national interest	10	8	4

Source: Norris, P. (2011).

Note

$n = 78$.

over the national interest. However, the table also shows that there is considerable variation in MPs' attitudes to this potential conflict in their representative roles by party type. Labour Party parliamentarians are most likely to perceive of their role as a party delegate, while the Liberal Democrats are the least likely. These findings also correlate with previous work undertaken by Rush and Giddings (2002: 11), who found that although all British MPs regarded themselves as representing their constituents first and foremost, 'Conservatives were more likely to place the nation second and the party third, whereas Labour respondents placed the party second and the nation third. This emphasis on party among Labour respondents permeated most aspects of their role perceptions'.

Using data from the 1993 Australian Candidate Study (ACS) sampling successful parliamentary candidates and incumbent MPs, Studlar and McAllister (1996: 76) reported that conservative legislators in Australia 'are less likely than their Labor counterparts to emphasize party factors and are more likely to emphasize the free mandate', echoing the British experience. Subsequent ACS have not included questions that enable a longitudinal comparison of the direct influence of party, parliament or the electorate on the role conceptions of parliamentarians. Nor is this evidence available for New Zealand MPs. However, some comparative data is available on the time MPs' devote to particular activities associated with the representative role. Table 7.2 draws together the results of candidate surveys in Australia, New Zealand and the UK conducted between

Table 7.2 Percentage of party MPs engaged in aspects of the representative task

Representative task	NZ Labour	NZ Greens	ALP	Australian Greens	Australian Democrats	UK Labour	UK Liberal Democrats
Hours per month spent attending local community functions							
<10	31	40	9	**90**	**93**	36	25
10–20	**44**	**60**	43	10	7	29	25
>20	25	0	**48**	0	0	35	**50**
Hours per month spent dealing with constituents' problems							
<10	12	0	6	**80**	77	9	**37.5**
10–20	**44**	40	15	0	8	23	25
>20	**44**	**60**	**79**	20	15	**68**	**37.5**
Hours per month spent speaking at public meetings							
<10	**56**	0	**70**	**90**	**83**	**83**	**75**
10–20	25	40	21	10	17	15	25
>20	19	**60**	9	0	0	2	0
Hours per month spent attending party meetings							
<10	**63**	40	**64**	**90**	**75**	**81**	**78**
10–20	31	40	25	10	25	19	11
>20	6	20	11	0	0	0	11

Sources: Birkbeck University of London (2011); New Zealand Election Study (2011); Australian Social Science Data Archive (2011).

Note: numbers in bold represent the highest values for each party.

2001 and 2005, which asked comparable questions of MPs on the allocation of their working time between hours spent at community meetings, dealing with constituents' problems, speaking at public meetings and attending party meetings. The first three activities are taken as components of the MPs' constituency role, whereas the last (attending party meetings) as an aspect of the party function of representation.

As the table indicates, parliamentarians, regardless of their party orientation, spend significantly less time attending party meetings than on other aspects of the legislative role. For example, more time is spent solving constituents' problems by social democratic party MPs, which amounts to more than 20 hours per month for 68 per cent of UK Labour and 79 per cent of the ALP respondents. Compared to zero UK Labour MPs and only 11 per cent of ALP parliamentarians spending more than 20 hours per month attending party meetings, this suggests that if party is a strong factor shaping conceptions of the representative task, this is not reflected by a disproportionately greater amount of time spent on party activities. With the exception of the Greens in New Zealand, parliamentarians of all parties also spend comparatively little time attending and speaking at public meetings.

Outside the parliament, the bulk of most parliamentarians' time is devoted to attending community functions and dealing with constituency concerns. It is only the MPs of the two smaller parties with a history of representation in Australia – the Greens and the Democrats – whose MPs spend less than 10 hours per month on these activities. This could be explained by the fact that these MPs are not elected to parliament by a local constituency (rather the electors of a state) and hence do not perform a constituency function. Further, questions to address the time spent on parliamentary activities (for example, committee work, debates, etc.) were not included in the ACS. Time spent on such parliamentary activities may have explained the relatively smaller timeshare allocated to constituency and party work by these parties, which have traditionally focused on exerting influence and securing governmental accountability through parliamentary means (see for example, Gauja 2008).

Interview evidence

Building on the results obtained through previous surveys of parliamentarians and looking more closely at the individual cases, the in-depth interviews conducted with MPs indicated that legislative independence was seen as the 'default' perception amongst members of Westminster-style parliaments. Although party is a significant socializing force and this perceived independence is subject to a number of organizational constraints such as party discipline and the resources and time available to members to form a considered opinion (discussed below), none of these influences was seen by interviewees as compromising their overall agency.

Table 7.3 illustrates the broad role orientations of the participants in this research. Interviewees were placed in one of four categories (party, qualified party, parliament, constituent), according to the emphasis placed on these respective interests during the course of the interview. Examples of statements that indicate a particular role orientation are provided in the section below. For most MPs, party does play the most prominent role. While many MPs claimed to act in the interests of the parliament/nation, interestingly, acting in constituents' interest was only clearly prioritized by one MP. Although the aim of the table is to provide some clarity and a basic indication of the frequency of particular representative conceptions, the results should not be interpreted conclusively as the representative function (by its very nature) is extremely difficult to categorize or quantify. For example, interviewees often expressed different and sometimes conflicting views as to their representative priorities during a single interview. The category 'qualified party' was adopted to incorporate this conflict. The analysis that follows will attempt to provide some explanation of how these inconsistencies are possible.

Partisanship amongst Labour Party parliamentarians

Perceptions of representation as a partisan activity occurred most frequently amongst Labour Party MPs in the sample, and reveal a sense of duty to the party that is based on the acceptance that the individual has been elected on the basis of a party platform, or political 'brand', both in terms of the voting effects of party identification and the resources the party was able to supply. An Australian Labor Party MP commented:

Table 7.3 Summary of role orientations emphasized by interviewees

Party	Qualified party	Parliament/Nation	Constituent
Stott-Despoja (Aus. Dem.)	Bartlett (Aus. Dem.)	Allison (Aus. Dem.)	Siewert (Aus. Greens)
Cohen (Aus. Greens)	Milne (Aus. Greens)	Cherry (Aus. Dem.)	
Hale (Aus. Greens)	Plibersek (ALP)	Greig (Aus. Dem.)	
Rhiannon (Aus. Greens)	MP2 (UK Labour)	Lees (Aus. Dem.)	
Albanese (ALP)	Barnett (NZ Labour)	Murray (Aus. Dem.)	
Arena (ALP)	Tanczos (NZ Greens)	Jones (Aus. Dem.)	
Hall (ALP)	Bradford (NZ Greens)	Chesterfield-Evans (Aus. Dem.)	
Lawrence (ALP)		Davey (Lib. Dem.)	
MP1 (UK Labour)		Howarth (Lib. Dem.)	
NZMP1 (NZ Labour)		Jones (Lib. Dem.)	
Dyson (NZ Labour)			
NZMP2 (NZ Labour)			
Moroney (NZ Labour)			
Pettis (NZ Labour)			
NZMP3 (NZ Labour)			
NZMP4 (NZ Labour)			

Note
'Qualified party' denotes primary allegiance to party, qualified by the option of a conscience vote in extraordinary circumstances.

Our philosophy is that people don't elect you to the Parliament. They elect the Labor Party in your seat to the Parliament. For the most part, a person's personal following in any seat is slim compared to the party identification and there's some areas where you will see people really jack up and refuse to enter the chamber for a vote, but it is very, very rare.

(Tanya Plibersek, interview, 11 July 2007)

Similarly, a NZ Labour parliamentarian explained that she was in the 'fortunate position' to be a member of parliament, 'but I'm not here because of my charm and good looks. It's because of all those people standing behind you and beside you that are helping to propel you here' (Jill Pettis, interview, 12 March 2008). However, interviewees revealed conceptions of party representation that were predicated upon different foundations. Plibersek (ALP) also saw party representation as the product of the collective will of like-minded individuals:

I think that you have to examine your own conscience and there are some things that no matter what the party decision was, I would not be able to vote for that thing in parliament. But if you're regularly making that decision [...] if you've made that decision more than once or twice in your lifetime you should seriously consider whether you should remain in the political party.

(Tanya Plibersek, interview, 11 July 2007)

Anthony Albanese, also of the ALP, highlighted the importance of party representation as providing political agency, in contrast to the place of an Independent or unaligned representative in what is essentially a two-party system:

I'm part of a political party, I'm bound by a political party, I support that political party and I don't decry from that. Because of that I have an opportunity to influence government rather than just be an individual shouting out things.

(Anthony Albanese, interview, 18 July 2007)

Albanese's response suggests that party representation, far from being dichotomous with constituency representation, can actually facilitate the latter.

Given that existing survey evidence indicates that labour parliamentarians are, for the most part, independent legislators, how can we account for the emphasis placed upon party representation by the interviewees? One possible explanation is provided by Katz, who suggests that the independent deliberations of MPs include considerations of political strategy and not only policy preferences – hence MPs can 'truthfully claim to be following their own judgement in preference to the views of their parties' (Katz 1999: 64). Another explanation may lie in the efforts that many Labour MPs make in attempting to reconcile the interests of their electorate with those of their party within the broader context of the parliamentary party organization, before an issue even enters the chamber.

Interviewees suggested that if they are presented with an issue that appears contrary to the party's platform or policy, they will often 'pursue the argument within the party', and 'take up constituents' views with ministers and get responses and justification', as 'being a member of the Labour Party does not exclude independent action and thought'. Interestingly, this is a strategy that was suggested only by the parliamentarians belonging to social democratic parties, and might represent a practical attempt by those legislators to accommodate different conceptions of representation within the framework of a tightly disciplined party structure.

Green parliamentarians

Overall, green MPs have mixed perceptions as to whether they see themselves as party or electoral representatives. When asked their view as to whether an MP should be able to vote with their conscience on issues they felt conflicted with the party's position, three of the 16 Green MPs holding public office in Australian federal and state parliaments felt strongly that they should, four were strongly opposed and the remaining nine felt that party MPs should be allowed to vote with their conscience, but that this would only happen very rarely in practice (Vromen and Gauja 2009). Green MPs who were in favour of the conscience vote cited their previous parliamentary experience as a strong factor influencing this preference, indicating that parliament may be a stronger socializing force than party in the case of the Greens, illustrated in the following three quotes:

> My thoughts have changed since I became more involved and an MP. There are some things I don't want the party to tell me how to vote on [...] I think it takes responsibility away from the MP [...] Sometimes you can put your own conscience on hold and go to the party and say – 'you make the decision'. I can't do that. And it's only since I've been put in this position that's it really come home to me that it is an unacceptable to bind people.
>
> (Rachel Siewert, interview, 14 July 2007)

> The majority of my work is about the work of the parliament, and the constituency [...] Less of my time is with the party [...] I will support things that the party asks me to support, but if you look at my overall work, that would not be very much compared to my parliamentary work.
>
> (Kerrie Tucker, cited in Vromen *et al.* 2009: 106)

> Basically I am a really strong supporter of all parliamentarians having a conscience vote and I wouldn't be in politics without one [...] In all my years in parliament I never voted against what the Greens had decided, but the fact that I know I can is very important for me because I cannot stand the herd mentality.
>
> (Christine Milne, interview, 14 July 2007)

Given that Green parties in Australia and New Zealand are located to the ideological left of Labour, this evidence presents a significant challenge to the hypothesis that MPs view their representational roles along the left–right dimension. However, this does not mean that political parties are not a socializing force. Rather than party ideology being the primary determinant, the political culture of a party and its organizational structure (as expressed in the party's rules and constitution) may provide a more convincing explanation.

The four parliamentarians who strongly opposed the use of conscience votes in the previously cited study all belonged to the New South Wales (NSW) State branch of the Green Party of Australia. Green Party interviewees commented that this branch has a very strong culture of regarding its parliamentarians as party delegates, and unlike the national Constitution of the party, the NSW Constitution outlaws explicitly the practice of conscience voting, regardless of the issue (Art. 41.5). As NSW Legislative Council MP Lee Rhiannon explained, 'we don't have a conscience vote, so we're bound by the policies of the party' (interview, 27 April 2005). We see the socialization effect of this constitutional and organizational imperative in the perceptions of NSW Senate MP, Kerry Nettle, who regards herself 'primarily as a representative of the party. It's the way I was elected, as a Green. In terms of prioritizing my time, and what I'm doing, a lot of that is prioritized around the goals that we, as an office, have set for ourselves' (quoted in Vromen and Gauja 2009: 106). In this respect, the culture of the NSW Greens is very similar to that of the labour parties, whose history is grounded in a strong discourse of membership sovereignty.

Diversity in attitudes to representation: Liberal democratic parliamentarians

Unlike the social democratic MPs, where a definite trend towards party representation is evident, the interviews with MPs from liberal democratic parties did not suggest that a common conception of representation was shared amongst MPs of this party type. Describing the character of his parliamentary party, one Australian Democrats Senator commented that 'my experience over four years is that we're not a united team of seven, we're seven Independents who share common values' (Brian Greig, interview, 4 February 2003). Two other Australian Democrats MPs gave almost polar opposite accounts of their roles as representatives:

> Who do you represent? Do you represent the people? Do you represent your committee? Do you represent your conscience? Do you represent the party? Who are you? That's a question that really has to be asked, and I think that most people – voters – think that you represent the voters. I think you represent the people. I don't think you represent the party.
>
> (Richard Jones, interview, 27 August 2005)

> There is a belief, albeit a non-constitutionally recognized one, that the party room is supreme [...] I don't have a problem with the notion that I'm the

person that they've selected to go into the parliament to make that final decision [...] but by the time I reach that point I should have consulted with my
members, I must be accountable to my members, I must be conscious of
party policy, conscious of what the President of the party says.

(Natasha Stott-Despoja, interview, 5 February 2003)

Given the liberal ideology of these parties, the diversity in parliamentarians' attitudes to representation is not surprising. However, as we have seen, this diversity also extends to parliamentarians from Green parties, whom, if the initial
hypothesis were correct, would almost all see themselves as party representatives given that green parties are commonly situated to the left of the ideological
spectrum (for example, see Miragliotta 2006: 586–7; Manning 2002: 17).

Dealing with conflicts in the representative role

Generally [the views of party members, constituents' interests and the
national interest] all pull in the same direction. At the end of the day, your
own judgement and conscience are the deciding factors, but your judgement
takes account of all the other factors.

(UK Labour MP, interview, 18 April 2007)

As the above quote illustrates, the question as to whether a parliamentarian conceives of himself or herself as a representative of the party, the electorate or the
parliament may actually be redundant. Although parliamentarians did acknowledge the possibility that these representative roles could conflict in theory, they
emphasized that in practice this rarely (if ever) occurs. For example, Australian
Democrat MP Andrew Bartlett did not see any tension in being a representative of
both the party and the electorate, as 'you're always weighing up a bunch of
factors' (interview, 8 July 2007). This lack of conflict concurs with the actual
balance that Australian and New Zealand MPs strike in allocating time and importance to parliamentary, constituency and party tasks (illustrated in Table 7.2).

In addition to the observation that tensions between different representative
roles are usually lost within a host of considerations that depend on the individual issue, there are a number of additional factors that promote consistency. One
cause is the difficulty of actually gauging the interests of a member of parliament's constituency:

The conflict would be a conflict between values and ideas on the one hand
and the interests of constituents on the other. It has not come up yet. One of
the reasons why it wouldn't come up very often is because the interests of
constituents are never one way or the other – there are a lot of varied interests. And it's unlikely that you will be in a situation where the interests of
everybody, or a large number of constituents, go in one direction or the
other.

(David Howarth, interview, 16 March 2007)

As discussed, Labour MPs will advocate for their constituents within the party room, thus negating conflict before it even gets to the chamber. Supporting the observations of Eulau *et al.* (1959: 745), given that MPs were elected to parliament with party endorsement, most considered they had a mandate to implement party policy and personally believed that party policy and principles coincided with what was best for the electorate. This was particularly true for the MPs of liberal democratic parties, who saw their organizations as representing broad values rather than detailed policy preferences, which are in many ways easier to reconcile with the interests of particular constituencies. Australian Democrat parliamentarians felt that considering their duty to the electorate within the broader principles and objectives of the party was enough (in the absence of actual policy) to satisfy both representative interests simultaneously. The only exception was a Senator who commented that being a representative of the party and the electorate could not easily be reconciled 'because our members tend to be, in left–right terms, more left, heavily critical of the government of the day, and we know that our voters are people who vote for the government of the day' (Lyn Allison, interview, 14 July 2007). The pragmatic solution devised by Green MPs to this potential conflict is to adhere to the principles of the party, but create a different 'sales pitch' to the party MPs' broader constituencies. As Rachael Siewert explained (interview, 14 July 2007): 'we understand where our base is coming from but we don't change our policy because of it. We sell it differently, or we'll pitch different aspects of it, but we won't change it'. In doing so, parliamentarians are able to pragmatically negate conflict that may arise within their legislative roles when the views of party members and constituencies differ.

Party influences on practical aspects of decision-making

Moving beyond attitudes to representation, another way in which we can analyse the impact of political parties upon legislative roles is to look at the range and importance of different influences and interests on the everyday decision-making processes of parliamentarians. In this section of the chapter I examine three such practical influences: the directives of the parliamentary party leadership, the views of the party membership and the impact and guidance provided by official party policy. Finally, I examine whether the method by which an MP is elected (single-member constituency or party list) has any discernable impact on partisan role perceptions.

Views and directives of the parliamentary party leadership

Previous research (see for example, Cowley 2002) has suggested that the advice (or directions) of the party leadership constitutes a significant influence upon the decision-making processes of party MPs. In Australia, New Zealand and the UK, parliamentary parties are tightly disciplined groupings and representatives of the same party vote together in 95 per cent of formal divisions (Bingham Powell 2000: 60). In complementing quantitative analyses, in-depth interviews with

MPs are able to provide valuable insights into why this is the case, and how the parliamentary party hierarchy operates to influence individual members' decisions.

All MPs interviewed, regardless of the party they belonged to, readily admitted in the vast majority of instances they would vote in the chamber according to the position that their party had predetermined. In his work on rebellions within the UK Labour Party, Cowley (2005) has emphasized the threat of discipline or demotion and the possibility of promotion as important mechanisms used within the party to promote unity. However, interviewees for this research project placed greater emphasis on ideological coherence and unity, political strategy and resource allocation as factors promoting discipline.

Political strategy is a paramount consideration shaping voting patterns. Several NZ parliamentarians suggested that members vote together for the simple reason that 'disunity is death'. Furthermore, as Liberal Democrat MP Ed Davey explained, 'by and large in the vast majority of situations it's obvious how everyone has to vote' – that is, MPs of a particular party will vote consistently with one another simply because they share similar ideological principles and values (interview, 23 May 2007). In this instance, the party leadership performs a co-ordinating role in aggregating the opinion of the caucus and directing party MPs to vote as they would anyway. Furthermore, while strong party discipline has been criticized as compromising parliaments as deliberative institutions (see for example Herman and Lodge 1978), if there is significant policy disagreement amongst MPs, this is resolved within the parliamentary party room rather than on the floor of the chamber:

> [Party] discipline doesn't necessarily mean lack of debate and in fact I think that good discipline comes from robust debate, because when you've had the debate and you've lost, or you've won – then collectively accepting that is where the discipline comes in, but it's not instead of robust debate.
>
> (Sue Moroney, interview, 13 March 2008)

Whilst it is possible that MPs' policy principles may come second to maintaining a strong political team, the opportunity for debate within the party caucus (as described above) constitutes one mechanism by which both policy preference and strategy can be reconciled.

The final reason MPs voted on the advice of the parliamentary leadership and the decisions of the caucus was simply a matter of time, legislative expertise and resource allocation. This was by far the most common explanation provided by MPs in the smaller parties: the Greens and the Australian Democrats. In dividing portfolio responsibilities amongst members of the parliamentary party, MPs were happy to defer to the advice of the relevant portfolio-holder on how to vote on a proposed piece of legislation. For example, Australian Democrat MPs will consult extensively with each other and consequently vote as a bloc. [Parliamentary] 'sitting days routinely incorporate at least one party room meeting [...] at which the position the Democrats will take on upcoming legislation is agreed'

(Ward 1997: 125). Each member of the parliamentary party will 'cover different areas and we basically follow the leader, the portfolio-holder' (Andrew Bartlett, interview, 8 August 2007).

A similar process occurs within the Australian Greens:

> We generally come to the same view on many matters and now that we've got the division of portfolio responsibilities, we certainly tend to say, well whoever is dealing with that matter [...] they're obviously more on top of it, they've had the opportunity to research more and to develop and to discuss with both Greens and members of the community and interest groups. So one will defer to their opinion.
>
> (Sylvia Hale, interview, 28 April 2005)

This evidence suggests that when analysing the causes of party cohesion, resource allocation, ideological similarities amongst elected members and political strategy are important factors and should be considered in addition to disciplinary measures designed to enforce the party line.

Views of the party membership

Another means by which to assess the impact of party on legislative roles and behaviour is to gauge the level of contact that MPs have with their party members and supporters, in contrast to their constituents. Parliamentarians were asked how they maintained links with their political parties. The amount of party activity undertaken and the importance accorded to this task varied significantly between individuals. Examples of continued links with the party included serving on policy committees, attending national conferences and distributing newsletters and parliamentary reports. Attending local and regional party meetings was by far the most common response, but the frequency of attendance varied from those MPs who went on a regular basis (for example, bi-monthly), to those who attended no more than two such meetings a year. Parliamentarians of all party types generally felt that such contact was worthwhile as a source of inspiration, ideas, or just to 'touch base' with the party organization.

However, a significant proportion of MPs will not prioritize consulting or meeting with their local party members any more than maintaining links with their broader local constituency, reflecting the fact that few Australian MPs will spend more than 10 hours a month attending party meetings and findings in the NZ context that local party meetings are a relatively unimportant aspect of the legislative role (Miller 2004: 101). The party meetings that MPs are most likely to organize and attend are usually open to the general public, consisting of general debates on topical issues, rather than following a party-led programme:

> I do a lot of consultations with non-Labor Party members as well; open forums usually organized by members of parliament in particular areas where they would write out to their constituency. Probably the ones that

were best attended were when I had childcare as part of my portfolio responsibilities. There would sometimes be a couple of hundred people in the room at any one time wanting to talk about childcare policy [...] I found those fantastically valuable in making up my mind about the best way to deal with some of the problems in the area.

(Tanya Plibersek, interview, 11 July 2007)

A Labour MP in the UK spoke of distributing feedback forms and questionnaires to his local party, but also stressed that he did the same 'area, by area, across the constituency with residents as a whole. I feel a strong sense of accountability to my constituency as well as to Party members' (interview, 18 April 2007). Liberal Democrat MP David Howarth did not find it necessary to prioritize, or deal with communications from the local party in a different way to those of constituents: 'we don't distinguish in that correspondence between party members and anybody else – so we deal with all the letters, emails and telephone calls in the same way' (interview, 16 March 2007). For those MPs that did consult with the party membership, this was generally done in a rather ad hoc way, with the ultimate responsibility for the decision resting with the individual parliamentarian:

If there's policy that the party's given guidance on we'd vote on that of course, but where the party doesn't have a position [...] I could talk to a few people, but it would just be the people I know [...] I probably would talk to a few people but at the end of the day it would be me making the decision based on what I think is right.

(Nandor Tanczos, interview, 13 March 2008)

Apart from the pressures of time, one reason for reluctance amongst parliamentarians to engage actively with their local parties is the perception that they fail to reflect the views of the party as a whole. As Liberal Democrats' Shadow Minister, Ed Davey, explained:

There's a monthly borough executive, which is not representative of the party. There's a council group meeting which is also not representative of the party. There are pappadams and politics, which are in my area and every other month we have a curry and a political discussion. That's still not representative of the party but there's more people at that so by definition it's more representative. So I'll go along to that.

(Davey, interview, 23 May 2007)

The Australian and NZ Greens are the only parliamentary parties that consistently emphasize the importance of ongoing consultation and communication between MPs and party members. However, the fact that we do not observe a similar trend among social democratic MPs indicates that there is no direct connection between levels of engagement with the party membership and partisan conceptions of representation.

The impact of party policy

Despite the constitutional position of MPs in Westminster parliaments as 'independent legislators', political parties will often use internal rules and procedures to influence the decisions of their elected representatives. Despite their legal unenforceability (see Gauja 2008), when viewed from the perspective of the MPs, these measures are quite effective and party policy does influence the legislative priorities of party parliamentarians – there would be little substance in the notion and practice of party government if it did not (however, see Caul and Gray 2000). The influence of policy was explained by an ALP parliamentarian as follows: 'if you're committed to something then you've got to make sure it's clearly and unambiguously in the platform. Resolutions are also binding, so [policy influence] can be through that, and with very few exceptions that is what occurs' (Anthony Albanese, interview, 18 July 2007). However, this relationship of influence is not based on a direct mandate. In practice, parties tend to formulate policy in very broad terms (in the language of aspirations and objectives) or they simply do not have policy on all the issues that come up for debate in the legislature, so it is only really the broad policy principles of the party that come into play. The influence of policy principles (as opposed to detailed directives) appears to be similar across all party types, regardless of the organizational relationship between the party and its MPs:

> What's in the Labor Party platform is sometimes different to [...] they're broad statements of principles rather than details of policy implementation, so I guess you'd say that the membership of the party is more likely to affect the direction of the party and its principles than to draft legislation.
>
> (Tanya Plibersek, ALP, interview, 11 July 2007)

> Obviously new issues crop up now and again and you just need to make a response in line with what you believe the principles of party policy to be. Obviously there will be very rapidly developing areas of policy and often you just don't have time to do that – you just have to react.
>
> (David Howarth, Liberal Democrats, interview, 16 March 2007)

NZ Greens MP Nandor Tanczos regarded 'broad-brush direction setting' as the most useful form of membership input into policy, allowing MPs a degree of flexibility to mould party policy to the issues at hand. Failing this, NZ Green MPs generally 'go back to the principles' (interview, 13 March 2008). An Australian Green MP explained the process as: 'if an issue comes up about which the Greens have no specific policy and of course there are thousands of issues that come up day to day on all manner of things, then the parliamentarians make the decision based on the principles of the Greens as they see fit' (Christine Milne, interview, 14 July 2007). The style and focus most common to MPs in this study was summed up nicely by Milne when she explained that the parliamentary party 'operates on a trustee model – we are the trustees of the Greens' philosophy and we are trusted to deliver on that and are accountable for that' (interview, 14 July 2007). Whilst the party remains the legislator's primary representational focus, unlike the party delegate (Thomassen 1994: 248) the *party trustee* has a greater degree of independence or agency to implement the broader principles and philosophies of his/her party rather than specific policy directives. This particular representative conception stems from the practical reality that parliamentarians must have some discretion to respond to changing circumstances:

> To what extent have we got freedom to adapt? We are supposed to react today to something the Prime Minister's just said – the detail of it – and we may not have any specific policies, so to what extent is it built on the policy that already exists or are we deviating? If the MPs step out of line too far of course our own party will turn on us. Learning how to ride that line is something that I guess all MPs have to do. The longer any of us are MPs I think the more we learn where the lines are and what you can do and not do, how much latitude you have.
>
> (Sue Bradford, interview, 5 May 2008)

The role conception of the 'party trustee' (adopted by most parliamentarians) provides a possible explanation and reconciliation for the seemingly inconsistent survey evidence that suggests that MPs view themselves as independent legislators, bound by a party mandate.

Does the method of election make a difference?

Previous studies have indicated that the method by which members of parliament are elected may have a significant impact upon their legislative role perceptions: those elected under a proportional representation system with a relatively closed list and multi-member districts are more likely to emphasize party service. Australia and New Zealand are excellent cases for testing this proposition as parliamentarians in each of these democracies are elected according to both PR and single-member plurality electoral systems. A mixed-member proportional system is used to elect parliamentarians in the New Zealand House of Representatives. In Australia, members of the Senate are elected through a variant of proportional representation, while their House of Representatives counterparts are elected under the alternate vote system in single-member electorates. Given that some MPs under both these systems need to be selected on a party ticket to ensure reselection, it could be argued that their primary allegiance would be to the party rather than to the electorate and that these electoral systems prioritise party rather than constituency service. As Karp (2002: 139) suggests, 'electorate MPs have a strong incentive to respond to local interests [...] whereas list MPs have a stronger incentive to respond to party leaders, and develop expertise that transcends local electorates'. For example, Studlar and McAllister (1996: 76) found that senators were more likely to endorse the responsible party model of representation than their House of Representatives counterparts.

Previous research based on results from the NZ Candidate Studies has suggested that there is a distinct difference in the legislative priorities of list and electorate MPs, with the latter group prioritising constituency activities to a greater extent (Gilton and Miller 2006: 182; Miller 2005: 207; Miller 2004: 100–2; Karp 2002: 140). However, MPs interviewed for this research generally disagreed with such a strong distinction. While not necessarily representing a geographic constituency, many list MPs assumed a responsibility to servicing the needs of a particular electorate based on a particular issue or ethnic grouping, which tied in closely to their parliamentary activities. Furthermore, Labour list MPs are still expected to maintain links with a regional area, 'they might even have two electorates that they are expected to keep in touch with' (interview with Jill Pettis, NZ Labour Party), and the party has usually insisted that they maintain a constituency office. As one MP explained, 'when I've been a list MP it's been expected that I can win a seat next time round, so I've carried on acting very much as if I were a constituency MP' (interview, 11 March 2008).

Labour list MPs who had previously been electorate MPs commented that they were still drawn into constituency work, by virtue of their previously higher profile amongst electors and the fact that they were still visible to the general public:

> Because my profile is still high, because I'm in the local electorate, because I've been around for 12 years, because most people don't know the difference between a list and a constituency MP, because those who are a bit more politically sophisticated have worked out that if I want someone to fix it, the government's going to fix it, and she's from Labour and they're the government, so I'll go to her.
>
> (Jill Pettis, interview, 12 March 2008)

One important aspect of the role of a list MP belonging to a governing party is addressing constituents' views in geographic electorates where the government may not hold the seat:

> For me, my list role has been about making sure that the non-Labour held electorates in our region have a Labour MP that those communities can connect with. So my role has been more geographically based. I wouldn't say that it would be aligned with the constituency MP role because I've been careful not to do one-on-one individual constituency work in those non-Labour held electorates. I've been focusing on instead making sure that the key community organizations in those non-Labour held electorates – that I visit them frequently, that they know who I am, that they know they can make contact with me if there are issues that they wish to raise. I think that's been quite useful given that we are in government, because it means they have access to a government MP even though their local member of parliament is not in the government.
>
> (Sue Maroney, interview, 13 March 2008)

If we combine this interview evidence with the fact that Australian upper house MPs (represented by the Democrats and Greens in this research) have very mixed perceptions about the extent to which they see themselves as party partisans, it appears as though parliamentarians elected by virtue of a party list or grouping are not necessarily more responsive to the party, nor do they prioritize party activities to any greater extent than constituency MPs. Consequently, method of election does not have a significant impact upon the integrity of the chain of policy trans-mission between party members and party parliamentarians; or if it does, this effect is mediated by other factors, such as MPs' experiences in the parliament.

Conclusions: the party dimensions of representation

The interviews conducted for this research, coupled with existing research on MPs' representative roles in Australia, New Zealand and the UK provided little evidence to support the hypothesis that partisan representation varies between parties according to the left/right ideological spectrum. MPs who belonged to social democratic parties did possess a stronger, more consistent identification with the role of a legislator as a party representative. This was also common to a specific subset of Green parliamentarians in Australia, who were subject to a specific constitutional dictate from their state party. However, MPs of liberal democratic parties and the majority of the Greens (both to the ideological left and right of social democratic parties) were individualist in their attitudes to their representative roles. This evidence suggests that political parties have the capac-ity to be a significant socializing force on MPs, despite their constitutional and legal independence in Westminster legislatures.

The concept of role orientations and the use of interviews and qualitative analy-sis are particularly useful in 'teasing out' this apparent paradox and analysing some of the generalized findings and contradictions uncovered by large-n studies in greater depth. Using the role framework, we learn that patterns of socialization and therefore the potential of MPs to respond to the views and policies of the party membership are more likely to vary with the specific culture of a party (for example, the prominence of the leadership, connections with the membership and the character of debate in parliamentary caucus) and the internal rules that regulate the relationship between the party and its elected MPs (for example, constitutional provisions that emphasize the subservience of the parliamentary party), rather than along a simple left–right spectrum. Parliamentarians' processes of reasoning and decision-making are also important: although some acknowledged the theoretical possibility, the different facets (party, electorate, parliament) of the representative role rarely came into conflict for MPs. Numerous strategies, such as advocating constituents' interests within the party room, and rationalization (that is, convinc-ing oneself that what one does is in the interests of both the party and the elector-ate) have been adopted by parliamentarians to resolve these potential conflicts.

The chapter also examined the salience of different aspects of party influence on MPs' decision-making processes: consultation and engagement with party members, the impact of party policy, advice of the party leadership and method of election. Although prioritized to a greater extent by the Green parties, consultation and maintaining connections with local party members are strategies that are utilized by MPs on an individual basis and there is little evidence to suggest that they provide a significant influence upon the behaviour or partisan attitudes of party MPs in social or liberal democratic parties. Party policy was deemed to have a significant impact in shaping legislative decisions along party lines. However, the degree of freedom party MPs possess in interpreting party policy and the fact that policy does not necessarily cover all issues that arise for debate in the legislature suggests that MPs could be viewed more as 'trustees' rather than 'delegates' of party policy. This may arguably weaken the transmission of policy preferences from party members to the parliament, but it is a more realistic role conception that accommodates political necessities, resource and time constraints, and acknowledges the general public duty of the parliamentarian in Westminster representative democracies.

The influence of the parliamentary party leadership is also an important dimension in shaping legislative roles. However, rather than MPs being coerced into following the decisions of the party, interviewees suggested that this was a conscious decision based on coincidence of ideological principles and policy preferences, political strategy, expertise, resource allocation and the division of labour within parliamentary party groupings. Finally, contrary to previous research findings, the evidence presented in this chapter suggests that MPs' method of election has limited impact on their representative role conceptions, as parliamentarians elected on party tickets do not seem to emphasize party representation to the detriment of constituency and parliamentary service. Overall, the findings highlight the importance of party in shaping, maintaining and analysing legislators' role orientations.

Notes

1 See for example Patzelt (1997); Wessels (1999); and Thomassen and Esaiasson (2006).
2 Under the Parliament Acts of 1911 and 1949 (UK), the House of Lords cannot block legislation passed by Commons, only delay it.
3 See for example Thomassen and Esaiasson (2006); Norris (2004); Thomassen and Anderweg (2004); Norton (2002); Esaiasson and Heidar (2000); and Klingemann and Wessels (2000).
4 Interviewees are identified where possible. However, some quotes are not attributed, to honour confidentiality agreements.
5 Rather than asking parliamentarians whether they felt they represented the interests of their party or constituency, the questions typically asked of MPs were more open: what was your reasoning on this piece of legislation? How does party discipline affect you?
6 Data available at Norris (2011).

References

Andeweg, R. (1997) 'Role specialisation or role switching? Dutch MPs between electorate and executive', *Journal of Legislative Studies*, 3: 110–27.
Australian Social Science Data Archive (2011) Australian Candidate Study. Available online at www.assda.edu.au/ (accessed 24 May 2011).

Barnes, S. (1977) *Representation in Italy: Institutionalized Tradition and Electoral Choice*, Chicago: University of Chicago Press.

Bingham Powell, G. (2000) *Elections as Instruments of Democracy*, New Haven and London: Yale University Press.

Birkbeck University of London (2011) British Representation Study 2005. Available online at www.bbk.ac.uk/politics/our-research/projects/past-projects/british-representation-study (accessed 24 May 2011).

Burnell, J. (1980) *Democracy and Accountability in the Labour Party*, Nottingham: Spokesman.

Caul, M. and Gray, M. (2002) 'From platform declarations to policy outcomes: Changing party profiles and partisan influence over policy', in R. Dalton and M. Wattenberg (eds.), *Parties Without Partisans – Political Change in Advanced Industrial Democracies*, Oxford: Oxford University Press.

Converse, P. and Pierce, R. (1986) *Political Representation in France*, Cambridge, MA: Harvard University Press.

Cowley, P. (2002) *Revolts and Rebellions: Parliamentary Voting Under Blair*, London: Politicos.

Cowley, P. (2005) *The Rebels: How Blair Mislaid His Majority*, London: Politicos.

Damgaard, E. (1997) 'The political roles of Danish MPs', *Journal of Legislative Studies*, 3: 79–90.

Dexter, L. (2006) *Elite and Specialized Interviewing*, Wivenhoe Park, Essex: ECPR Press.

Emy, H. (1975) *The Politics of Australian Democracy: An Introduction to Political Science*, South Melbourne: Macmillan.

Esaiasson, P. and Heidar, K. (2000) *Beyond Westminster and Congress: The Nordic Experience*, Columbus, OH: Ohio State University Press.

Eulau, H., Wahlke, J., Buchanan, W. and Ferguson, L. (1959) 'The role of the representative: Some empirical observations on the theory of Edmund Burke', *American Political Science Review*, 53: 742–56.

Fontana, A. and Frey, J. (2005) 'The interview: From neutral stance to political involvement', in N.K. Denzin and Y.S. Lincoln (eds), *The Sage Handbook of Qualitative Research*, 3rd edn, Thousand Oaks, CA: Sage.

Gauja, A. (2008) 'State regulation and the internal organisation of political parties: The impact of party law in Australia, Canada, New Zealand and the United Kingdom', *Commonwealth and Comparative Politics*, 46: 244–61.

Gilton, G. and Miller, R. (2006) 'Role of an MP', in R. Miller (ed.) *New Zealand Government and Politics*, 4th edn, Oxford: Oxford University Press.

Heidar, K. (1997) 'Roles, structures and behaviour: Norwegian parliamentarians in the nineties', *Journal of Legislative Studies*, 3: 91–109.

Herman, V. and Lodge, J. (1978) 'The European Parliament and the "decline of legislatures" thesis', *Australian Journal of Political Science*, 13: 10–25.

Judge, D. (1999) *Representation: Theory and Practice in Britain*, London: Routledge.

Kam, C. (2009) *Party Discipline and Parliamentary Politics*, Cambridge: Cambridge University Press.

Karp, J. (2002) 'Members of Parliament and Representation', in J. Vowles, P. Aimer, J. Karp, S. Banducci, R. Miller and A. Sullivan (eds) *Proportional Representation on Trial: The 1999 New Zealand General Election and the Fate of MMP*, Auckland: Auckland University Press.

Katz (1999) 'Role orientations in parliaments', in R. Katz and B. Wessels (eds), *The European Parliament, the National Parliaments and European Integration*, Oxford: Oxford University Press.

Klingemann, H.D. and Wessels, B. (2000) 'The political consequences of Germany's mixed-member system: Personalization at the grass roots?', in M. Shugart and M. Wattenberg (eds.) *Mixed-Member Electoral Systems. The Best of Both Worlds?*, Oxford: Oxford University Press.

Manning, H. (2002) 'The Australian Greens and the handicap of left legacies', *Australian Quarterly*, 74: 17–20.

Marsh, I. (2006) *Political Parties in Transition?*, Sydney: Federation Press.

Miller, R. (2004) 'Who stood for office, and why?', in J. Vowles, P. Aimer, S. Banducci, J. Karp, and R. Miller (eds.) *Voters' Veto: The 2002 Election in New Zealand and the Consolidation of Minority Government*, Auckland: Auckland University Press.

Miller, R. (2005) *Party Politics in New Zealand*, Melbourne: Oxford University Press.

Miragliotta, N. (2006) 'One party, two traditions: Radicalism and pragmatism in the Australian Greens', *Australian Journal of Political Science*, 41: 585–96.

Navarro, J. (2005) 'Converging patterns of behaviour in the European Union? The limited impact of socialisation on the Members of the European Parliament', Paper presented at the 3rd ECPR Conference, Budapest, September.

New Zealand Election Study (2011) New Zealand candidate study 2002. Available online at www.nzes.org/exec/show/2002, (accessed 24 May 2011).

Norris, P. (2004) *Electoral Engineering: Voting Rules and Political Behaviour*, Cambridge: Cambridge University Press.

Norris, P. (2011) Shared dataset – British representation study 1997. Available online at www.pippanorris.com/ (accessed 23 May 2011).

Norton, P. (2002) *Parliaments and Citizens in Western Europe*, London: Frank Cass.

Norton, P. (1997) 'Roles and behaviour of British MPs', *Journal of Legislative Studies*, 3: 17–31.

Page, B., Shapiro, R., Gronke, P. and Rosenberg, R. (1984) 'Constituency, party, and representation in Congress', *Public Opinion Quarterly*, 48: 741–56.

Pattie, C., Johnson, R. and Stuart, M. (1998) 'Voting without party?', in P. Cowley (ed.), *Conscience and Parliament*, London: Frank Cass.

Patzelt, W. (1997) 'German MPs and their roles', *Journal of Legislative Studies*, 3: 55–78.

Rasmussen, M. (2008) 'Another side of the story: A qualitative case study of voting behaviour in the European Parliament', *Politics*, 28: 11–18.

Rush, M. and Giddings, P. (2002) 'Parliamentary socialisation: The UK experience', Paper presented at the ECPR Workshops, Turin.

Searing, D. (1994) *Westminster's World: Understanding Political Roles*, Cambridge, MA: Harvard University Press.

Studlar, D. and McAllister, I. (1996) 'Constituency activity and representational roles among Australian legislators', *Journal of Politics* 58 (1): 69–90.

Thomassen, J. (1994) 'Empirical research into political representation: Failing democracy or failing models?', in M.K. Jennings and T.E. Mann (eds), *Elections at Home and Abroad: Essays in Honor of Warren Miller*, Ann Arbor, MI: University of Michigan Press.

Thomassen, J. and Andeweg, R.B. (2004) 'Beyond collective representation; individual members of parliament and interest representation in the Netherlands', *Journal of Legislative Studies*, 10: 47–69.

Thomassen, J. and Esaiasson, P. (2006) 'Role orientations of members of parliament', *ActaPolitica*, 41: 217–31.

Turnbull, N. and Vromen, A. (2006) 'The Australian Greens: Party organisation and political processes', *Australian Journal of Political History*, 52: 455–70.

Vromen, A. and Gauja, A. (2009) 'Protesters, parliamentarians, policy-makers: The experiences of Australian Green MPs', *Journal of Legislative Studies*, 15: 87–110.

Ward, I. (1997) 'Party organisation and membership participation', in J. Warhurst (ed.) *Keeping the Bastards Honest: The Australian Democrats' First Twenty Years*, St Leonards: Allen & Unwin.

Wessels, B. (1999) 'Whom to represent? Role orientations of legislators in Europe', in H. Schmitt and J. Thomassen (eds), *Political Representation and Legitimacy in the European Union*, Oxford: Oxford University Press.

8 Parliamentary roles of MPs in sharp and soft focus

Interviews and behavioural record compared

Marcelo Jenny and Wolfgang C. Müller

The lay observer of politics tends to see parliamentary work as the main or even sole task of MPs. Work in parliament in general and giving speeches in particular is the yardstick that some Austrian news media apply when hunting down the laziest MP of the year and putting all others in pecking order at the end of a parliamentary year. They should know better. It is no secret to politicians and professional observers of politics, whether journalists or academics, that parliamentary work in the narrow sense is only part of their many obligations resulting from public office. Indeed, for some MPs it may not be among their most important tasks. While the floor of parliament in many ways is the most important arena in which MPs act, their contribution to the collective goals of both the nation and their party may be greater if they adhere to some division of labour and concentrate the greater amount of effort on their activities in less visible arenas. These other arenas include constituency rallies, media events such as talk shows on national or regional TV and radio stations, attending meetings of their party organization, visiting administrative agencies and businesses, attending events organized by interest group, and having contacts with ordinary citizens. Notwithstanding that the job of an MP includes such a broad spectrum of often essential tasks this chapter confines itself to analysing what MPs do in parliament.

We choose Kaare Strøm's definition of parliamentary roles as "routines, regular patterns of behavior" (Strøm 1997: 158) as the conceptual anchor of our study. Behavioral data should thus be an excellent, if not the best source of data to capture the roles of MPs. The alternative methodological approach that is used by most classic contributions and is still dominant in the research field on parliamentary roles is the analysis of interviews with MPs (see e.g. Müller and Saalfeld 1997). In this chapter we combine the two approaches. We compare roles or types of Austrian national MPs derived from behavioural data with the role descriptions derived from personal interviews.

The MPs are from the twentieth legislative period (1996–1999) of the National Council, the lower and dominant chamber of the Austrian parliament. We describe the two interview questions most relevant to the topic and the patterns of answers given. Then we present data on MPs' parliamentary activities and develop our typology of MPs based on their behavioural record in parliament. We analyse the match between the behavioural data and the interview data, show where they differ or concur and draw some conclusions on how the different sources of data impact on the roles and types of MPs found in empirical research.

Theory: roles and types of MPs

Modern research on representatives begins with *The Legislative System* by Wahlke, Eulau, Buchanan, and Ferguson (1962). This landmark study distinguished between "role orientations" – its main focus – and "role behavior". "Role orientations" constitute a "coherent set of 'norms of behavior'" while "role behavior" refers to "overt actions which result from legislators' acting in conformity with some norms included in the role" (1962: 8–9). This study's conception of role orientations has been criticized severely because of its underlying functionalistic assumptions. Hence, role-related attitudes and behaviors are considered to be coined by the expectations of the individual's social environment rather than by the actors themselves. Moreover, widespread consensus is assumed about the contents of such roles that may or may not exist (Searing 1991: 1245). Yet first and foremost, the roles developed in *The Legislative System* suffer from being theoretical constructs "that were not operationalized as roles that exist in the minds of politicians" (Searing 1991: 1250). When this is not the case, the question remains why we should expect representatives to behave according to these roles.

In his work, culminating in the magisterial *Westminster's World*, Searing (1994) moved forward the research on parliamentary roles by developing the "motivational approach". Accordingly, political roles are "particular patterns of interrelated *goals*, *attitudes*, and *behaviors* that are characteristic of people in particular positions"(1994: 18). In line with Rational Choice theorizing, Searing considers cognitive career goals as central ("prominent part") for parliamentary roles (1994: 19). Career goals are more important the more explicitly the tasks are defined that come with a particular parliamentary position. Leadership positions – including ministers and junior ministers in the British case and presiding officers, committee chairmen, and all kinds of whips everywhere – clearly come with a long list of tasks that need to be fulfilled (1994: 19). They constitute what Searing calls "position roles". Yet career goals are only part of the story. Searing also includes "emotional incentives" – which provide the "passion" – into his "motivational core" of political roles (1994: 19). Secondary components of political roles are "characteristic attitudes" (or "beliefs") and "characteristic behaviors" (or "actions") (1994: 19). While political leadership positions largely confine MPs to "position roles", backbenchers can chose roles that "have nearly as much to do with the preferences of the role players as with the established rules of the institution" (1994: 13, 395).

Searing's study clearly is a landmark and has moved our understanding of political roles in the right direction. Yet, it may not have gone far enough. We concur with Strøm (1997: 157) that it is not convincing to include motivational incentives as part of the role definition. Rather we prefer to separate individual preferences, (institutional) constraints, and actual behaviour. The preferences held by politicians are not part of their roles, but they exercise influence on the choice and shaping of such roles. Political roles, then, are "routines, regular patterns of behavior" (Strøm 1997: 158). Patterns of behaviour, in turn, are designed to help politicians to reach their goals. The choice of particular behavioural patterns is hence strategic. Individual preferences ("emotional incentives", "passions") and the institutional environment influence the choice of these goals. Unconstrained actors, as assumed in influential first-generation Rational Choice studies, would follow only their individual preferences. Yet no MP is unconstrained by his or her institutional environment. As Searing (1994) points out, there are differences between backbench and leadership positions with incumbents of the former having more freedom to define their roles than those of the latter. In any case, the behaviour that is likely to help in achieving the goals is chosen deliberately by the MPs and thus represents "roles that exist in the minds of politicians" (Searing 1991: 1250). Finally, the behaviour relevant here involves the use of scarce resources such as time, attention, and effort on the part of the MPs.

The conceptual shift in the definition of roles, what the term includes or excludes from Searing to Strøm, makes it much easier to use the terms "roles" and "types" of MP interchangeably. By using Strøm's definition of roles as routinized behaviour we can talk of a typology of MPs and easily build a bridge towards multivariate statistical methods like cluster analyses that are commonly used to find groups of similar cases in the data.

Searing developed the roles or types of MPs from interviews in the 1970s with MPs for the British parliament. There are many system differences between Great Britain and Austria – in particular party system and institutional differences – that suggest that a straightforward transfer of Searing's MP roles to other national parliaments would not work. Back then Great Britain had a true two-party system resulting in alternating single-party governments. In contrast, Austria in the 1990s had a multi-party parliament (with very different sized parties) and a grand coalition government comprising the two major parties, the Social Democratic Party (SPÖ) and the People's Party (ÖVP). As we will demonstrate below, party size has a tremendous effect on the "patterns of behavior" of the respective MPs, even more so when party size is combined with the party's status as a government or an opposition party. The next section describes our research design and data.

Research design and data

From the fall of 1997 to the spring of 1998 in-depth interviews with all 183 Austrian MPs in the Austrian National Council were conducted by a research team of academics and PhD students (Müller *et al.* 2001: 36). Interview partners were assured complete anonymity in publications. Each interview opened with two general questions about the respective MPs' tasks and activities. During the course of the interview we followed up with more specific questions about the various arenas and dimensions of their behaviour: in the constituency, in parliament, in the parliamentary party group, activities to reach out to the public, and the MPs' relations with interest groups. We also asked about changes that occurred during their career as MPs. In the interviews we did not confront the MPs with prefabricated response items. However, for some of the more specific questions the interviewers had a list of sub-dimensions to be used as prompts if the MPs did not mention them in their initial responses. Notes were taken during the interviews and they were transcribed immediately after their conclusion to arrive at close to verbatim protocols. Each of the interviews was subsequently coded independently by two members of the research team. Coding differences were identified and resolved by discussion between the two coders or, if necessary, among the entire research team. These codings formed the basis for quantitative analyses.

Our second source consists of behavioural data on parliamentary instruments that were selected to match with the self-descriptions of parliamentary behaviour from the interviews. They include the number of parliamentary questions, private member's bills and motions introduced by each MP, committee rapporteurships held and speeches given to the plenary between January 1996 and July 1997, which corresponds roughly to the first half of the twentieth legislative period and thus constituted the time immediately preceding the interviews. The period of data for bills and amendment motions as well as committee rapporteurships was somewhat shorter than for other parliamentary instruments, covering January 1996 to the beginning of October 1996 (Müller *et al.* 2001: 264–5). The aim was to have enough data to be able to differentiate activity levels of individual MPs rather than the complete coverage of parliamentary activity.

As already mentioned the political context of the interviews and parliamentary behaviour was the grand coalition government of the SPÖ and ÖVP (S and V in the tables, respectively). Our study covers the last of four consecutive legislative terms of this coalition, which had been governing together since 1986. Initially, the grand coalition comprised 85 per cent of the seats. In the last term, beginning in January 1996 and ending in February 2000, the government parties still held more than two-thirds of the seats between them. Yet, compared to the situation at the beginning of their cooperation in 1986 the opposition was considerably strengthened by the spectacular rise of the Freedom Party (FPÖ, F) and the establishment of two new parties, the Greens (G, from 1986) and the Liberal Forum (L), a 1993 break-away from the FPÖ. Table 8.1 provides the basic information about the government status and parliamentary strength of the parties during the period of this study.

The recorded parliamentary behaviour occurred before our interviews were undertaken. Therefore there can be no observer-induced effect on what the Austrian MPs did in parliament. Rather, any influence worked the other way. We expect that the MPs in formulating answers to our questions drew on their own behaviour in the most recent past.

Table 8.1 Government status and size of parliamentary parties (1997)

	Governing parties	Opposition parties	(n)
Large parties	Social Democrats (S) (71), People's Party (V) (52)	Freedom Party (F) (42)	(165)
Small parties		Liberal Forum (L) (9), Greens (G) (9)	(18)
(*n*)	(123)	(60)	(183)

Note
Number of parliamentary seats given in parentheses.

Parliamentary activities: the MPs' perspective

The following two tables provide information based on the interviews with all 183 MPs who were asked questions about their parliamentary priorities and the parliamentary instruments they deemed most important to their work. The often quite extensive answers given were coded by the research team based on a common coding scheme. The first question we present in Table 8.2 puts the focus on the arenas that the MPs prioritize in parliament. Deliberations in committee are given the most frequent emphasis, followed by dealings with their own party. Only one-tenth of the MPs put their emphasis on activity in the plenary – e.g. giving speeches, being a rapporteur, asking questions. About the same number of MPs mention inter-party negotiations or said "somewhere else". The latter coded statement, given by many liberal MPs, …went outside the scope of the question, which was meant to deal only with intra-parliamentary activity. The answer referred to the MP's dealings with important actors situated outside of parliament, e.g. with the media or interest groups.

Another small group of MPs, among them many Green MPs, say that ranking is impossible, and that everything they do in parliament is equally important.

Table 8.3 shows what the MPs identified as the most important parliamentary instruments for their work. The relevance of parliamentary instruments for MPs is largely balanced between the parties. Yet, predictably, we recognize two imbalances, relating to committee work and parliamentary questions.

Altogether, 56 per cent of the MPs mentioned committee work, but there is a large gap between the answers from government and opposition MPs: 69 per cent of the former, but only 29 per cent of the latter mentioned committee work. Some opposition MPs complained about the futility of tabling their own legislative proposals in committee, as these would be voted down routinely by the government parties.[1]

Parliamentary questions exhibit the opposite pattern: Government MPs are much less inclined to introduce parliamentary questions than those from opposition parties. Plenary speeches were mentioned by about a third of the MPs, by government and opposition MPs in equal proportion. Bills and motions were mentioned overall by slightly less than a third of the MPs, but more often by opposition than

Table 8.2 Most important emphases of parliamentary activity (%)

	S	V	F	L	G	Large parties	Small parties	Gov. parties	Opp. parties	Parliament
Committees	66	65	59	29	29	64	29	66	51	61
Own parliamentary party	43	35	34	14	29	38	21	39	31	37
Plenary	3	6	27	0	14	10	7	4	22	10
Inter-party negotiations	10	14	2	14	0	9	7	12	4	9
Somewhere else	7	6	7	57	0	7	29	7	13	9
No ranking possible, equally important	6	10	5	0	43	7	21	8	9	8
(n)	(68)	(52)	(41)	(7)	(7)	(161)	(14)	(120)	(55)	(175)

Notes
The question was: "Where do you put the emphases in your parliamentary activity?" Additional question asked participants to name the most important ones in case of multiple answers. Coding of answer in up to three different categories allowed. Numbers are column percentages.

government MPs. Note that most bills introduced in parliament are government bills. Moreover, introducing Private Member bills requires party approval and their chances for success, or even of only receiving a considerable amount of attention, is usually slim. Thus it is reasonable that fewer government than opposition MPs call Private Member bills an important item in their parliamentary toolbox.

Parliamentary activities: objective data

In Table 8.3 we have reported responses to a question on the importance MPs attach to parliamentary instruments. The answers are, of course, subjective and include an evaluation component, as instruments can be important even if rarely used. We now turn to the actual behaviour of MPs (as reconstructed from the official record). We measure the amount of parliamentary work of individual MPs with a range of behavioural data. For each MP we measure (1) the number of bills and other material motions, (2) the number of parliamentary questions asked, (3) the number of rapporteur reports to the plenary meeting when bills return from committee deliberations (to be followed by debate and final voting), and (4) the number of plenary speeches per session. Whenever parliamentary instruments require the support of more than one MP, in accordance with common knowledge of experts on Austrian parliamentary practice, we count only the first one to sign.[2]

All of these indicators are "hard" quantitative ones that we have generated from the parliamentary records. Together these indicators cover the range of instruments provided by the standing orders of parliament. They include the most relevant indicators of individual MPs' parliamentary work that can be extracted from publicly available sources for the time immediately preceding our interviews. As access to committee deliberations is restricted, only the successful legislative and non-legislative initiatives of MPs coming out of the committees could be extracted from the official parliamentary records. This introduces a bias towards observing the behaviour of MPs from the two government parties at the committee stage. Proposals introduced at the committee stage make up less than one-fifth of the total number of 689 bills and motions in our study. If anything, these limitations in data access introduce a small bias towards overstating the government MPs' activities.

Austrian MPs differ widely in their actual use of parliamentary instruments. Table 8.4 and Figure 8.1 reveal substantial differences between the MPs for all activities. More than two-thirds of the MPs (69 per cent) have never acted as a committee rapporteur on a bill, but 10 per cent of the MPs gave more than five such reports. Forty-four per cent of the MPs introduced neither a bill nor a motion, but 3 per cent (six MPs) introduced 20 or more. Seventeen per cent never asked a parliamentary question, but 4 per cent introduced 40 or more such questions. Two per cent (three MPs) gave no speech in the plenary, but three MPs at the upper end of the activity scale spoke more than 100 times each. In terms of data structure, the distribution for the plenary speeches comes closest to a normal distribution whereas the reports on bills, the bills and motions, and parliamentary questions look more like negative binomial distributions.

Table 8.3 Parliamentary instruments most important to MPs (%)

	S	V	F	L	G	Large parties	Small parties	Gov. parties	Opp. parties	Parliament
Committee work	70	67	30	22	33	59	28	69	29	56
Parliamentary Questions	31	26	50	22	44	34	33	29	45	34
Plenary speeches	29	39	35	22	22	34	22	33	31	32
Bills and motions	24	28	38	33	33	29	33	26	36	29
Other	21	14	13	11	22	17	17	18	14	17
No ranking possible, instruments are equally important	6	6	15	22	0	8	11	6	14	8
(n)	(70)	(51)	(40)	(9)	(9)	(161)	(18)	(121)	(58)	(179)

Note
The question was: "Which parliamentary instruments are most important to you?". Coding of answer into multiple categories allowed. Numbers are column percentages.

A typology of MPs derived from behavioural data

We ran a two-stage cluster analysis with the four indicators of parliamentary indicators presented above to arrive at a typology of the MPs based on objective data. The resulting typology is shown in Table 8.5. The first stage of the cluster analysis included three activities: parliamentary motions/bills, written questions, and reports on bills. Clustering was done via Ward's method, a standard hierarchical clustering procedure, using squared Euclidean distances as the measure of proxim-

Table 8.4 Descriptive statistics of parliamentary activity data (1996–1997)

	Reports on bills	Bills and motions	Oral and written questions	Plenary speeches
Median	0	1	3	17
Mean	1.5	4.0	7.3	23.6
Standard deviation	3.6	6.2	13.1	23.8
Minimum	0	0	0	0
Maximum	27	31	111	132
Sum (183 MPs)	276	734	1,338	4,348

Note
Period covered: 15 January 1996 to 31 July 1997.

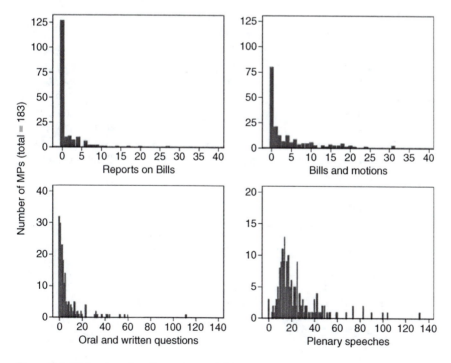

Figure 8.1 Histogram of parliamentary activities.

ity. All variables were range-standardized to the range 0–1 ahead of entering the clustering algorithm. In the second-stage cluster analysis, the five groups resulting from the first stage were entered plus the range standardized number of plenary speeches per session. The two-stage cluster analysis gives more weight to plenary speeches relative to the other three parliamentary activities. The rationale for doing so is that speech making is the most constrained parliamentary activity. Each party has only a very limited number of slots for speakers in most debates. Hence, giving greater weight to parliamentary speeches seems substantively justified.

A cluster solution is always the result of a set of variables run through a specific clustering algorithm equipped with a specific distance or proximity measure. Whether the outcome is, from a substantive perspective, a good cluster solution or the most appropriate for a research question is mostly outside the realm of the methodological literature on cluster analysis. Cluster analysis is an exploratory method of multivariate data analysis that has been weak in giving advice on criteria like "optimality" or "stability" of a cluster structure found (Kettenring 2006). There is thus considerable leeway for researchers with regard to the cluster solution they extract from the data.

The result we present here consists of five types of MPs that we label the Spectator, Rapporteur, Showhorse, Workhorse, and Exemplary MP.[3] Even though these five types result from a cluster analysis, at the same time they seem to approximate a generalized scaling of the MPs from low to high parliamentary activity as shown in Figure 8.2 below. The five groups are of very unequal size: the higher the activity patterns, the fewer MPs. Almost half of the MPs (47 per cent) are classified as Spectators, and only 7 per cent as Exemplary MPs. The distribution resembles a pyramid with a broad base at the first two levels of activity and a narrow peak at the higher levels of activity.

Spectators justify their name by displaying the lowest activity with regard to three of our four indicators. Reporting on bills to the plenary is the only item where they fare on average slightly ahead of Showhorse MPs. Reporting bills to the plenary is the core activity of the Rapporteurs. It is there that they outdo all other groups and they tend to be slightly more active than Spectators in the other realms. Showhorses beat the Spectators and Rapporteurs in all activities except rapporteurships.

Table 8.5 Means of parliamentary activity by type of MP

Parliamentary activities	Spectator	Rapporteur	Showhorse	Workhorse	Exemplary MP
Parliamentary motions/bills	0.4	3.4	5.4	16.9	20.7
Parliamentary Questions	1.9	6.8	8.9	26.7	30.7
Reports on bills	0.8	3.8	0.0	1.0	0.1
Plenary speeches per session	0.2	0.2	0.6	0.5	1.1

Note:
Numbers are mean activity values for MPs belonging to the same type.

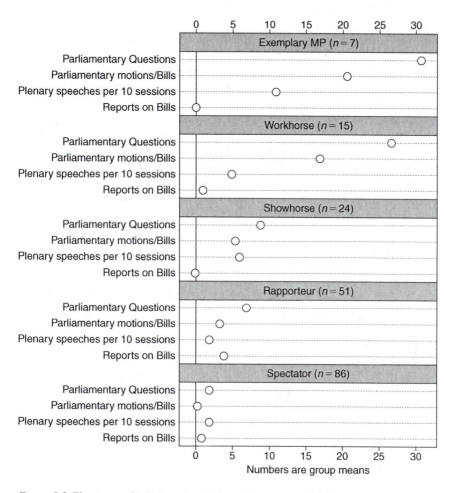

Figure 8.2 Five types of MPs based on their parliamentary activities.

The group label Showhors stems from contrasting this type's behavioural pattern from that of the Workhorses: MPs of the Workhorse type introduced on average many more parliamentary questions, motions and bills. They were behind only in giving speeches. Therefore we labelled them Workhorses and the former group of MPs Showhorses. A small group of seven MPs, named here Exemplary MPs, introduced more parliamentary questions, motions, and bills, and delivered more speeches than the Workhorses. However, the Exemplary MPs did not engage in reporting bills to the plenary. Rapporteurships therefore seem to be a necessary, yet not particularly highly esteemed activity in the Austrian parliament.

Our cluster analysis is deliberately blind or agnostic toward the MP's party membership and includes no variables measured at the party group level. Neither the size of the five parliamentary parties nor their status as a government or an opposition party entered the clustering algorithm. Yet Table 8.6 shows that these two variables exhibit a systematic relationship with the types of MPs. Recall that the five types approximate a dimensional scaling of parliamentary activity. The two small parties, the Liberals and Greens, have a much higher share of high-activity types of MPs than the three large parties. We see that none of the Liberal or Green MPs is a Spectator or a Rapporteur and that none of the Social Democratic or People's Party MPs is classified as an Exemplary MP. The comparison of the three opposition parties – the FPÖ, the Liberals, and the Greens – with the two government parties – the SPÖ and ÖVP, exhibits directionally the same association, though it is slightly weaker. Opposition MPs seem to do more on average than government MPs and we thus find them more often among our Exemplary MPs, Workhorses, and Showhorses. Parliamentary activity and party size show a similar pattern of association as parliamentary activity and party status. Dividing the five parties with these two criteria into binary groups results in a strong overlap. With the exception of the Freedom Party all parties turn up in the same grouping twice.

We nevertheless maintain that these two variables at the party level are separate influences on an individual MP's pattern and amount of parliamentary activity he or she undertakes. Party size directly bears on the division of labour between MPs. Clearly, MPs in a small party have to shoulder a much bigger relative burden of their collective project while parliamentary demands on parties in many respects are not bound to party size. MPs in small parties simply cannot throttle their individual level of activity down to the level of a Spectator without risking their party's presence in the parliamentary arena. In contrast, MPs from large parties are neither required nor allowed by their leaders to use parliamentary instruments to the same extent as their colleagues from small parties. While all MPs from small parties understand that they carry a heavy burden, some would not want to do without these possibilities for a showing in parliament.

The government status of parties also exerts a strong influence on their MPs' parliamentary activities. MPs from government parties have fewer incentives to ask parliamentary questions to government minister as they can use informal

Table 8.6 Parliamentary types by party size and party status

	S	V	F	L	G	Large parties	Small parties	Gov. parties	Opp. parties	Parliament
Exemplary MP	0	0	5	22	33	1	28	0	12	4
Workhorse	3	2	17	11	44	6	28	2	20	8
Showhorse	1	4	31	67	22	10	44	2	35	13
Rapporteur	28	42	21	0	0	31	0	34	15	28
Spectator	68	52	26	0	0	52	0	61	18	47
(*n*)	(71)	(52)	(42)	(9)	(9)	(165)	(18)	(123)	(60)	(183)

Note
Number of cases given in parentheses.

channels of communication. And they enjoy much less leeway with regard to introducing bills and motions as the parliamentary leaders of government parties exercise control to avoid (unwanted) conflict between the coalition parties and the displaying of intra-party differences between MPs and their ministers.[4]

Classifying MPs according to their actual behaviour is based on objective data and should produce an accurate picture of the parliament in the given period. However, the distribution of types of MPs, derived from behaviour, may be very different only a few months later, if the government and opposition status change and party strengths in parliament alter significantly. Our interviews have produced massive evidence that changes in government status and party size led to shifts of focus and tasks among MPs (Müller *et al.* 2001: chapter 10).

Comparing the perspective of MPs with their behaviour

In the final step of our analysis we compare the two different data sources – interviews and data derived from the parliamentary records. We approach the interview answers from the perspective of the types of MPs we have extracted from objective data that cover the months preceding the interview period. Figure 8.3 provides the relative frequency of the different emphases given in the interviews. Specifically, we asked the MPs where the centre of their activities is and offered them the alternatives in the figure. If MPs mentioned several priorities, we urged them to name only the most important ones.

Our interpretation concentrates on the data points of the three most important arenas for the MPs' activities as identified in Figure 8.3: committee work, own parliamentary party, and the plenary of parliament. While we do not have an explicit ranking of these three priorities by importance, we can still draw conclusions about their relative importance based on the frequency of mentioning them as the most important arena. As only small minorities of MPs mentioned the remaining alternatives, we will not pay much attention to them.

The most noticeable result is the similarity in the overall emphasis profiles of the two types with the lowest levels of parliamentary activity, Spectators and Rapporteurs. They score similarly on ranking committee work, their own parliamentary party, and the plenary of parliament. A very large majority of these two types of MPs records the committee stage as taking priority in their parliamentary work. More than half of the MPs from both types also see their own party as an important priority. Less than a third identifies the plenary as their centre of activity. Comparing the two data sources, we can conclude that the patterns derived from actual behavioural data and the interviews do not conflict with each other. Yet, due to a lack of objective data with regard to specific arenas – work in committee and, above all, within the respective parliamentary parties – we cannot conclude that they are fully in accord with each other.

A larger share of Showhorse MPs – who are more active than Spectators and Rapporteurs according to our objective indicators – mentioned the plenary as a central arena for their work than these two reference groups. Showhorse MPs

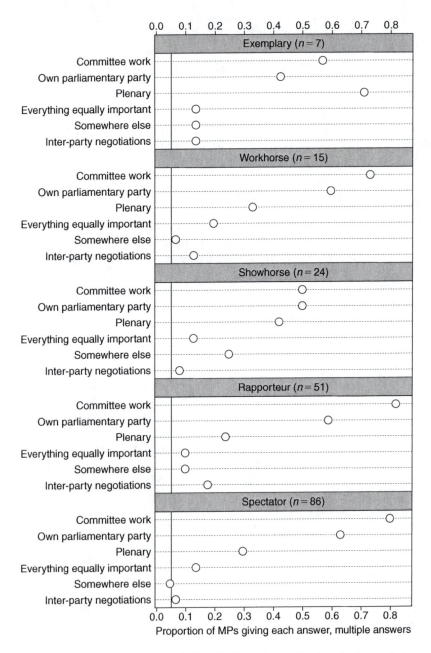

Figure 8.3 Behavioural types of MPs (derived from objective data) and their most important arena for activities as MPs (as revealed in interviews).

mentioned the two arenas that are closed to public observation – committees and work in their own party – less often. The interview answers and our image of a Showhorse MP thus fit nicely. The behavioural pattern derived from objective data also fits well when matched with the interview answers of Workhorse MPs. Workhorse MPs mentioned the plenary slightly less often than Showhorse MPs, but they stressed their work in the committees and in their own parliamentary party much more often.

The relative frequencies for the Workhorse MPs are quite similar to the emphasis patterns of Spectators and Rapporteurs. This is surprising. As we mentioned before, measuring the amount of work in two of the three arenas is problematic and we might have underestimated the overall parliamentary activity of Spectators and Rapporteurs. However, for most of these MPs a distinct bias in the answers is the more credible alternative. They might have chosen these non-observable arenas exactly because they knew that their record on publicly observable indicators is not particularly strong relative to some party colleagues. And participation in committee work and in the internal deliberations of their own party are both commendable activities for MPs.

The pattern of emphases that Exemplary MPs revealed in the interviews is distinct. They have the strongest focus on the plenary – which accords well with their record in giving speeches – followed by emphasizing committee work. Note however, that they hardly mentioned their own party as the locus of their activities. We have seen from their behavioural record, that this group is highly active in parliamentary proceedings. Does this mean that they put less value on their own party? That would probably be the wrong conclusion. Their activities – introducing bills and motions, putting parliamentary questions, giving speeches on behalf of their party – require previous approval by the leadership of the parliamentary party. Most of the Exemplary MPs are from small opposition parties, thus the task of convincing their colleagues of their own ideas seems a small one compared to that of MPs in the larger parliamentary groups, and even smaller compared to that of MPs from a parliamentary group in government. Indeed, they will often be the only ones in their party who are really informed about the policy substance of pending legislation and the only participant observers of committee deliberations, and hence the only ones who can really make an informed decision. And such monopolies tend to create relationships of mutual non-interference among MPs.

Conclusion

Our behavioural data provided precise measurements that allowed us to extract distinctive types of MPs. Indeed, we would have been hard pressed to develop these or any types of MPs without access to such data. The interview data gave a much more blurred, soft-focus image of MPs' roles. Does this imply that interview data are not reliable or are of less value than behavioural data derived from the parliamentary record? Certainly not! And there are many reasons why this is true and our concluding discussion will not cover them all.

To begin with, these two types of data maximize different virtues. They give different information: intentions (from the interviews) and objective evidence (from actual behaviour). Indeed, without evidence from interviews our conclusions from objective data would have been heavily based on mere assumptions. In the same vein we note that the interviews were extremely useful in interpreting the behavioural patterns we found. Data on actual behaviour relate to a specific time period. They begin with the first observation day and end with the last one. We can thus tie behaviour precisely to time-variant objective conditions such as the MPs' offices, whether they belong to a small or large party (when this varies dramatically), or whether their party is in government or opposition. Such precise data cannot be obtained from interviews. Even when interview questions try to specify similarly precise periods, human beings will never manage to respond adequately. Yet, this lack of precision is almost balanced by getting responses that relate to people's life experience under perhaps very different conditions.

Finally, there are many arenas that are – according to all that we know about politics – truly important, but can only be researched using interviews. Most committee and parliamentary party meetings, for instance, are closed to outside observers. Leaving such arenas out of the picture for the sake of precision in studying the remaining ones would lead to a grossly distorted picture of the roles of MPs. As so often, the silver bullet to understanding what MPs do in their job as representatives is to combine empirical evidence generated by different methods.

Notes

1 Seasoned MPs explained that the majority's voting-down of opposition proposals does not necessarily mean rejecting their "substance". At least occasionally, parts of their content make it into subsequent proposals of the coalition parties. The weaker the opposition MPs' ownership claims for an idea, the better are its chances of being adopted by the committee majority. A quote from an interview with an opposition MP illustrates the trade-off of visibility against policy influence: "Plunking a finished proposal on the table is a demonstrative act. Then one can claim: I have made 36 proposals. That's a kind of proof of activity. However, if one wants to move something, one needs to do it differently."
2 Parliamentary bills, motions, and written questions require the support of five MPs. It is generally agreed that the first MP to sign any of these is the one who is most active with regard to the issue at stake and the measured activity.
3 We borrow the labels Spectator (Searing 1994) and Showhorse and Workhorse (e.g. Langbein and Sigelman 1989) from the literature but have our own operational definitions. To the best of our knowledge the remaining labels have never been used before.
4 Although there are no formal incompatibility rules, Austrian ministers, with a few exceptions, have not been Members of Parliament since 1983.

References

Kettenring, J.R. (2006) "The practice of cluster analysis", *Journal of Classification*, 23: 3–30.

Langbein, L.L. and Sigelman, L. (1989) "Show horses, work horses, and dead horses", *American Politics Quarterly*, 17: 80–95.

Müller, W.C. and Saalfeld, T. (eds.) (1997) *Members of Parliament in Western Europe. Roles and Behaviour*, London: Frank Cass.

Müller, W.C., Jenny, M., Steininger, B., Dolezal, M., Philipp, W. and Preisl-Westphal, S. (2001) *Die österreichischen Abgeordneten. Individuelle Präferenzen und politisches Verhalten*, Vienna: WUV Universitätsverlag.

Searing, D. (1991) "Roles, rules, and rationality in the new institutionalism", *American Political Science Review*, 85: 1239–60.

Searing, D. (1994) *Westminster's World. Understanding Political Roles*, Cambridge, MA: Harvard University Press.

Strøm, K. (1997) "Rules, reasons and routines: Legislative roles in parliamentary democracies", in W.C. Müller and T. Saalfeld (eds.), *Members of Parliament in Western Europe. Roles and Behaviour*, London: Frank Cass.

Wahlke, J.C., Eulau, H., Buchanan, W. and Ferguson, L.C. (1962) *The Legislative System. Explorations in Legislative Behavior*, New York: Wiley.

9 Role stability in the context of institutional and positional change

Gabriella Ilonszki

Introduction – the aims and context of this exploration

The Hungarian parliament and the political context in which it has been in operation have been thoroughly transformed since 1990.[1] Is this reflected in the roles of MPs? How do MPs learn their roles in the first place, and how are roles affected by a changing environment? These questions will be the main focus of this chapter. Preliminary analysis has shown that despite this fundamental transformation MPs' roles have remained relatively stable. How to explain this phenomenon – can the function of institutional transformation be adjusted to role stability? This is what the chapter seeks to prove.

In order to do so, first the context and range of transformation will be introduced together with an understanding of the role concept. Then in subsequent sections learning roles, stabilizing roles and the evolution of role types will be presented. These developments and their potential implications for roles will be examined for the 1990–2010 period: that is, from the first to the sixth free elections, in six parliaments, which occurred at normal, regular intervals, in 1990, 1994, 1998, 2002 and 2006.

In addition to learning about representative roles this chapter seeks to connect this question to the broader issue of representation: can representative roles draw our attention to the general state of the representative linkage? This question might well be justified in a new democracy.

The context

Stability and role change are most pertinent issues, considering that substantial changes have taken place in both *personnel* and *institutional* terms. Table 9.1 provides a summary of the transformation with respect to the dimensions that might have had a significant impact on MPs' roles. Regarding personnel, after the first free elections in 1990 an entirely new group of parliamentarians was elected. Continuity with the former period was a mere 3 per cent and the prior political experience of the new MPs was very limited. In 1990, parliament was an entirely new terrain for the overall majority of the MPs in Hungary, and for most of them politics itself was also an unknown field. Very few among the MPs had any political experience in the former regime and opposition organizations had only a short pre-transition history. For the newly established parties it was difficult to run candidates who were mainly inexperienced 'amateurs', a word widely applied to the new political group at that time.

The first parliamentary group had to establish their own representative role. Consolidation was reflected in increasing continuity patterns until 2010, with incumbency rising to 70 per cent. As a result of the 2010 elections a party system change occurred and parliamentary continuity dropped to below 50 per cent. Do these groups define and approach their roles differently? In terms of roles one should certainly take into account the fluctuating dimension of novelty or incumbency.

Table 9.1 provides further information on institutional transformation as well as on the positional changes of MPs. Change in the party system should be considered the most important institutional transformation. From moderate multipartysm in the early 1990s through increasing bipolarity and block politics for more than a decade, in 2010 the Hungarian party system was characterized by one dominant party with a two-thirds majority in parliament comprising smaller parties and including an extreme right-wing party. Party system consolidation has progressed at quite a speed, and the thesis of early freezing has been formulated (Ágh 2002). Have parliamentary roles become more strictly partisan during this period? Does a higher proportion of MPs tend to consider and acknowledge the power of the 'party king'?

In addition to party system change, organizational change in political parties will be considered in the following sections: not only the number and positioning of the parties but also their organizational features have an impact on MPs' roles. At the beginning of the systemic change, party organization was loose – with the possible exception of the successor Socialists. Centralization and strong leadership have become the norm. This was not simply the result of party consolidation but also of increasing partisanship (Enyedi 2006a). From the end of the 1990s onwards the party elite began to play the game of symbolic politics and most of society followed suit (Tóka 2006). The personality of the party leader, and his attitudes towards the past, and to nationalism, have become increasingly important issues, the party system has bipolarised on this basis and block politics has formed (Enyedi and Bértoa 2011).

The extent of party consolidation and the developments of bipolarization and partisanship can be demonstrated by some plain facts. The effective number of parties was 6.71 in 1990: by 2010 it was just 2.82. The number of parties has diminished not only in parliament but also in the electoral context. The number of national lists is the most telling sign that the party system is closing down. To establish a national list a party should be able to run at least seven regional lists (out of 20) and in 2010 only six parties could do so – as opposed to 12 in 1990 and 15 in 1994. Earlier, many more parties had a national spread and thus a fair chance to get into parliament.

The stabilization of parties can be observed in the parliamentary arena. Parliamentary tourism was not particularly high in Hungary – at least in comparison to other post-communist countries (Shabad and Slomczynski 2004; Ilonszki and

Table 9.1 Institutional and personnel transformation, 1990–2010

Year	Effective no. of parties	No. of parliamentary parties	No. of national lists	Newcomer MPs (%)	Floor crossing of MPs	No. of MPs with mayoral position	Party leaders (%)	Women (%)
1990	6.71	6	12	92.8	91	n.a.	5.8	7.3
1994	5.23	6	15	61.9	49	14	18.4	11.1
1998	4.46	5	12	48.6	25	29	23.2	8.3
2002	2.84	4	8	34	19	60	34.5	9.1
2006	2.69	5	10	29.3	6	74	27.8	10.6
2010	2.82	4	6	45.3	3*	85	35	9.1

Source: www.valasztas.hu, MKA, 2010.

Note
* Until February 2011.

Edinger 2007) – and the trend of stabilisation has also been obvious. In the first parliament 91 MPs left their Parliamentary Party Group (PPG), in the second parliament this number was 49, in the third parliament 25, in the fourth 19, and in the 2006–2010 term a mere six MPs (putting aside the dissolution of a PPG) left their party group.[2]

In addition to party transformation a major constitutional change might also influence the study of MPs' roles. A constitutional amendment has made the accumulation of mandates possible: that is, since the second parliament (1994) MPs have been able to occupy several mandates: in addition to a parliamentary seat they can now serve as elected mayors and members of the regional councils. Can we assume that these positions inspire change in MPs' roles?

Altogether, between 1994 and 2010, 262 MPs served as mayors and 352 MPs were members of regional councils in addition to their parliamentary mandate (Várnagy 2008: 52–4, and MKA 2010). These tendencies have gathered strength over time: a mere 14 MPs in 1994, then 29 MPs in 1998, 60 MPs in 2002, 74 MPs in 2006, and 85 MPs in 2010 were also mayors. That is, by 2010 more than 20 per cent of MPs served as mayors and even more in the regional councils. One can rightly assume that accumulated mandates matter in understanding MPs' representative roles.

Last but not least legislation has become extremely overloaded by partisanship. While the partisan nature and the 'government versus opposition mode' is a natural working style of parliaments (King 1976), cross-party legislation is virtually absent, not to mention other more flexible modes (Andeweg and Nyzink 1995), and the party vote is very high. Individual MPs' legislative activity has decreased. In the first term close to one-third of all bills was initiated by an individual MP. This number has shrunk to a handful of bills, and legislation has been taken over by the party in government (Ilonszki and Edinger 2007: 52).

The approach

This chapter will focus on the representative role of MPs – that is, their views about their connectedness to those actors that potentially appear as their principals, whose opinion and interest they should forward to the parliamentary arena and represent to their best knowledge. How do parliamentarians see their connection to the broad social and political environment in terms of representing parties, voters, particular social groups or other assumed actors?

Since it is largely in consolidated democracies that MPs' roles have been examined, the Hungarian case can be instructive from the perspective of how roles reflect change. How constant (stable) are roles? When do they stabilize and altogether how fast are they formed? Are roles connected to concrete (and changing) institutional contexts or do they have some constant elements that remain intact and possibly change over much longer periods than we are able to examine over 20 years?

These questions are related to two other issues: 1) what gives roles their structure, on what grounds are they formed and 2) what are their consequences: that is, are roles and concrete behaviour connected? What representative focus do MPs think to maintain and, in concrete or even conflict-ridden situations, whom and what do they really represent?

We hypothesize that roles influence behaviour: that is, they are not simply attitudes or opinion or views – but they do not influence behaviour in an indirect way. For example, we cannot assume that if an MP reports a constituency focus he/she will not consider party as an influential actor and its potential consequences on his/her career perspectives and future opportunities. Roles cannot be directly translated into behaviour – rather they have to be placed in context, which implies a strategic consideration of the role – and a strategic consideration of the behaviour that results.

Thus the approach of the chapter follows Strøm's perspective (1997) – with some modification, however. While acknowledging the importance of the institutional context Strøm regards roles as 'behavioural strategies conditioned by the institutional framework' (Strøm 1997: 157). Thus this approach maintains that MPs will form their roles according to the goals that they want to achieve and on the basis of the resources that are available to them. Role does not equal behaviour; rather it is a comprehensive strategic consideration about goal achievement. More concretely, MPs will attest roles that support their career expectations (an obvious one being reelection) and help them reach posts that are necessary to perform their tasks, whether in the party hierarchy or a parliamentary office.

This approach can be applied effectively in the Hungarian case because it takes into consideration the changing institutional framework. Since institutions 'constrain and enable behaviour' (Strøm 1997: 162) transformations – whether in a constitutional context, such as the opportunity to hold parliamentary and local positions in parallel, or an organizational change like party institutionalization – are part and parcel of this approach. At the same time in order to be able to operationalize the institutional framework, the positions of MPs also have to be considered. Institutions and positions are closely intertwined but are not identical. For example, in an institutional context the consequences of highly centralized and leader-oriented parties on candidate selection are easy to recognize – but in forming roles it is essential to understand how the role-holder (the MP) regards his/her role. We assume that positions – or rather the combined effects of positions – will also explain representative roles. The institutional context and the positional context are equally important from the perspective of roles.

In addition to broadly understanding institutions and concretely considered positions as a third explanatory variable, this chapter will examine norms and expectations that are assumed to influence MPs' views and attitudes. This approach is largely missing from more recent role theories, because in the neo-institutional literature – which provides a foundation for the renewed interest and analysis of roles – roles are embedded in and are institutions themselves. In a neo-institutional perspective, roles are informal constraints. For example, as North (1990: 9) notes: 'Institutions consist of formal rules, informal constraints (norms of behaviour, conventions, and self-imposed codes of conduct) and the enforcement characteristics of both.' According to this, norms and expectations are structured by institutions and they are also institutions themselves. Still, in the Hungarian case there are two reasons why norms should be examined separately, or at least somewhat independently from the institutional framework. In the first place, the institutions were born only in 1990 – from the electoral system, through parties to a democratic parliament – they did not exist before, which makes the following question legitimate: were there expectations before the institutions could give birth and create norms and conventions? Second, representative roles are structured not only by the institutions among which the MPs operate but also by wider society, citizens and voters, whose expectations concerning roles can also be regarded as role-creating momentums. These societal expectations, particularly when they can be observed before the institutional set-up begins to operate, demonstrate that not only institutional determinants but also cultural expectations influence role formations. These cultural expectations and norms are most probably embedded in older formalities and institutional set-ups; that is, we cannot regard them as if they follow from the present reality. Then these expectations and norms may either reinforce the new institutional constraints and opportunities or are modified (or might even evaporate) in the face of new strategic considerations. All in all, an attempt will be made to find the explanatory value of these approaches.

This chapter seeks to test how these diverse approaches can be spotted and identified in the evolution of MPs' roles in Hungary. Indeed, we assume that these different dimensions are equally present – but possibly to different strengths and degrees depending how far the different roles have evolved. At the beginning of the democratic period when institutions were still feeble (or at least not firmly consolidated) one could not expect to find a powerful institutional explanation, and the career routes and perspectives were not clear either. Thus cultural explanations and public expectations as well as the MPs' own socialization patterns and motivations will have an impact on the way they understand their place in the new framework. Then, in parallel with institutional consolidation, institutional constraints might gain importance in outlining MPs' roles, although we assume that the impact of cultural norms will always prevail.

Unfortunately, scarce resources made it impossible to examine representative roles regularly and systematically with the same research questions and survey methods. Nevertheless five survey results can be compared. The data used in this chapter are taken from several research projects.[3] This chapter attempts to combine and apply these diverse sources so as to illuminate the role concept dimensions discussed above and their relative strength in its formation and development.

Learning roles in the context of expectations and new institutions

In 1990, the electoral system was the most stable institutional element – and it has not been modified since (although electoral system reform has been on the agenda from the second half of the 2000s). The impact of the electoral system on

MPs has been acknowledged (Bogdanor 1985), although the ambivalences of this impact will be explored below. Still, from the perspective of role formation, the impact of the electoral system will be placed in focus first. As mentioned above, in addition to the electoral system, social expectations and norms will be examined. This is because when an institution (such as the electoral system) is new, the function of inherited norms might be instructive in understanding role formation. The first surveys concerning role expectations took place before the first democratic elections, thus in this respect we do indeed have pre-institutional norms.

The electoral design itself responds to and is partially related to an understanding of the representative role (Bogdanor 1985). This is nicely proven in Hungary if we examine the considerations behind the new electoral system. The new electoral system created three types of mandates on the basis of single majority districts (SMDs), regional lists and a national list. The electorate cast two votes: one for the SMD candidates and the other for the regional list candidates, while national list mandates are distributed according to the fragmented votes on the former two tiers (Benoit 2005).

The post-communist and opposition forces hammered out this mixed system because the former thought that their candidates would have better electoral opportunities in SMDs, being better known than the new faces of the new parties, while the latter hoped to level out their disadvantages in this respect by the list system.

The representational impact of the mixed electoral system seems self-explanatory: still, researchers have been engaged in providing a proper academic analysis. Regarding Germany, the 'closest' example to the Hungarian case, academic literature long assumed that the type of mandate does not affect the roles of MPs. With reference to earlier research Klingeman and Wessels (2001) argue that until the 1980s the difference between the two types was not considered, because candidates normally ran in both tiers, and thus their dual identity was obvious. One can add that this is also true in the Hungarian case: after some initial learning, candidates tend to run in an increasing number of tiers on average (Sebestyén 2003). Although in Germany MPs often run in both tiers and parties expect close constituency ties from the MPs, from the 1990s onwards the differences between the two types of mandates have become visible. The types of mandate seem to count in role orientations (Klingemann and Wessels 2001: 292).

Interestingly, in Lithuania, which also applies a mixed system (71 persons are elected in SMDs and 70 on a national list) academic research found differences between the two mandates but not in the expected direction (Clark et al. 2008). The expectation – a higher level of party discipline among list MPs versus a higher level of free voting among constituency MPs – was not supported by their parliamentary voting behaviour. Clark et al. (2008: 335) claim that constituency MPs are not connected to their district to the expected degree. This experiment cannot be processed in Hungary due to the very high level of PPG discipline.

These examples demonstrate that the impact of the electoral system is not self-evident: several other contextual factors, such as party development, relations to territoriality, and the power of tradition have to be considered. These perspectives are instructive in analysing the Hungarian case. Differences in mandate type are important, but they do not provide an exclusive explanation for representative roles.

This is strengthened from another perspective by the certainly 'remote' example of New Zealand, which changed its electoral system after a referendum in 1993 from a SMD majority system to the mixed pattern. Analysing the impact of the new system has revealed that legacies – i.e. expectations embedded in former rules – have a greater impact than the new electoral system (McLeay and Vowles 2007).[4] This case draws our attention to the importance of former norms and experiences. Irrespective of the introduction and existence of the list tier, district effects remained predominant.

All in all, on the basis of various examples, one can conclude that the impact of the electoral system on representative roles depends on the context. Still, we shall consider the potential representative consequences of the mandate type first, because the electoral system has provided a stable institutional dimension from the very beginning of the democratic period.

The first survey among MPs took place in the Spring of 1992. Table 9.2 shows significant representational differences between list and SMD MPs (list MPs include both the regional and the national list MPs.) Close to half of the SMD MPs named their constituency, town or region as the most important representative focus, while nearly one-quarter of the list MPs named the party. Representing all citizens of the country proved to be important in both groups (35 per cent and 28 per cent respectively), that is, the trustee style of representation. Overall however the delegate style of representation and, among SMD MPs, representating the constituency and the region remain predominant.

We argue that the positions (mandate types) of MPs are complemented by the norms that the MPs have encountered and internalized during their political socialization. It would exceed the scope of this chapter to include lengthy historical explanations about how representation and political democracy have been harmed – with potential consequences for the current situation. Still we have to note that since representative government was established in Hungary in 1848,

Table 9.2 Focus of representation by type of mandate in 1992 (%)

	SMD n = 56	*List* n = 61	*All* n = 117
Town, region	3.6	15	9.4
Constituency	44.6	3.3	22.2
Party	8.9	23.3	17.1
Social layer/group	3.6	18.4	10.3
Interest group	0	3.3	1.7
All citizens of the country	37.4	27.8	32.5
Other, don't know, no answer	3.9	8.9	5.8

Note
The question was "Whom do you primarily represent?"

the chain of representation was always more or less broken, democratic norms were not observed and pork barrel politics have served as a substitute for proper democratic representation.

This was the case during the communist period as well. Law III (1966) created territorial constituencies and thus replaced the former list system and thereby acknowledged the general expectation that region and locality should be represented. This meant that although MPs (candidates) had to be party-faithful the new electoral system responded to public demand by acknowledging local interests. The change accepted the presence and legitimacy of special – in this case, local – interests and ensured constituency service for the people when interests other than those of the communist party and the proletariat were not part of the official ideology.

As a further symbolic gesture Law III (1970) made nomination possible within local constituencies – of course under the supervision of the communist party (Judge and Ilonszki 1995: 163). The impact was clear: in the 1980s most interpellations covered local affairs (Kerekes 1987: 132), MPs sought to respond to local expectations in this way, and according to a representative survey in the Spring of 1988, 84 per cent of respondents agreed that those MPs whose parliamentary work was not satisfactory should be recalled (Kurtán et al. 1990: 499).

Other early (pre-democratic) opinion polls also strengthen this view. In October 1989, citizens were asked how MPs should vote. Ten per cent of respondents thought they should vote according to their own conscience while 70 per cent expected that they vote according to the will of the voters and the others thought they should consider both (Kurtán et al. 1989). As to the question 'what the MPs should focus on?', a relative majority (38 per cent) named the representation of local interests, thus coming ahead of those voting for national affairs (29 per cent) while the others (33 per cent) regarded the representation of both levels as important. With respect to the personal traits of potential (prospective) MPs, even before the first democratic elections in March 1990, respondents expected locally and nationally well-known politicians in almost equal proportions (35 per cent and 36 per cent respectively), while the others did not regard this as an important issue. To another question, half of the respondents said that they would prefer a locally based MP (Kurtán et al. 1990). These data demonstrate how deeply rooted the expectation concerning the representation of the local interests was.

Historical experiences strengthened the perspective of local representation into an expectation – and we should add that these expectations have hardly changed during the past two decades. In 2009, 49 per cent of respondents (in a representative national survey) claimed that MPs should represent their town, region or local constituency, 31 per cent named 'all citizens of the country', 12 per cent named the party, and another 5 per cent named a societal group as the focus of representation (Róna 2009). These societal views and opinions certainly influence representative roles. The stability of expectations should be particularly noted.

Parliamentarians brought some pre-cooked roles with them and these roles were then implanted and also reinforced by the institutional setting. Early roles were cemented and – as we shall see – they are not in harmony with the institutional transformation, at least at a first glance, particularly with the consolidation of the parties and the party system. In the next section we shall examine how institutional consolidation and the positional changes of MPs influenced MPs' roles and how they can be understood.

The new MPs in 1990 were not locally based. As candidates they were found ad hoc and under the pressure of election (and campaign) time. They were not connected to the constituency in any considerable degree. Moreover, at that time they were not allowed to occupy local positions in parallel with the parliamentary mandate. Yet despite such remoteness from the local field, differences between the types of mandate were acknowledged from the start in terms of the representative focus. The historical legacy helps to account for this. All in all, it seems that MPs already had roles when they entered Parliament for the first time, and certain role patterns could be observed from very early on. Representing the locality is a strong political tradition, which appears to be a norm – more explicitly for SMD MPs but also for list MPs. Public expectations also reinforce this tradition.

Stabilizing roles: changing institutions and positions

This section will analyse whether institutional and positional changes made their impact – and what differences could be observed with respect to representative roles between the first and later parliaments. As mentioned above the democratic transition was party-driven and party consolidation was quick. The party basis of the political system is unquestionable. Does this imply that party focus, that is, representing the party will assume importance in an MP's role? Is the assumption justified at all that, due to the party-centred nature of the political system, parties will appear as dominant among the representative foci? If not, what are the reasons, and explanations behind them?

In this respect we have to acknowledge the differences between the parties – both in terms of their organization and their political place. MPs' views and opinions are influenced first and foremost by whether their party is in government or opposition. Government MPs have wider opportunities to pursue their representative agenda, but at the same time they have to adjust more to discipline and to accept the party agenda. Second, organizationally it is important to know whether the external party or the PPG is in the dominant position. At the beginning of the transition, with the exception of the successor Socialist party, the other parties were all weak externally, and the PPGs were at the centre of programme and image formation. In the second decade the Conservative Fidesz also managed to strengthen its party organization. At the same time, we know that the party is highly centralized, which appears among other things in candidate selection. Personal decisions in this respect are concentrated at the top hierarchy of the party elite. During the 2010 elections, among the parliamentary parties, it was possibly only in the Socialist Party that the local organization had some say in selecting their candidate – and even in their case this was the result of party disintegration and the emasculation of the party centre.

We can rightly assume that under these circumstances when party discipline prevails within the House and re(s)election depends on the party, the party/PPG connection would and should be indispensable in the formation of MPs' representative roles: MPs should be highly partisan and regard the party focus as most important. Is this assumption justified by data? Thus our first question is: 'how is the (centralized) parties' elevated role reflected in representative roles?'

At the same time the MPs' positional transformation has also to be considered. As mentioned above, from the second parliamentary term (1994), elected local government positions became compatible with parliamentary mandates. Initially this served the Socialists well on the basis of their former organization's embeddedness but later, as a result of the Conservatives' campaign, which also aimed at acquiring local government posts, both big parties had a similar share of MPs with cumulated mandates. This local 'activism' is connected to other phenomena as well. Since Hungarian parties are poor (Enyedi 2006b) they badly need local resources not only in political but also in economic terms. But local resources are also necessary to MPs: they will use them partly for their own purposes but can also support the party and thus gain safer positions in the selection process. This bilateral context of scarce resources, which hits both the party and the candidate/MP, is demonstrated by the fact that of the MPs with accumulated mandates there are two trajectories representing an equal share: half of the group obtained their parliamentary mandate first and the local mandate second, and the other half got into parliament only after occupying a local post (Várnagy 2008: 53). This implies that MPs (even some on the top of the party hierarchy) reach out for locality. These are strategic decisions that have transformed the positions of MPs – possibly with an effect on representative roles.

The growing importance of local ties can be observed in another positional change as well. In 2006, one-third of MPs gained their mandate in the same SMD, one-seventeenth on the same territorial list as before (Papp 2008: 99), and similar proportions prevailed in 2010 despite a larger level of general turnover owing to the appearance of two new parties and the failure of two old ones. We can rightly claim that the candidate pool of the parties has stabilized and got a local flavour. Local posts and SMD mandates do often overlap although this connection is not exclusionary. Certainly, mayors are overrepresented among MPs with SMD mandates, underrepresented in the territorial list mandates and largely underrepresented in national list mandates. It seems that locality has increasingly become an asset for MPs: they can create a non-party image for themselves and find electoral and financial resources above and outside of the party. A mayor's position might become more stable either in parliament or in the party, as a result. How are these developments (growing partisanship and increasing local connectedness) reflected in representative roles?

Table 9.3 provides an answer to this question showing the results of the 1999, 2007 and 2010 surveys (we shall not return to the first survey, see Table 9.2).

Table 9.3 Focus of representation by type of mandate in 1999, 2007 and 2010 (%)

	1999		2007		2010	
	SMD n = 47	List n = 50	SMD n = 36	List n = 44	SMD n = 116	List n = 116
Town, region	15.2	12.2	}60	}26.8	}67.2	}23.3
Constituency	45.7	4.1				
Party	13	24.5	8.6	19.5	3.4	18.1
Social layer/group	0	10.2	14.3	9.8	1.7	9.5
All citizens of the country	23.9	42.9	17.1	43.9	26.7	48.3
Other, don't know, no answer	2.2	6.1	0	0	1	0.8

These years are a good selection from the MPs' perspective: 1999 can be regarded as the peak of consolidation, with the stabilization of the party system and the MPs themselves; in 2007 the signs and consequences of 'over-stabilization' could be observed with front lines cemented and the political class closing down; while 2010 is a new beginning, from the party and political perspective: both new parties and new MPs emerged.

The broadest focus of representation, representating all citizens of the country – which can be tied to the trustee style of representation – is present at a relatively high level (about one-third) in each survey, and is overrepresented among list MPs. Interestingly, it is at the highest level in the 2010 parliament: even higher than in the first parliament, which is not covered in this table. An explanation might lie in the relatively high level of newcomers: half of the new MPs are close to the trustee style while one-third of the incumbents claimed representing all citizens of the country as the most important part of its role. Nevertheless the impact of 'novelty' could not be observed in the first parliament, where almost everybody was a newcomer. This implies that the impact of the party should also be considered. In 2010, many newcomers could be found in the two new parties. Modest local ties and less developed party organization in their case were reinforced by radical right and new left political orientation. Representating a social layer/group is a privilege of list MPs, with the exception of the 2007 House. It must also be noted that representing interest groups does not appear at all among the answers, thus it has been left out of the table/analysis.

In terms of the party focus, two developments must be considered: although the difference between list and SMD MPs is maintained (it is always the list MPs that claim 'party representation' in higher proportions), it is significant that party representation tends to decrease in both mandate types. Moreover, in both 2007 and 2010, list MPs name territorial representation (either town or regional constituency) as more important than party representation.

The importance of territorial representation has grown dynamically. It increased by 10 per cent among SMD MPs between 1992 and 1999 and by the same proportion among list MPs between 1999 and 2007. It can be assumed that in the former case existing norms have further strengthened as a result of the electoral system and increasing resources available in constituency work, and of the opportunity to accumulate mandates. In the latter case however the strength of the territorial focus among list MPs' views about representation warns us that representative roles cannot be understood exclusively on the basis of mandate types. Altogether, by 2010 the party focus occupied third position among list MPs and was almost irrelevant among SMD MPs. At first glance, the extent of the decrease is astonishing in the face of the highly partisan nature of the political system. If, however, we understand roles as behavioural strategies in accordance with the academic literature referred to above, these developments can be explained, and are revealing.

Above all, MPs have tended to reflect social expectations and norms in their roles. This has been confirmed by the elevated presence of local representation orientation in a period when the institutional context was not yet fully blown.

This could be one source of MPs' ambivalence about party representation. The tendency has persisted, however. Following rapid particization people increasingly distanced themselves from political parties. By the middle of the 1990s confidence in parties had fallen away even more sharply and they became the least trusted of all political institutions, a phenomenon confirmed by international comparative results (Rose and Munro 2003). With diminished party importance in their role orientation MPs could show themselves as being independent (i.e. not party dependent), and responsive to public views, the low level of public confidence in parties, and so on.

In addition, this role orientation has also become rational by institutional and positional conditions: resources (from reelection to media presence) can generally be understood in the context of party connections and party dependence. For example, selection and nomination are guaranteed increasingly by local positions – they are also badly needed by parties. Thus, the diminishing party focus reflects strategic behaviour from the perspective of MPs. Partisanship and party dominance are suppressed by social expectations and anti-party attitudes as well as by the mutual interests of parties and MPs embodied by their local political position.

Amongst the positional developments we must also consider the stabilization of the parliamentary group and its potential impact on roles. From 3 per cent in 1990, incumbency continuously increased to 70 per cent by 2006 and dropped to below 50 per cent in 2010 (see Table 9.1). Are there differences in terms of role orientations between newcomers and incumbents? Can it be rightly assumed that role orientations are stabilized as a result of the socialization process and consequently new and old MPs report different role perceptions? Table 9.4 demonstrates some of the answers. In the 1992 survey each MP was regarded as new, not only because of the very low level of incumbency, but also because even for the few incumbents democratic parliamentarism was a novelty.

Table 9.4 Focus of representation among newcomers and incumbents in 1992, 2007 and 2010 (%)

	1992	2007		2010	
		Newcomers	Incumbents	Newcomers	Incumbents
Town, region	9.4 } 35		} 44.6	} 32.1	} 51.1
Constituency	22.2				
Party	17.1	10	16.1	12.3	11.7
Social layer/group	10.3	20	8.9	8.5	5.1
Interest group	1.7	–	–	–	–
All citizens of the country	32.5	35	30.4	47.2	32.1
Other, don't know, no answer	5.8	0	0	0	0

Note
Concerning the newcomers of 2007, the number of cases is small in this group, thus percentage proportions should be evaluated with care.

Interestingly, the proportion of the territorial focus has hardly changed among the newcomers; it remained at around one-third throughout 1992, 2007 and 2010. However, while this group included all MPs irrespective of mandate type in the first parliament (they were all new!), in 2010 the majority of newcomers had a list mandate (this is exclusively the case with the two new parties). The very similar territorial focus in 1992, in 2007 and then in 2010 conceals a larger share of territorial/constituency representative orientation among the newcomers. Thus there is an obvious difference in role orientation between incumbents and newcomers, which follows in part from the larger proportion of SMD MPs among the incumbents. The importance of territorial focus among incumbents has increased between the two most recent elections, strengthening our former argument: this implies a safer place according to the expectations of the public and the party alike. In parallel with this, the level of party orientation is almost the same among incumbents and newcomers. General role orientation (representation of all citizens of the country) has always been higher among newcomers but the difference has become spectacular. The effect of mandate type, length of service and type of party reinforce each other.

Typology of MPs

With the help of institutional, positional and normative considerations we were able to explore and explain the background of the development and transformation of representative roles. We combined them with some important characteristics of the political system, like partisanship and locality. We could observe why and how regional–territorial focus of representation has increased and party orientation diminished. It has to be noted that the explanatory value of the type of mandate has diminished particularly in these two respects, however. Mandate type remains important in the delineation of roles but does not suffice in itself to create a relevant role typology.

One limitation of the exclusively mandate based role typology is that candidates run regularly in more than one tier. Thus, even if they 'lose' in the SMD and get a list mandate they will regard the lost constituency as their own, will maintain some of their services, partly in the hope of a future victory and partly by the encouragement of their party. In addition, even a list mandate could and will require the performance of some 'constituency service' on the list level, which is also a well-outlined regional entity.

Another limitation of the exclusively mandate-based role typology is that MPs could gain different types of mandates in successive elections. Although the increasing coherence of mandates has been observed above, this type of continuity and coherence has its own limitations due to the success of new candidates, new parties, and altogether changing electoral fortunes. Finally, the analysis of role behaviour itself, which aims to explore the foundations of strategic behaviour, requires that several perspectives be included (considered) in the formation of the relevant role typologies.

In the following we shall attempt to create the role typology in the Hungarian parliament. We understand that established representative roles prevail when representative role orientations have a relatively stable and predictable group character among members of parliament, and they also tend to explain the behavioural strategies of the MPs. A well founded role typology can demonstrate the relevance and explanatory character of the representative role.

On the basis of the former analysis, three dimensions are included: the relative importance of the type of mandate has to be acknowledged; local positions are important because of mandate accumulation and widely spread local interest representation; and party positions have a function in role definition/perception in the context of highly centralized parties. On this basis three groups of parliamentarians have been created: the party group, the constituency group and the combined group as indicated in Table 9.5.

The constituency group contains MPs who have local posts and are not party leaders, in combination with either list or SMD mandates, and also those who have neither party nor local positions but their SMD mandate clearly reflects a constituency-centred career. The party group contains party leaders who have no local posts, in combination either with list or SMD mandates, and also those who have neither of these positions but their list mandate indicates their party base: they are important for the party and have been selected for a winning place on a list. Finally, in the combined group, those MPs who have both party leadership and local posts irrespective of mandate type can be found. Because in the end the combined group contained only a handful of MPs (eight), they have been replaced into one or the other category, as appropriate.

In addition to the two remaining categories – party group and constituency group – length of service has been added to differentiate between newcomers and incumbents. Newcomers have become a separate group on their own right: they are hardly ever party leaders and, even for those who happened to have local posts before entering the House, the novelty of the context seems to be a more important contextual factor than their local status. The differences between newcomers and incumbents in Table 9.4, with respect to regional versus party focus, also support this argument. In this way three groups have been identified: the party group, the constituency group and the group of newcomers.

Table 9.5 Typology of MPs

Not party leader + list mandate + local post	Constituency group
Not party leader + list mandate + no local post	Party group
Not party leader + SMD mandate + local post	Constituency group
Not party leader + SMD mandate + no local post	Constituency group
Party leader + list mandate + no local post	Party group
Party leader+ SMD mandate+ no local post	Party group
Party leader + list mandate + local post	Combined group
Party leader + SMD mandate + local post	Combined group

According to our assumption the above groups – based on the positions of the MPs – explain significantly the roles of MPs. This assumption is tested in Tables 9.6 and 9.7.

The pattern is the most straightforward in case of the constituency group: 80 per cent among them reports a constituency focus. This is also strong (actually the strongest) in case of the party group with 40 per cent, while another close to 40 per cent among them mentions 'all the citizens of the country' as the most important focus of representation.

At the same time only 15 per cent of the party group reports a party focus, which is high in comparison to the other two groups, but low if we consider that it includes party leaders. Nevertheless it is in harmony with our former argument about understanding roles as strategic behaviour: this response – particularly the response rate – responds to expectations and norms while also regarding locality as a safeguard to the mandate. The constituency group does not consider group representation important, unlike the other two groups. Overall, there is a significant connection between the groups and representative focus. The relevance of the typology has been tested with a more concrete question as well, with respect to views about parliamentary voting behaviour (see Table 9.7).

In answering the question 'how should an MP vote if the opinion of the voters and the party diverge?', 60 per cent of the party group would prefer the party line while more than three-quarters of the constituency group would decide in favour of voters. Newcomers are more inclined to vote according to voters' opinion. The connections are significant, thus roles reflect and correspond to the basis of group foundations. Roles prove to be relatively well founded, and could be well connected to political–institutional–positional contexts. Altogether it has been found proven that roles are a working concept, and can reveal the foundations of the strategic behaviour of MPs.

Conclusions

Early and quick role learning and the relative stability of early roles are an obvious conclusion of the two-decade overview. From the first moment,

Table 9.6 Whom should an MP represent? By type of MP (nos and %, 2010)

Whom should an MP represent	Groups of MPs			Total
	Party group	Constituency group	Newcomers	
Constituency	38 (40.9%)	32 (80%)	34 (35.4%)	104 (45.4%)
Voters of his/her party	14 (15.1%)	1 (2.5%)	10 (10.4%)	25 (10.9%)
A social group	6 (6.5%)	0	6 (6.3%)	12 (5.2%)
All citizens of the country	35 (37.6%)	7 (17.5%)	46 (46.9%)	88 (38%)
Total	93 (100%)	40 (100%)	96 (100%)	229 (100%)

Note
($p < 0.01$).

Table 9.7 How should an MP vote if the opinion of the voters and the opinion of the party are in conflict? By type of MP (nos and %, 2010)

How should an MP vote if the opinion of the voters and the opinion of the party are in conflict?	Groups of MPs			Total
	Party MP	Constituency MP	Newcomers	
Should vote according to party line	45 (60%)	9 (23.7%)	32 (38.1%)	86 (43.7%)
Should vote according to voters' opinion	30 (40%)	29 (76.3%)	52 (61.9%)	111 (56.3%)
Total	75(100%)	38 (100%)	84 (100%)	197 (100%)

Note
($p<0.01$).

representative roles could be distinguished by the type of mandate, and the power of territoriality could be observed. This early role formation, which preceded not only consolidation but in some respects even institutionalisation, has drawn our attention to the potential relevance of norms and expectations in role formation, an approach only rarely reflected upon in role research. The stability of societal expectations – demonstrated by opinion poll surveys over more than twenty years (beginning before the democratic transition) – has also underlined the importance of this approach. Local interest representation and the local embeddedness of MPs have been and remain the overarching preference of the public. Early role perceptions have proved stable, although the explanatory value of mandate types has decreased; and most importantly party representation focus has diminished while territorial representation focus has become dominant.

Overall, several components are at play in determining roles: institutional factors, the concrete positions that MPs occupy, and norms, which latter are embedded via public views in MPs' opinions. For example, the low level of party focus – despite and amongst the conditions of excessive partisanship – can be explained by the low level of confidence in political parties – a culturally coded historical legacy, which has by now been reconfirmed: systemic underperformance can be connected to parties, although it is always the party of the 'other camp' that is blamed and does not undermine the desire to have strong and popular party leaders (Tóka 2006). At the same time, although the party hierarchy controls the most important entry point – that is, candidate selection – local resources can contribute to this, which could be a stepping stone for party positions (such as PPG leadership posts) or for further resources (such as media publicity).

Altogether the dominance of the regional/territorial focus of representation has been constructed and maintained by the parties, it often happens that the most successful local politicians are forced to enter national politics to bring new resources into the party – under the potential threat that their local post might be lost if the party hierarchy finds somebody else more suitable (and more open to persuasion) for the post.

Role orientation has consequences however: the actors have to respond to and adapt to their roles. At the beginning of the chapter we argued that representative roles are an ideal terrain to investigate the state of democracy. In our case, local/ territorial interest representation has become a general requirement while at the same time it tends to hide the partisan agenda. This situation has a negative impact on the roles of MPs in general. MPs are expected to fulfil many roles, the representative role being only one of them (Saalfeld and Müller 1997). From passing legislation to government scrutiny there are many tasks that cannot be performed only on territorial logic. Earlier research has confirmed that the volume of PPG work has decreased as opposed to party and local 'business' (Kurtán and Ilonszki 2008: 30). Positions that MPs occupy in addition to their parliamentary mandate do influence their parliamentary work (e.g. they spend less time in parliament) while they increase their income from extra-parliamentary sources (Juhász 2008). We can rightly argue that representative roles in their concrete existence in the Hungarian case impoverish parliamentary roles – and thus also the functions of parliament. If national affairs are devalued and if party affairs are disguised in local robes, the parliamentary institutional framework is losing ground and the general principle of representation is harmed.

The roles we have found and the role typology we have established can indeed be understood as the strategic role perception and role behaviour of MPs. This rational strategy hides role inconsistencies, however. On the part of MPs, for example, this becomes evident when we note the level of party cohesion and party discipline that are exceptionally high even by international standards (Ilonszki and Jáger 2011). In addition, role inconsistency emerges with respect to the MPs' and their voters' connections. Although we have found an apparent harmony between social expectations and parliamentarians' responses in terms of the elevated role of locality some empirical findings hint at fundamental linkage problems. While voters expect the representation of 'the local', their connection with MPs is exceptionally low – lower than most countries with a similar mixed electoral system. A mere 7 per cent of the Hungarian voters could report on any connection with their MPs while this proportion was 11 per cent in Germany, 15 per cent in Lithuania, and 24 per cent in New Zealand, the countries referred to at the beginning of the chapter (Norris 2004: 241). Even if the New Zealand case is omitted due to the country's long experience with parliamentarians' strong local connections, the problematic nature of the Hungarian representative context cannot be overlooked.

The diagnosis of representation deficit has been confirmed by revealing the roots and foundations of the role concept. Society does not work according to its advocated norms and expectations about representation. MPs, on the basis of a strategic choice, namely to enter and then remain in the political game – weaken the foundations of representation by impoverishing parliament with reference to the local – but under strong party constraints. It must also be noted that the other – more structured – dimensions of representation have virtually disappeared during the last two decades. In the first parliament the representation of certain social groups was greater than in the most recent ones and the representation of interest groups has entirely disappeared from the MPs' representative focus. This contradicts the working reality of representation, in which non-transparent forms of interest representation cast doubts on parliamentarians' roles.

Notes

1 I would like to thank the help of TÁMOP-4.2.1.B-B-09/1/KMR-2010-0005 support scheme in preparing the analytical work of this chapter.
2 When the number of the MDF PPG decreased to less than 10, the members had to be moved to the independent benches.
3 Surveys are:

Survey date	Parliamentary term	Survey method	Number of respondents	Project
1992 spring	1990–1994	Postal survey	117	DKMK (Centre for Democracy Studies, Corvinus University of Budapest)
1999 spring	1998–2001	Postal survey	97	As above
2007 spring	2006–2010	Face-to-face interviews	80	FP6 (INTUNE), CES (Centre for Elite Studies)
2009 spring	2006–2010	Face-to-face interviews	100	PARTIREP (Brussels), CES, as above
2010 summer	2010–2014	Face-to-face interviews	240	MVKP (Centre for Democracy Studies)

Hereafter the survey date will be signified throughout the text when a survey is referred to.
4 For a recently changed electoral system, what is accepted as legitimate behaviour for an MP is the product of the norms and values of the past as much as the characterstics of the present structures (McLeay and Vowles 2007: 92).

References

Ágh, A. (2002) *Demokratizálás és európaizálás: a korai konszolidáció keservei Magyarországon*, Budapest: Villányi Úti Konferenciaközp. és Szabadegyetem Alapítvány.

Andeweg, R.B. and Nyzink L. (1995) 'Beyond the two-body image: Relations between ministers and MPs', in H. Döring (ed.) *Parliaments and Majority Rule in Western Europe*, Frankfurt: St. Martin Press.

Benoit, K. (2005) 'Hungary: Holding back the tiers', in M. Gallagher and P. Mitchell (eds) *The Politics of Electoral Systems*, Oxford: Oxford University Press.

Bogdanor, V. (ed.) (1985) *Representatives of the People? Parliamentarians and Constituents in Western Democracies*, Gower: Aldershot.

Clark, T. D., Martinaikis, Z. and Dilba, R (2008) 'Electoral mandate and party cohesion: Does it matter in Lithuania?', *Journal of Communist Studies and Transition Politics*, 24: 317–37.

Enyedi, Zs. (2006a) 'A befagyott felszín és ami alatt van. A 2006-os választás és a magyar pártrendszer', in G. Karácsony (ed.) *Parlamenti választás 2006. Elemzések és adatok*, Budapest: DKMKA BCE.

Enyedi, Zs. (2006b) 'Accounting for organisation and finance. A contrast of four Hungarian parties', *Europe–Asia Studies*, 58: 1101–17.

Enyedi, Zs. and Casal Bértoa, F. (2011) 'Patterns of party competition 1990–2009', in P. Lewis and R. Markowski (eds) *Europeanising Party Politics? Comparative Perspectives on Central and Eastern Europe after Enlargement*, Manchester: Manchester University Press.

Ilonszki, G. and Jáger, K. (2011) 'Hungary: Changing government advantages – challenging a dominant executive', in B. Rasch and G. Tsebelis (eds.) *The Role of Governments in Legislative Agenda Setting*, London: Routledge.

Ilonszki, G. and Edinger, M. (2007) 'Members of Parliament in Central Eastern Europe: A parliamentary elite in the making', *Journal of Legislative Studies*, 13: 142–63.

Judge, D. and Ilonszki, G. (1995) 'Member–constituency linkages in the Hungarian Parliament', *Legislative Studies Quarterly*, 20 (2): 161–76.

Juhász, G. (2008) 'A fele nem tréfa. Parlamenti képviselői jövedelemlista', *HVG*, April 19.

Kerekes, Zs. (1987) 'Válaszúton az Országgyűlés', *Medvetánc*, 120–43.

King, A. (1976) 'Modes of executive–legislative relations: Great Britain, France, and West Germany', *Legislative Studies Quarterly* (1) 1: 11–34.

Klingemann, H.-D. and Wessels, B. (2001) 'The political consequences of Germany's Mixed-member system: Personalization at the grass roots?', in M.S. Shugart and M.P. Wattenberg (eds.) *Mixed Member Electoral Systems. The Best of Both Worlds?*, Oxford: Oxford University Press.

Kurtán, S., Sándor, P. and Vass, L. (eds) (1989) *Magyarország politikai évkönyve. Opinion Poll 1989*, Budapest: DKMK.

Kurtán, S., Sándor. P. and Vass, L. (eds) (1990) *Magyarország politikai évkönyve. Opinion Poll 1990*, Budapest: DKMK.

Kurtán, S. and Ilonszki, G. (2008) 'Munka, foglalkozás, hivatás – a képviselői professzionalizáció többszempontú elemzése', in G. Ilonszki (ed.) *Amatőr és hivatásos politikusok. Képviselők Magyarországon II*, Budapest: Új Mandátum Kiadó.

MKA (2010) Magyar Képviselői Adatbázis (Hungarian Representation Database).

McLeay, E. and Vowles, J. (2007) 'Redefining constituency representation: The roles of New Zealand MPs under MMP', *Regional and Federal Studies*, 17: 71–95.

Norris, P. (2004) *Electoral Engineering: Voting Choices and Political Behaviour*, Cambridge: Cambridge University Press.

North, Douglass C. (1992) 'Transaction costs, institutions and economic performance', San Francisco, CA: International Center for Economic Growth.

Papp, Zs. (2008) 'A stabilitás forrásai a képviselők megválasztásában', in G. Ilonszki (ed.) *Amatőr és hivatásos politikusok. Képviselők Magyarországon II*, Budapest: Új Mandátum Kiadó.

Róna, D. (2009) 'Kit képviselnek? A magyarországi képviselet elemzése a reprezentációs megközelítés alapján', unpublished manuscript, Corvinus University of Budapest.

Rose, R. and Munro, N. (2003) *Elections and parties in New European Democracies*, Washington: CQ Press.

Saalfeld, T. and Müller, W.C. (1997) 'Roles in legislative studies: A theoretical introduction', in W.C. Müller, and T. Saalfeld (eds) *Members of Parliament in Western Europe: Roles and Behaviour*, London: Frank Cass.

Shabad, G. and Slomczynski, K.M. (2004) 'Inter-party mobility among parliamentary candidates in post-communist East Central Europe', *Party Politics*, 10: 151–76.

Sebestyén, I. (2003) 'Országgyűlési választások: pártok, stratégiák, képviselőjelöltek és mandátumok', in S. Kurtán, P. Sándor and L. Vass (eds.) *Magyarország politikai évkönyve 2003*, Budapest: DKMKKA.

Strøm, K. (1997) 'Rules, reason and routines: Legislative roles in parliamentary democracy', *Journal of Legislative Studies*, 3: 155–74.

Tóka, G. (2006) 'Vezérek csodálói. A magyar választói magatartás nemzetközi összehasonlításban', in G. Karácsony (ed.) *Parlamenti választás 2006. Elemzések és adatok*, Budapest: DKMKA BCE.

Várnagy, R. (2008) 'Az országgyűlési képviselők helyi beágyazottsága', in G. Ilonszki (ed.) *Amatőr és hivatásos politikusok. Képviselők Magyarországon II*, Budapest: Új Mandátum Kiadó.

10 The cognitive rationality of role choices

Evidence from the European Parliament

Julien Navarro

The concept of role, defined as a configuration of goals, attitudes and behaviours that are characteristic of people in particular positions (Searing 1991, 1994), is critical to understanding and explaining parliamentary activities. It enlarges the analysis of parliamentary representation by extending the range of activities taken into account, beyond the traditional focus on voting behaviour. In this sense, the concept allows one to question the relationship between a representative and its principals, the parliamentarians' emphasis on their different tasks and duties, or the interpersonal interactions between MPs and other social actors such as interest groups. Second, and more specifically, the concept of role moves research one step further by demonstrating how various activities combine around the unique position of parliamentarian, and thus by challenging the constitutive tension between individual agency and institutional constraint. Third, analysing parliamentary roles contributes to the broader understanding of institutions and their transformation: parliaments are not only governed by *ex ante* constitutional arrangements, they also depend on their members' activities. Analysing how MPs perform their role offers a better insight into the political system as a whole.

The concept of role proves particularly instrumental in studying parliamentary representation at the European level. The interactions between the European Parliament (EP) and other EU institutions, the intergovernmental or supranational nature of parliamentary work or the capacity of the representatives to legitimate the European political system are linked closely to the way the Members of the European Parliament (MEPs) endorse their function. Several studies have already addressed issues such as the focus of representation in the EP, the impact of institutional socialisation or the interactions with the national political parties (Hagger and Wing 1979; Katz 1999; Scully and Farrell 2003; Blomgren 2003). One remaining question concerns the explanation of role orientations. Why do politicians endorse a role model? Why do they endorse one role orientation instead of another? The origin of individual role orientations is a major challenge that role theory has to face. In this perspective, individual parliamentary roles are regarded as 'dependent' variables that need to be explained. In the literature on roles, several 'independent' variables have been considered.

A first approach emphasises the cultural and social dimension of roles: role orientations are predetermined by cultural and social inheritance – parliamentarians play roles that are consistent with their culture, education or social class (Viet 1960). A second theory relates roles to processes of institutional socialisation; the attribution of a position leads automatically to the internalisation of expectations about the behaviour of its holder (Dahrendorf 1968). Both views tend to underestimate the individual margin that individuals, in particular parliamentarians, have when they endorse a new function, and they also fail to explain interpersonal differences amongst role holders. A third approach views roles as behavioural strategies of rational actors trying to maximise their interest (Strøm 1997). In this utilitarian perspective, parliamentarians adopt role models, which, in a given institutional context, maximise their chances of fulfilling their individual goals – to be re-elected, to reach another position outside the parliament, or to gain leading positions within the parliament.

Beyond these career goals that are part of the 'motivational core' of roles, Searing adds another important dimension: the 'emotional incentives' (Searing 1991 and 1994). In *Westminster's World* (1994) roles are explained mainly by the psychological gratifications that they provide. According to Searing 'only desire can supply the motivation for which reason seeks paths to satisfaction' (Searing 1991: 1253). For instance, the role of constituency member is linked to such emotional incentives as 'the desire for a sense of competence', that of policy advocate to the emotional incentive of 'rectitude and hubris' (Searing 1991: 1253–4). In line with the motivational approach promoted by Searing, this chapter will defend the thesis that utilitarian conceptions of rationality are too narrow to account for parliamentary roles. Unlike him, however, it does not emphasise the psychological aspect of role choices, but proposes to broaden the concept of rationality in a cognitive direction.

According to Boudon (1999), actions are not all oriented towards external ends or objectives (consequential action); some derive from normative or cognitive principles. One prominent example of such action is the act of voting, which utilitarian theories have the greatest difficulties in explaining. According to Boudon (2002), people vote not because it is in their interest to do so but because they believe in the virtue of democracy and their vote is a way to manifest this belief. In this perspective, norms are not only 'transmission belts for interests' (Moravcsik 2001: 229) – they are at the root of action itself. This theory resembles closely the weberian concept of *Wertrationalität*, according to which social agents sometimes act in conformity with 'imperatives' or 'expectations' which they feel obliged to follow (Weber 1968). What Boudon adds to the weberian concept of value-rationality is the idea that the normative principles underpinning action can be founded rationally. According to Boudon, an actor frequently believes that doing something is good, fair, true, legitimate, etc. not on the basis of instrumental reasons but because his experience and knowledge make him believe that it is so.

Following this line of thinking, I will investigate whether the choice of a parliamentary role might emanate – beyond self-interest and strategic considerations – from what Boudon calls 'good reasons'. What, then, could the 'good reasons' behind role orientations in the EP be? I will hypothesise that these norms and cognitions are substantively significant in defining a legitimate European political order. Considering the continuous debate on the course of European integration, ideas about European integration should influence how MEPs conceive of the EP as an institution and therefore of their own role within it. Discussions on the future of the EU are driven by contrasted definitions of democracy, the most accepted principle of contemporary government in Western Europe. MEPs should thus hold ideas about democracy that are consistent with their role orientation. To sum up, I hypothesise that MEPs' role orientations can be explained, on the one hand, by strategic considerations – career goals – and, on the other hand, by contrasted ideas about democracy and European integration. The empirical part of the chapter will be based on the study of the fifth term of the EP (1999–2004) relying on a mixed-research design combining interview and quantitative data analysis.

The first section is devoted to describing four role models in the EP – the animator, the specialist, the intermediary, and the outsider. The second and third sections serve to test our hypotheses about the origins of role orientations, starting with the impact of career trajectories in the second one and continuing with the importance of norms and cognitions in the third one. The fourth, concluding section discusses the meaning of these findings for role theory.

The repertoire of roles in the European Parliament: an overview

There are four major role types in the EP – the animator, the specialist, the intermediary, and the outsider[1] – which are directly derived from in-depth interviews with 78 MEPs.[2] The following description of parliamentary roles is inspired by Max Weber's ideal-type methodology: they are intellectual constructs in which some features are deliberately emphasised in order to highlight their defining characteristics and specificities. As a consequence, strictly speaking, no individual parliamentarian should be said to belong to one given role orientation to the exclusion of the others. In what follows, however, MEPs are dispatched according to the different models (i.e. to the one they appear to resemble the most) in order to test for the coherence of discourses and observable behaviours.

The animator

'Animators' ('*animateur*' in French), following the expression of a Spanish Conservative MEP (interview 19, French),[3] are those MEPs who are fundamentally attached to *politics*, not as the management of things, but as a way to decide about general social ends. They 'animate' in the sense that they strive to enliven the political debate within and beyond the EP in order to politicise Europe. Animators conceive of the EP as 'a democratic forum where all subjects – even without legislation – are debated and given an orientation' (interview 43, PES, DE, French) or as 'a place for reflection, for discussion' (interview 26, PES, ES, French). They are often very critical of the petty business the Parliament must get involved in: 'When we are requested to dissert about neon ballasts to determine how much gas they should contain, I am not sure that I entered politics to decide about that' (interview 15, Green, FR, French).

Animators especially appreciate their function as Euro MPs as they see it as an historical task to contribute to building peace and prosperity for the continent (interview 52, EPP, DE). They feel they are doing something 'that can be useful for your children and grandchildren' (interview 19, EPP, ES, French). On the personal level, the social gratifications that accompany the function of MEP are particularly valued: 'I like very much the internationalized approach and I like to be with people from different parts of Europe, even from different parts of the world, and try to see where we meet'. This MEP confesses getting 'a lot of satisfaction by discussing with colleagues from other member states and trying to understand how they see things and trying to see where there is common ground'. Being an MEP is a rewarding personal experience: 'aside from the culture and spiritual wealth, I must say that has taught me a way of living and a way of addressing issues' (interview 56, EPP, GR).

Typically, the animators' discourses emphasise the deliberative function of parliaments, such as debating in plenary sessions and exercising responsibilities within party groups. This is reflected in their activities. Compared to the whole sample, animators are particularly active during plenary sessions where they are the most assiduous (with an attendance of 86.3 per cent as compared to 84.5 per cent for the whole sample) and where they speak the most (117.3 speeches during the parliamentary term as compared to 88.7 for the whole sample) (Table 10.1). Compared to their colleagues, they table slightly more resolutions (29.2 on average), a typically deliberative tool; but they produce fewer questions and reports (12.4 written questions, 3.6 questions at question time, two reports).[4] The contrast with the model of specialist, which is described below, is especially striking: the specialists write on average three times more reports than the animators, who in turn speak twice as much in the plenary sessions.

Affinity with the model of the animator can also be seen in the choice of parliamentary committees (Table 10.2). During an interview, an Italian Conservative MEP made explicit the connection between her membership of the Foreign Affairs committee and her conception of the European mandate as 'an experience of high politics' (interview 64, French). As a matter of fact, the animators are largely over-represented in the Foreign Affairs committee, the Culture committee, the Constitutional Affairs committee and the delegation to the Convention: 16 of the 21 interviewed animators (76.2 per cent) belong to one of these bodies as compared to 28.2 per cent in the sample as a whole (Table 10.2). On the other hand, animators are totally absent from the Budget Control committee, the committee on Regional Policy and the Petitions committee.

Accordingly, MEPs who depict themselves as animators tend to prefer responsibilities in the bureau of the EP or in that of party groups where they can 'contribute to the organisation of a European public space' (interview 39, PES, FR, French), rather than in committees, which are deemed more technical. In the sample, one-third of the animators belong to the EP or group bureau, whereas

Table 10.1 MEPs' activities during the fifth term (averages)

	Reports	Written questions	Questions with territorial dimension	Question time	Declarations	Resolutions	Speeches in plenary	Attendance record
Animators (n = 21)	2	12.4	24.1	3.6	0.8	29.2	117.3	86.3
Standard deviation	2.2	13.9	18.9	6.9	1.1	33.7	181.7	8.3
Specialists (n = 28)	5.9	33.4	24.4	6.5	1	31.4	64	83
Standard deviation	5.1	42.4	22.9	13.7	1.4	31.5	40.5	9.4
Intermediaries (n = 23)	4.3	22.4	32.5	9.4	0.7	15.8	98.6	86
Standard deviation	3.5	22.6	24.4	17	1	17.9	97.3	7.8
Outsiders (n = 5)	0	8.4	37.4	6.8	1.2	7.2	78.8	80.4
Standard deviation	0	7.4	15.8	10.9	1.6	8	34.4	6.6
Sample total (n = 78)	3.9	22.6	26.9	6.5	0.8	24.3	88.7	84.5
Standard deviation	4.1	30.2	21.7	13.1	1.2	28.5	111.8	8.6
EP total (n = 626)	3.6	33	–	6.8	0.6	27.1	82.5	85.1
Standard deviation	3.8	63.4	–	15.2	1.2	43.5	132.2	53.4

Source: for 'Attendance record': www.europarliament.org.

Note
For 'Attendance record', n = 22 for the intermediaries and 624 for the Parliament as a whole. 'Questions with territorial dimension' present the percentage of written questions that include a reference to a specific region or country. MEPs who asked two questions or less are not included in the calculus; the number of MEPs taken into account (n) is thus respectively of 19, 25, 16, 3 and 64.

Table 10.2 Responsibilities held by MEPs during the second half of the fifth term (% in brackets)

	COCOBU, RETT, PETI***	AFET, CULT, AFCO, CONV*,***	Members of EP and/or group bureau*	Committee chair and/or coordinators***
Animators (*n* = 21)	0 (0)	16 (76.2)	7 (33.3)	2 (9.5)
Specialists (*n* = 28)	3 (10.7)	5 (17.9)	3 (10.7)	14 (50)
Intermediaries (*n* = 23)	9 (39.1)	0 (0)	3 (13)	4 (17.4)
Outsiders (*n* = 5)	1 (20)	1 (20)	0 (0)	0 (0)
Sample total (*n* = 78)	13 (16.7)	22 (28.2)	13 (16.7)	20 (25.6)
EP Total (*n* = 626)	101 (16.1)	153 (24.4)	59 (9.4)	128 (20.4)

Notes

Acronyms: Committee on Budgetary Control (COCOBU); Committee on Regional Policy, Transport and Tourism (RETT); Committee on Petitions (PETI); Committee on Foreign Affairs, Human Rights, Common Security and Defence Policy (AFET); Committee on Culture, Youth, Education, the Media and Sport (CULT); Committee on Constitutional Affairs (AFCO); European Parliament Delegation to the European Convention (CONV).

Cramer's V significant at $p < 0.01$ (***), $p < 0.05$ (**) and $p < 0.1$ (*).

the proportion for the whole assembly is only 9.4 per cent. Besides, no animator is a coordinator and the only two who belong to a committee bureau are members of the 'political' committee on Constitutional Affairs. Animators display behavioural and discursive patterns clearly distinct from the pragmatic approach adopted by the specialists.

The specialist

The specialist, another well-identified type in the MEPs' discourses, is characterised by his efforts to put his imprint on the day-to-day decision-making process. The label does not mean that these MEPs are necessarily recognised experts in one given narrow field (although this is often the case and probably the most telling examples of specialists): the specialists are MEPs who give priority to the technical and practical attributes of their position and agree to limit their scope of action in order to gain in competence and efficiency. As a Finnish Conservative (interview 11) puts it, specialists 'come to the EP to do normal parliamentary job: to do legislation'; this same politician, who explains that she would not seat in the EP if it was only a 'talking-shop', regards herself as belonging to this category of parliamentarians 'who normally concentrate on one particular field or [who] concentrate very much on legislation, making real changes to the articles [of directives or regulations]'.

When asked to describe their most important tasks and duties as Euro-parliamentarians, some specialists mention just one specific policy: 'Well, I'm in research and technology. So I'm very interested in promoting good research programmes' (interview 41, EPP, DK). In the most extreme cases, every activity is subordinated to their specialisation field: 'For me, it is – without a doubt – the social question. It is the social question which encompasses several issues, several related tasks, that is employment policy, social policy, equality, diversity, non-discrimination, fight against poverty, social exclusion, all that' (interview 45, PES, BE, French). Most specialists mention the legislative process at its different stages: agenda setting, consultation of interest groups, committee work, negotiations with the other institutions, implementation.

This description is confirmed by quantitative data. As Table 10.1 reveals, during the fifth term, MEPs who have been identified as specialists have written more reports (six on average) and asked more questions than any other category. Despite this intense activity, their attendance record at plenary sessions puts them behind animators and intermediaries, and the same is true of speeches. Any political field can call for some sort of specialisation, and specialists can be found in any committee. However, given their inclination towards practical outcomes, it is not surprising that they are under-represented in the so-called non-legislative committees on Foreign Affairs, on Culture, on Constitutional Affairs and the Convention.

Unlike animators, specialists do not resent having to get into the details of legislation. They even see it as a form of gratification and a sign of the importance of their role. Asked about what she finds the most satisfying in her role, a

Danish MEP responded: 'the fact that you actually can be influential. I've seen a number of amendments that I feel were very important, where I felt: "okay, if I hadn't been in, this wouldn't have been made in this respect"' (interview 16, ELDR, DK). A very similar comment was made in another interview: 'most of the proposals I've made have been carried through by a sensible majority, which means that, in my area of expertise and interest, I believe that I've had a sizeable influence' (interview 41, EPP, DK).

Specialists often mention committee responsibilities when talking about their role: 'I am the spokesperson of my delegation in a committee that works a lot and has many competencies: the committee on regional policy and transport' (interview 7, EPP, ES, French); 'I am here four days a week. As every member, I am on a committee. I am the coordinator of my group on the agriculture committee. The role of coordinator is to make sure that we reach a common position on the different reports ... on proposals that we must make, and also in public expression ... this is what is mobilizing my energy' (interview 75, PES, FR, French). As far as leading positions are concerned, whereas the majority of specialists have little interest in the bureau of the Parliament (none is a member) or group bureau (10.7 per cent), half of them are either members of a committee bureau or its coordinator (Table 10.2).

Whereas animators and specialists focus on the European level, intermediaries are more concerned with building bridges with citizens.

The intermediary

The ideal-type intermediary can best be compared to the spokesperson, the advocate or the ambassador of a population or a territory. Although this is something that all parliamentarians do to some extent, only some MEPs really give priority to this function. Intermediaries are especially attentive to the work of linking citizens and political leaders, and 'to be the voice of the citizens within the European Union' (interview 38, ELDR, FIN, French). The metaphors of the transmission-belt or dash are well appropriate to describe this situation: 'it is really us who are the transmission-belts and the dashes between the European thing, the institutions at large, the Parliament, and the citizens, because they are the ones who put us here and who chose the people they want to represent them' (interview 51, ELDR, BE, French).

This role orientation means both to speak in the name of the represented and to defend their interests: 'I see my role first and foremost as defending the interest of the Dutch people and, of course, particularly the people who voted for my party, at the European level' (interview 20, PES, NL). For intermediaries, the parliamentary function literally corresponds to the exercise of a mandate. 'In the tradition of my country, you are obviously representative of the individual people in your constituency, equally representative of the administration in this area and businesses. So, you have a constituency job' (interview 27, EPP, UK).

Contrary to specialists, intermediaries do not focus exclusively on one policy area because 'it is very, very important to deal with subjects that are interesting for the citizens' (interview 38, ELDR, FIN, French). Intermediaries are generalists who take care of all the questions relevant for their voters, as explained by one of them: 'you're working in the constituency very hard; but also you're keen to represent those people whenever you're dealing with different policy areas' (interview 74, PES, UK). This role implies direct contacts with the citizens:

> Representing the people of my region is more or less meant in a broader sense: not by my membership in the parliamentary committee, but I'm taking care even of individual concerns that people have. I make contacts with firms, schools, other institutions in my region, who want to have contacts on certain programme funding from the European Commission. I inform them about European legislation; I communicate to people about what the European Union is all about, what it does; this is everything.
>
> (Interview 53, PES, DE)

Consequently, the intermediaries are keener than the specialists and animators to put questions with a territorial dimension (Table 10.1).

From a quantitative point of view the 23 intermediaries in the sample stand somewhere in between the animators and the specialists (Table 10.1). On average, during the fifth term, each wrote 4.3 reports, asked 22.4 questions to the Commission and the Council, made 98.6 speeches, and had an attendance record of 86 per cent at plenary sessions. However, they initiate far fewer resolutions than their animator or specialist colleagues: as a consequence of their strong focus on their constituency, intermediaries seem to have difficulty mobilizing their colleagues and obtaining the necessary support for their resolution proposals.

The inclination of some MEPs towards the model of the intermediary is very obvious in the choice of committees (Table 10.2). None of the intermediaries belongs to the committees on Foreign Affairs, Culture, Constitutional Affairs, or to the delegation to the Convention; but many sit in the committees on Budget Control, Petitions, and Regional Policy. The first two are committees that clearly have a function of control characteristic of the archetypal intermediary. As for the committee on Regional Policy, it deals with questions that are particularly relevant at the local level. Unlike the specialists, there are only few intermediaries who are members or coordinators of a committee bureau: the four exceptions are found in the committees on Petitions, Regional Policy, Budgetary Control, and Fisheries.[5]

The outsider

The model of the outsider represents not only a different way of endorsing the role of an MEP; it also shows a rupture with the conventional interpretations of this role embodied by the animator, the specialist and the intermediary. Outsiders are unsatisfied by the institutional working of the Parliament and want to manifest it as much as possible. The term 'outsider' is borrowed from Huitt, who analysed the 'compulsive independence' and the disrespect for established parliamentary rules by one US Congressman (Huitt 1961). Outsiders do not consider the EP as import-ant in itself: it only provides them with an opportunity to publicise their positions. More than other MEPs, outsiders highlight that the EP has no real power (but they do not support projects to grant it these missing powers).

In a sense, the outsiders share with the animators the idea that politics is about debating general ideas. 'The relevant point for us is to bring political issues; I don't think that I can have much influence on the policy process' (interview 70, EUL/NGL, DK). This conception of parliamentary work is expressed provoca-tively by one MEP from the National Front: 'What is missing is democratic life: people standing, private conversations, lobby talks, lobby rumours, plots … things that we love!' (interview 78, NI, FR, French). As a consequence outsid-ers' endeavours are as much oriented towards the 'outside' as towards the EP as such. The efficiency of their actions must be measured according to how much publicity they receive and not according to the legislative results that they can get. Thus the editorial activities are particularly important, since they allow MEPs to express their views without compromising with the institution and their colleagues (interview 72, EDD, FR).

Outsiders also think that, within the Parliament, the decisions are appropri-ated by the EPP–PES majority, which seeks to marginalise and even silence dis-sident voices. This animosity towards other MEPs is obvious in some of what they say: 'There are extremely arrogant people [in the EP]: they really do believe they're little gods. In fact, the MEPs have very little power, but you wouldn't think that from the way they behave!' (interview 65, EDD, UK). In sharp con-trast to other interviewed MEPs, outsiders have little trust in MEPs who belong to a party group other than theirs. To the question, 'In your experience in Parlia-ment, to what extent can one trust and rely on members of the other groups? How confidently can you work with them personally and politically?', no out-sider answers 'always' or 'most of the time', compared to the very large major-ity of animators (66.7 per cent), specialists (65.4 per cent) and intermediaries (76.2 per cent) who do so.

The relationship of outsiders to the institution and their conception of their mandate have a direct impact on their behaviour. Typical activities of outsiders belong to the register of denunciation and anti-conformism. They must act in a dramatic way so as to gain attention. As can be seen from Table 10.1, they do not try to influence the decision-making process. The five outsiders in the sample have a limited output in terms of legislation (they did not write any reports) and they ask few written questions to the Commission and Council (8.4 on average, compared to an average of 22.6 in the whole sample). Despite this weak legisla-tive output and a lower rate of attendance at the plenary sessions, these MEPs made a significant number of speeches (78.8 on average, more than the special-ists) and they tabled more declarations. This demonstrates that the outsiders prefer the deliberative dimension of the parliamentary function. In the sample, no outsider belongs to the bureau of the Parliament, groups or committees, and none is a coordinator: this is particularly in keeping with the distance they keep with the institutional charges of the Parliament. Through his behaviours and discourse, the archetypal outsider intends to contest the established order: he claims to be speaking the truth against the official vision.

Having quickly introduced the role models in the EP, I shall investigate their individual sources.

Individual trajectories and role orientations

As hypothesised a number of factors need to be taken into account to explain parliamentary roles. Before turning to ideological factors, we test for the impact of career patterns. The analysis is based on logistic regressions with the MEPs' role orientations as the dependent variable: three separate regressions were run with the major role models as dichotomous variables. The independent variables relate to the nationality, the party group, previous national mandates, and seniority in the EP. On the whole, the regressions have a fairly strong explanatory capacity although they are not statistically significant.

In contradiction with earlier studies which found nationality to be the most important factor in explaining MEPs' roles (Hagger and Wing 1979, Wessels 1999, Katz 1999), our multi-varied analysis shows that, compared to other variables, nationality has no significant overall impact on role choices in the EP fifth legislature (Table 10.3). It is noticeable, however, that Greek and Italian MEPs are more likely to adopt the model of the animator, Danish MEPs that of specialist, Spanish MEPs that of intermediary, and Dutch MEPs that of specialist or intermediary. Looking more qualitatively to outsiders (for which a regression is not applicable due to the sample size), they are concentrated in the French delegation (three out of five). One difficulty in interpreting the impact of the national factor, however, is that it mixes cultural features and institutional constraints.

Party affiliation is the other 'usual suspect' in explaining role orientations. With the exception of the outsiders, the distribution of roles in the conservative EPP and centre–left PES groups reflects predominantly that of the Parliament as a whole. Liberal representatives from the ELDR group prefer the model of the intermediary. The far left and green MEPs are more likely than any other to fall in the category of the specialist, while the models of animator and intermediary are more popular amongst the UEN parliamentarians. The EDD representatives tend to adopt the model of the outsider: three out of five fall into this category. One of the two remaining outsiders belongs to the non-attached. This is extremely meaningful since it shows that marginal parties opposed to the process of European integration are not trying to influence the decisional process but simply to manifest their disagreement.

The conjunction of institutional and political constraints can help to explain role orientations in some specific cases. The many intermediaries from Catalonia and the Basque country tend, for instance, to strengthen a strategic–utilitarian interpretation of roles at the expense of one that emphasises a cultural divide, in which representation styles in Northern Europe (intermediation and specialisation) differ from those in Southern Europe (oriented towards politicisation). It is because they have specific regional interests to defend that they endorse the role of intermediary.

Outsiders provide another relevant example of how institutional constraints explain role orientations. For MEPs who are dissatisfied by the opportunities offered in the institutional system of the EP (either because they disagree with European integration or because they consider that they do not receive sufficient recognition) but who encounter difficulties in establishing themselves at the national level, especially when electoral rules prevent any career perspective at this level, it is tempting to maintain a protesting presence on the European scene. This is explained by a Danish MEP:

> The main reason [for being an MEP] is an internal reason. We want to be part of the political agenda in Denmark: the debate is whether to continue with integration or to withdraw from the EU. There is a law in Denmark which gives access to the media, television, radio, etc. to every party which has representatives. That is the main reason why we are here. The EU is financing us. Without the MEPs, our party wouldn't exist in Denmark.
>
> (Interview 70, EUL/NGL, DK)

In countries where it is difficult for the small or protesting parties to exist on the national stage, the EP offers a good alternative. In France where the electoral rules strictly limit access to the National Assembly, many small parties do not have the opportunity to be represented and defend their ideas at the national level; the EP makes this possible. This helps to explain why there are so many outsiders in the French delegation: 23.1 per cent (three MEPs out of a total of 13), the largest proportion in the sample.

Political experience – measured by the mandates held at the local, regional or national levels – and seniority are other predictors that can be interpreted in terms of individual goals and strategies. Due to the lack of any direct indicator of personal ambition, we rely on the MEPs' actual political career trajectories. Past positions are potentially important in understanding the kind of resources that MEPs dispose of and their commitment towards the European mandate. Almost half of the MEPs who held no electoral mandate before 1999 (17 out of 37, i.e. 49.9 per cent) follow the model of the specialist, and the regressions show that the more political experience they have the more MEPs tend to opt for the intermediary model.

Tenure has a significant impact in the category of animators: MEPs with an older mandate tend to fall into this category, which corresponds to a seniority selection process (Navarro 2009: 198). A longer tenure demonstrates a special relationship with the parliamentary institution – it is thus logical that these MEPs want to coordinate activities within the assembly and that their colleagues trust them to do so. MEPs who entered the Parliament after 1999 are correlated to the models of intermediary and outsider – these models seem to reflect a greater proximity to the electorate. All in all, however, past experience and seniority have a limited impact on role orientations, but they give an indication of individual trajectories.

As a matter of fact, MEPs' role orientations can be understood not as resulting from past influences but as revelations of career ambitions. MEPs must anticipate the expectations of those who are going to select them in their future

Table 10.3 Determinants explaining role orientations (logistic regressions)

Dependent variable[1]	Animators exp(B)	Specialists exp(B)	Intermediaries exp(B)
Country (reference category: UK)			
BE	1.70	1.09	0.18
DK	0.00	2.11	0.53
DE	1.45	0.86	0.89
GR	4.85	1.55	0.00
ES	1.74	0.58	1.17
FR	3.14	0.34	1.05
IT	19.14	0.50	0.00
NL	0.00	1.75	2.37
FIN	2.37	0.61	0.81
SV	1.63	1.22	0.52
Party (reference category: EPP)			
PES	0.51	0.99	2.63
ELDR	0.18	0.67	7.60*
GUE	0.27	2.48	0.00
Greens	0.89	2.83	0.40
UEN	902.31	0.00	5,223.07
EDD	0.00	0.00	1.43
NI	0.84	0.00	0.00
Political experience[2]	0.84	0.61	2.56*
Seniority[3]	1.15**	0.92	0.94
Model chi-squared	24.918	19.640	27.820*
Prediction success (%)	82.05	69.23	78.21
Nagelkerke R^2	0.39	0.31	0.43
N	78	78	78

Notes
1 The dependent variable is a dummy opposing one given category to the others (including outsiders and dilettantes).
2 Ordinal categories: No elected mandate before 1999; local or regional mandate before 1999; national MP or minister before 1999.
3 Number of years in the EP before 1999.
Country abbreviations: BE: Belgium; DK: Denmark; DE: Germany; GR: Greece; ES: Spain; FR: France; IT: Italy; NL: Netherlands; FI: Finland; SV: Sweden; UK: United Kingdom.
Parliamentary groups abbrevaitons: EPP: European People's Party; PES: Party of European Socialists; ELDR: European Liberal, Democrat, and Reform Party; GUE/NGL: European United Left/Nordic Green Left; UEN: Union for Europe of the Nations; EDD: Europe of Democracies and Diversities.
Significance levels: **$p<0.05$; *$p<0.1$.

positions: 'Our ambitious politician must act today in terms of the electorate of the office which he hopes to win tomorrow' (Schlesinger 1966: 7). As regards the three most important role models in the EP, we can formulate the following hypotheses. MEPs who are about to retire have more freedom vis-à-vis their principal in determining their behaviour (Fisher and Herrick 2002): they will be less likely to endorse the model of intermediary. On the contrary, the MEPs who want to pursue their career at the local or national level must care for their electorate and political party: we expect more of them to be intermediaries than the other MEPs. Finally, the MEPs who hope to gain a higher position within the Parliament must demonstrate their efficiency by their work inside the 'house', as animators or specialists. Since it is very difficult to obtain reliable information on the real career ambitions of politicians, we take actual career patterns as a proxy indicator.

Figure 10.1 represents the career pattern of the interviewed MEPs according to their chosen role orientation. Starting with the incumbent MEPs who left the Parliament after 2004, we can distinguish between those MEPs who voluntarily quitted their function in order to pursue a career elsewhere and those who retired or failed to be reelected. Among the latter, all roles seem to be involved. Thirteen politicians retired from all political or professional activity for personal reasons such as health and age; these include six animators, five specialists and one intermediary who did

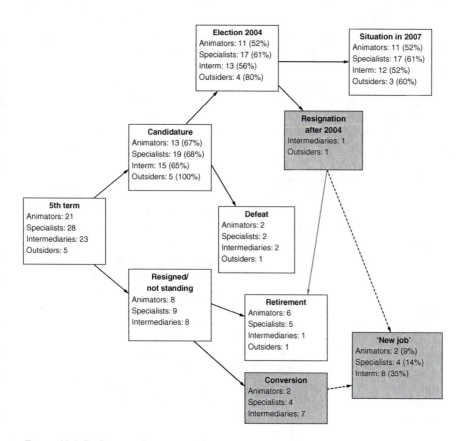

Figure 10.1 Trajectory after 1999 of the 78 interviewed MEPs.

Note
All percentages relate to the initial population (frame '5th term'). The situation of the outsider who resigned in 2006 is equivalent to that of a retiring MEP because it followed a road accident. The frame 'new job' corresponds to the sum of the frames 'conversion' and 'resignation since 2004'.

not stand again for election in 2004, and one outsider who resigned in 2006 following a road accident. The under-representation of intermediaries in the group of politicians who retired in 2004 confirms our hypothesis that retiring politicians are less worried about satisfying their principals. The 14 MEPs who quitted the EP voluntarily to exercise other political or non-political functions ('new job' box) are very interesting because of the over-representation of intermediaries.

The fact that incumbent MEPs who access a regional or national mandate are almost all intermediaries (seven out of eight) is particularly striking. The role orientation of intermediary can therefore be interpreted as a stepping-stone to a regional or national power position (an incumbent MEP even managed to become the chairperson of his national party). In a similar way, the role orientation of animator seems to be popular among older, experienced politicians who want to achieve their career without exercising heavy executive responsibilities; however, against our expectations, some retiring politicians followed the model of specialist.

The underlying logic of role choices is also apparent in the trajectory of MEPs who were reelected in 2007 and still sat in the EP three years later. Table 10.4 distinguishes between three situations: the 'ascending trajectory', which includes the MEPs who earned new responsibilities in the fifth and sixth terms (bureau of Parliament, of groups, of committees, coordinator) or who maintained a top position (e.g. presidency of a group); the 'stable trajectory' for those who maintained their previous responsibilities (e.g. coordinator) or whose position is only slightly higher (e.g. member of a group bureau at a slightly higher rank); and the 'mediocre trajectory' for MEPs who remained without responsibility or who lost any that they had. If many MEPs reached higher positions within the institution, their career prospects depend partially upon their role orientation in the previous term. Animators and, to a lesser extent, specialists were more successful in attaining leading positions than intermediaries (and outsiders).

The positions held in the sixth term are also an indication of the stability of role choices. Of the 25 MEPs who held a hierarchical position in 2007, only five have one other than that predicted by our typology (namely group or Parliament bureau for the animators, committee chair or coordinator for the specialists). If we look in more detail, it appears that three intermediaries and one animator became members of a group bureau, that one animator became member of the

Table 10.4 Career patterns of reelected MEPs (% in brackets)

	Mediocre trajectory	Stable trajectory	Ascendant trajectory
Animators ($n = 11$)	5 (45.5)	0 (0)	6 (54.5)
Specialists ($n = 17$)	5 (29.4)	6 (35.3)	6 (35.3)
Intermediaries ($n = 12$)	7 (58.3)	5 (41.7)	0 (0)
Outsiders ($n = 3$)	1 (33.3)	2 (66.7)	0 (0)
Total ($n = 43$)	18 (41.9)	13 (30.2)	2 (27.9)

Note
Cramer's V = 0.40; $p < 0.05$.

bureau of the Foreign Affairs committee, that another animator became chairman of the Constitutional Affairs committee, and that three specialists kept their previous position in their respective committees. These observations are consistent with the descriptions of role types in the previous section.

By and large, the choice of a role is definitively linked to career goals and opportunities; this utilitarian logic does not exhaust our interrogations about role orientations.

The cognitive rationality of parliamentary roles

In the introduction, I argued that norms and cognitions are important factors behind the role orientations of the parliamentarians. In this section, I will confront the MEPs' conceptions of European integration and democracy with their role choices as reflected in the interviews.

Conceptions of European integration and parliamentary roles

European integration is a prominent issue for MEPs. Since they have the double task of shaping the institutional framework and taking part in the daily decision-making process, each one's behaviour has significance for the future of the continent. The hypothesis of a link between ideas about Europe and the MEPs' roles was first formulated by Katz:

> When thinking about European level politics, MPs at both [national and European] levels must confront not only the question of their individual roles within their institution, but also the question of the role of the EP and the national parliaments as institutions within the broader European political system.
>
> (Katz 1999: 61)

Here a distinction between general attitudes towards European integration and specific issues of institutional reform must be made. Starting with the MEPs' position on integration, it appears that most of the outsiders are predominantly opposed to further integration, whereas other MEPs are much more divided. On a −1 to +1 scale positing MEPs on the integration dimension,[6] the mean score is −0.75 for outsiders (standard deviation 0.06), 0.09 for animators (s.d. 0.44), 0.04 for specialists (s.d. 0.40), and 0.08 for intermediaries (s.d. 0.42). The fact that the standard deviation is far higher in the case of specialists, animators and intermediaries shows that MPs following these role types have no uniform attitude towards the EU. On the contrary, rejection of EU integration is a defining feature of the model of the outsider: Euroscepticism implies a disagreement with the working order of the EU (Eurosceptics believe that decisions should be taken at the national level and not by supranational institutions such as the EP): the lack of involvement in the conventional work of the Parliament is a way to express this rejection and to avoid giving their consent to European integration.

Turning to more specific issues about Europe, it appears that there are differences among animators, specialists and intermediaries.[7] The answer to an open-ended question asked in the interviews will help to gain a better knowledge of how MEPs see the situation of Europe. The question was: 'According to you, what are the main problems that the EU is facing today?'. The most quoted items are: the reform of EU institutions and the work of the Convention (49.3 per cent), enlargement (47.8 per cent), and the international situation (47.8 per cent). Other answers relate to the coherence and identity of Europe (33.3 per cent), economic and social matters (31.9 per cent) and the issue of democracy (24.6 per cent).[8]

Apart from enlargement, which figures at a similar level on the agenda of all role models, there are important differences in the MEPs' answers. Animators tend to mention the institutional reform much more often than the other MEPs. Those who are the most worried by international affairs tend to opt for the model of the animator and, to a lesser extent, that of the specialist. Of the MEPs who mention economic issues 63.6 per cent are intermediaries, whereas the intermediaries are more likely to be found among respondents stressing the lack of cohesion and identity in Europe. Three times as many MEPs who mention the democratic issue are animators as are specialists and four times as many are intermediaries as are specialists.

These divergent judgements are also reflected in MEPs' views about alternative options for the future of Europe. The intermediaries, who are the most worried about the lack of coherence in the EU and the democratic deficit, are also logically more opposed to the adhesion of Turkey to the EU[9] and they are keener to plead for limiting the scope of EU competencies and even renationalizing some of them.[10] Regarding the revision of the treaties in the future (either unanimously or by a majority vote), intermediaries are the most numerous advocates for keeping unanimity (nine of them, i.e. 40 per cent, as compared to six specialists, 22.2 per cent, and seven animators, 35 per cent; $n = 67$). Intermediaries are much more cautious than other MEPs about the Europeanization of foreign policy: only 38.9 per cent of them want such a step to be taken (as compared to 72 per cent of the specialists and 88.2 per cent of the animators). Rather than opposition to European integration, this reflects their view that the EU should concentrate on the immediate problems of the citizens.

Animators are much more eager to transfer prerogatives from the national to the European level – as many as 55 per cent believe that in the future unanimity should not be required for modifying the treaty/constitution.[11] Significantly, they have an internationally oriented vision of the EU: they are more likely to support the project for an EU presidency, they overwhelmingly wish to see the Europeanization of foreign policy and they defend the accession of Turkey in order to give more weight to the EU and allow it to influence Middle East affairs. Their opinion on the idea of having an EU president shows that they want Europe to have a personified presence on the international stage.

The specialists expressed a 'careful' stance on many issues relating to the constitutional debate. For instance, they stand somewhere in between the animators

Table 10.5 Most often mentioned problems facing the EU ($n = 69$) (% in brackets)

	Reform of institutions***	Enlargement	International situation***	Coherence and identity of Europe	Economic problems**	Problem of democracy within EU
Animators	15 (75)	9 (45)	12 (60)	6 (30)	5 (25)	6 (30)
Specialists	14 (50)	14 (50)	17 (60.7)	7 (25)	14 (50)	3 (10.7)
Intermediaries	5 (23.8)	10 (47.6)	4 (19)	10 (47.6)	3 (14.3)	8 (38.1)
Total	34 (49.3)	33 (47.8)	33 (47.8)	23 (33.3)	22 (31.9)	17 (24.6)

Note
Cramer's V significant at $p < 0.01$ (***) and $p < 0.05$ (**).

and the intermediaries on the questions of renationalizing some EU competencies and of European Foreign policy. However, they are more likely than the other MEPs to defend a constraining status for the Charter of Fundamental Rights.[12] Regarding the mode of revision of a future treaty or constitution, the specialists' most popular answer is an intermediate solution combining unanimity and qualified majority voting:[13] 13 of them (48.1 per cent) prefer this solution, as compared to two animators (10 per cent) and five intermediaries (25 per cent).' As for the accession of Turkey, as many specialists as animators are in favour of it, but they are more likely to respond that they 'tend to be in favour' (64 per cent as opposed to 37.5 per cent of animators) rather than they are 'strongly in favour' of it (4 per cent as opposed to 31.3 per cent of the animators).

As can be seen from the interviews, different views about the future of Europe guide the type of role that MEPs follow. What about contrasted conceptions of democracy?

Conceptions of democracy and parliamentary roles

Self-definitions of roles are also directed by contrasted visions of a legitimate European political order and, in particular, by different interpretations of democracy. There are at least two reasons for giving so much importance to conceptions of democracy. First, in European societies, democracy is more than a mere political system: it is a value that everyone is supposed to accept and respect. As Sartori puts it, 'in the final analysis, our political behaviour depends on our idea of what democracy is, can be, and should be' (Sartori 1965: 5). Second, from an analytical perspective, there is a logical link between definitions of democracy and parliamentary roles because, in a representative political system, the definition of democracy entails a description of the function of the parliament and the individual role of parliamentarians.

Although all MEPs originate from liberal parliamentary regimes, they do not share the exact same definition of democracy and they do not all perceive the EU democratic deficit in the same way. Questioned about it, three MEPs out of four respond that there is such a deficit: this figure is slightly higher in the cases of the specialists (78.6 per cent) and the intermediaries (80 per cent) than in that of

Table 10.6 Perceptions of the democratic deficit ($n = 68$) (% in brackets)

	Weakness of Parliament*	Organization of Council	Absence of demos
Animators	5 (27.8)	8 (41.2)	6 (31.6)
Specialists	15 (53.6)	11 (39.3)	11 (39.3)
Intermediaries	11 (57.9)	7 (36.8)	3 (15.8)
Total	31 (47)	26 (39.4)	20 (30.3)

Note
* Cramer's V significant at $p < 0.1$.

the animators (70 per cent).[14] The most significant differences appear if we consider how the interviewed MEPs define this deficit (Table 10.6). Three aspects are very often pointed out: the weakness of the EP (47 per cent), the working rules of the Council (39.4 per cent) and the absence of a genuine European demos or shared identity (30.3 per cent). The intermediaries are most sensitive to the fact that the EP has limited prerogatives in the decision-making process and cannot properly control the Commission (57.9 per cent). This problem, which is also taken seriously by 53.6 per cent of the specialists, is mentioned less frequently by animators (27.8 per cent). More than half of the MEPs who think that the democratic deficit has to do with the citizens who do not have a sense of shared destiny and abstain at European elections are specialists.

In other words, intermediaries, who feel strongly that they are speaking in the name of citizens, are less keen to blame them for the democratic deficit: they prefer to pinpoint the Parliament's institutional lack of power. Specialists consider that two links in the chain of delegation are faulty: one between the citizens and the parliamentarians and the other between the parliamentarians and the executive. As for animators, they are singled out by the fact that they do not strongly resent the weakness of the Parliament: as they conceive of their role as dominantly deliberative, they do not feel the need for an increase in the decision-making powers of the Parliament. Evaluating the democratic deficit is not only a problem of perception: it also depends on the chosen criteria, i.e. the definitions of democracy.

In order to have a better understanding of their conception of democracy, MEPs were asked to define this concept. The question was identical to the one asked by Putnam in *The Beliefs of Politicians*: 'The word "democracy" is often loosely used in talking about politics and government. What seem to you personally to be the essentials of a real democracy?' (Putnam 1973). Instead of establishing a typology of definitions, the most frequent features are listed.

More than any other category, animators take the rule of law and the balance of powers seriously: these are mentioned by 65 per cent of them as opposed to one-third of the other MEPs (Table 10.7). For intermediaries, the most frequent answers relate to the election (90 per cent) and the existence of a parliamentary system (55 per cent). The definitions of specialists show more variety; however, it can be noted that they are especially attentive to individual rights (36 per cent), transparency (32 per cent) and direct democracy (33 per cent). These responses about democracy reveal some convergence with ideas about European integration and they help to explain the choice of specific parliamentary role orientations.

The way the intermediary typically conceives of democracy is distinct from both that of the animator and that of the specialist. As already noted, intermediaries stress the importance of the electoral link in democracy, and they mention the crucial place of the parliament more than MEPs following the other role models. On the other hand, they do not mention individual rights or the direct participation of citizens as principles of genuine democracy. This indicates that, for them, democracy is above all 'government of the people', hence their emphasis on the delegation link, which the centrality of parliament in the political system embodies best.

Table 10.7 The essentials of a real democracy (*n* = 67) (% in brackets)

	Election*	Rule of law*	Parliamentary system	Individual rights	Transparency	Direct democracy*
Animators	12 (60)	13 (65)	8 (40)	5 (25)	3 (15)	5 (25)
Specialists	17 (60.7)	9 (32.1)	9 (32.1)	10 (35.7)	9 (32.1)	9 (33.3)
Intermediaries	18 (90)	7 (35)	11 (55)	4 (20)	6 (30)	1 (5)
Total	47 (69.1)	29 (42.6)	28 (41.2)	19 (27.9)	18 (26.5)	15 (22.4)

Note
* Cramer's V significant at *p*<0.1.

The way institutions are interrelating is a decisive factor of democracy. And concerning this, I'm advocating a strict and unbroken chain of legitimacy that is from the voter to members of the parliament, and there the decision has to be made who should form a government, and this government should be responsible to the parliament. I think this is the essence of a democracy.

> (Interview 53, PES, DE)

This view is perfectly consistent with intermediaries' ideas about European integration, since they notably emphasise the importance of increasing the role of the Parliament. Furthermore, the archetypal intermediary does not feel that he/she belongs to the elite. He sees himself/herself as the spokesperson of the citizens vis-à-vis the real elites that are, according to him/her, the Commission and the governments:

The main problem is to get acceptation from the European people to the project, to the all project [of European integration]. Because I think this is a project from the political elite and *they* don't have sufficient support.

> (Interview 71, EDD, DK, emphasis added)

Since they believe that they are siding with the citizens and not the elite, intermediaries tend to see the democratic deficit not as a failure in the relationship between the representatives and their electors but as citizens – and their representatives – lacking influence over the 'elites'. They wish to increase the influence of representatives globally, but not to have to deal with the small details of legislation. Their view about democracy is very much procedural: it is about *input* legitimacy and not about *output* legitimacy – which is the concern of specialists.

Of course, specialists – as all MEPs – recognize the importance of elections as an essential principle of democracy; but unlike the others they rank individual rights (freedom of opinion, of the press, human rights, etc.) in second place among the defining features of democracy. In other words, they appreciate very much the effectiveness and substantive dimension of democracy. They also advocate transparency and the direct involvement of stakeholders in the decision-making process; this means that majority rule is less important for the specialists than for other MEPs:

To me, democracy also includes very much the protection of minorities [...] the most democratic decision making is decision making which reflects some kind of consensus, which is why I like the way the EP works. Now, I do accept that consensus decision-making may be the lowest common denominator, but I still think that it's more democratic.

> (Interview 76, ELDR, UK)

In their speeches, specialists do not stress the division between the 'elites' and themselves: 'all those who have public responsibilities, in my opinion, have a responsibility towards the understanding of Europe, its functioning and its project'; they see their task as one of making Europe develop '*for* and *with* the citizens' (interview 75, PES, FR). If specialists are very supportive of an increased European integration, they often express a very balanced and careful view about it; this reflects their pragmatic approach to politics, which separates them from animators.

The fact that animators, when qualifying the democratic deficit, complain less about the weakness of the Parliament than other MEPs does not mean that they do not have a high opinion of this institution: it indicates rather that they believe that participation in the day-to-day decision-making process is less decisive for the Parliament than its moral influence on the political debate. According to the archetypal animator, democracy is first and foremost an institutional system based on the balance of powers, the rule of law and respect for constitutional principles. In this framework, the role of the parliamentarian is to maintain a political dialogue with the Commission and Council.

> There is a democratic deficit ... the democratic deficit exists and ... Democracy: what is democracy? Democracy is about political discourse in society about major issues and this trans-national discourse is not well organised. So, we lack two things: European political parties [...] and cross-border communications. The media and all the communication, which is part of this discourse, are under-developed.
>
> (Interview 43, PES, DE, original in French)

This conception reflects well the tendency of animators to hold 'political' responsibilities in party groups and in the bureau of the Parliament. The animators want to enable Europe to have more influence on the world stage: more than the other MEPs, they support having a president of Europe, of giving more power to the EU in foreign policy and of allowing Turkish membership. The focus of animators on the international and institutional problems (Table 10.7) is consistent with the committees in which they choose to sit. It more broadly reflects their understanding of what politics is about.

Concluding remarks

The aim of this chapter has been to explain why some MPs choose different particular parliamentary role types. Based on an empirical study of the EP's fifth term, I have contended that politicians do not choose their role only according to selfish interests – defined in terms of career goals – but also take into account normative principles and values. Relying on Boudon's concept of cognitive non-instrumental rationality, attention has been drawn to the impact that contrasted conceptions of European integration and democracy can have on how MEPs define their duties and tasks within the European parliamentary system. This approach draws heavily on Searing's motivational theory of roles by relying on the politicians' own conceptions and discourse. However it tries to overcome the overly descriptive nature of the motivational approach of roles (Searing 1994: 8) and to establish a clearer distinction between the emotional incentives (that are part of the 'motivational core' in Searing's conceptualisation) and the 'external' factors orienting role choices.

The cognitive–rational approach of role choices has a number of advantages in comparison with rival sociological and psychological theories. First, it does not produce the kind of 'black boxes' inherent to socialisation theories (Boudon 2002): role types in the EP have been connected to ideas about democracy and European integration, which help to make sense of role choices *but* are analytically distinct from them. Second, it is not based on the 'ad hoc' explanations that motivational approaches sometimes rely upon. For instance, it is more simple and convincing to explain the role of an intermediary by referring to specific ideas about democracy and career opportunities than by assimilating a specific *habitus* or by the 'desire for a sense of competence' (Searing). In fact, psychological explanations of roles – such as those relied upon by Searing – sometimes pose a problem of endogeneity: motivations are derived directly from discourses, actual behaviours and attitudes, which are part of the 'motivational core' of roles. Could not the 'sense of competence', even completed by a 'sense of duty' (Searing 1994: 147), be as good an explanation for the role of 'constituency member' (in Searing's typology) as for that of 'policy advocate' (another major role type)?

The strength of rational interpretations of roles is their inner but not circular logic: someone who thinks that democracy is about making the voices of the citizens heard will act in a way that is consistent with this view; in the same vein, someone who considers that European integration is about peace, international relations and high politics will adopt a role orientation appropriate to this conception – a role orientation that will be different from the one chosen by a parliamentarian for whom politics is about problem-solving. It should be noted here that utilitarian and cognitive rationalities are complementary: the outsider, for instance, has some *reasons* to act the way he does because he does not agree with the course of European integration *and* because he has limited opportunites of obtaining leading positions at the national level. In most cases, both types of rationality even tend to reinforce each other.

Finally, an analysis of roles based on the concept of cognitive rationality is superior to the narrow utilitarian perspective, because it can account for behaviours that do not involve individual interests and because it does not rely on a given fixed exogenous set of interests. According to Boudon, indeed, cognitions, norms and values do not have to be considered as exogenous variables (or as the result of biological, cultural or psychological forces): they are logical deductions based on the individual's experience and knowledge (Boudon 1999). In other words, the theory of cognitive rationality foresees the possibility of changes in the goals and representations of the actors and, therefore, changes in role orientations. For instance, a politician who is elected to the EP with great ideas about getting immersed in high politics across nations may discover that European integration is actually about dealing with small concrete issues and passing compromises, and then adopt the model of the specialist. This should not be interpreted as the result of inculcating a constraining behavioural pattern, but as the rational deduction from an experience in a context different from that expected. To take the cognitive–rational analysis of parliamentary roles further, it would be necessary to question MEPs not only about their conception of democracy and European integration but also about their broader understanding of politics.

Notes

1 A fifth type – that of the dilettante – which was identified to one interviewed MEP and presented in an earlier study (Navarro 2009) is not dealt with in this chapter.

2 In order to delineate roles making sense for the actors, the methodology was inductive rather than deductive. Semi-structured interviews (completed by a closed-ended questionnaire administered directly at the end of the interview) were carried out with 78 MEPs between 2001 and 2003. Interviewed MEPs came from 11 countries and all political groups. The sample is representative of the whole EP in terms of nationality, party group, gender, age, and tenure (see Navarro 2009: 267–73 for a detailed description). Besides, MEPs in the sample have practices and responsibilities fairly similar to those of other MEPs (Tables 10.1 and 10.2). All interviews were conducted on a non-attribution basis and tape-recorded. The most important question in elaborating the typology of roles was adapted from Searing's seminal work: 'Thinking of your broad role as a Member of the European Parliament, what are the most important duties and responsibilities involved?' (Searing 1994: 484). The other issues dealt with included the future of Europe, the concept of democracy, the institutional reforms debated in the Convention, and their personal satisfaction with their experience as an MEP.

The qualitative analysis of the interviews followed a three-step process. A first 'mapping' of the interviews, which were entirely transcribed in their original language, aimed at delineating alternative role models: the main themes and key words used to describe an MEP's tasks and responsibilities were identified and highlighted. This verbal material was then reused to elaborate our role types, which are therefore not *a priori* theoretical constructs or imported categories, but descriptions of how the MEPs conceive of their position, tasks, and responsibilities. In the second stage of the analysis, MEPs were identified to a specific role orientation by going back to the interviews verbatim and matching individuals to the role patterns, which their discourse predominantly reflected. In the third, confirmatory step, textual data were confronted to behavioural indicators as reported in the second section of this chapter. This shows that, although there is a great variety in the actual behaviour of MEPs within each attributed category, the MEPs' conduct is globally consistent with their subjective descriptions.

3 To preserve the anonymity of the interviewed MEPs, I indicate only their party and delegation. The language of the interview was English unless another language is mentioned.

4 The fact that standard deviation be high for some of the activities emphasises that these are not monolithic categories but ideal types. More precisely, some of the available indicators of activity are somewhat rough. Reports, like other parliamentary tools, can serve different purposes: it would be interesting for example to distinguish better between legislative and non-legislative reports. Additionally the high standard deviations can also be explained by the differences in the global level of activities within each category: not all intermediaries, to take one example, are equally involved in parliamentary business and not all are equally eager to write questions, prepare reports, etc.

5 This last case can be explained by the fact that the MEP in question was elected in a region where fisheries are very important.

6 We rely on NOMINATE, an algorithm based on roll-call votes, which establishes the position of MEPs on the left–right dimension (dimension 1) and on the integration dimension (dimension 2). Scores go from –1 to +1 on both dimesions. The data are provided by the European Parliament Research Group (London School of Economics). See Hix 2001.

7 In what follows, I will concentrate on the cases of animators, intermediaries and specialists, because they are the most numerous and because the role of outsiders has already been accounted for.

8 Other answers are not taken into account since they are given only by very few MEPs. As all responses were coded, the total is more than 100 per cent.

9 Sixty-five per cent of intermediaries declare that they are opposed to the adhesion of Turkey; the figure is 31.3 per cent for animators and 32 per cent for specialists.

10 In the interviews, some open-ended questions related to this issue. Out of 62 respondents, four animators (23.5 per cent), seven specialists (26.9 per cent) and six intermediaries (31.6 per cent) agreed that some EU policies should be handled at the national or regional level.

11 The proportion is only 30 per cent for specialists and intermediaries.

12 This was a closed-ended question in which the MEPs had to say how far they agreed with the statement that the Charter should be legally binding: 22 specialists (78.6 per cent) say that they strongly agree, as opposed to 13 animators (61.9 per cent) and 12 intermediaries (52.2 per cent). This is an important observation as it highlights the connection between conceptions of democracy and ideas about Europe, which will be discussed in the next section.

13 The question was open-ended and some MEPs suggested to distinguish between the different parts of the then constitutional treaty or to introduce possibilities to opt-out.

14 The question was worded as follows: 'As regards the European Union it is often said that it suffers a "democratic deficit". According to you, what is this democratic deficit about?'

References

Blomgren, M. (2003) *Cross-pressure and Political Representation in Europe: A Comparative Study of MEPs and the Intra-Party Arena*, Umeå: University of Umeå.

Boudon, R. (1999) *Le sens des valeurs*, Paris: Presses Universitaires de France.

Boudon, R. (2002) 'Utilité ou rationalité? Rationalité restreinte ou générale?', *Revue d'Economie Politique*, 112 (5): 754–72.

Dahrendorf, R. (1968) *Essays on the Theory of Society*, Standford, CA: Stanford University Press.

Fisher, S. and Herrick, R. (2002) 'Whistle while you work: Job satisfaction and retirement from the U.S. House', *Legislative Studies Quarterly*, 27 (3): 445–57.

Hagger, M. and Wing, M. (1979) 'Legislative roles and clientele orientations in the European Parliament', *Legislative Studies Quarterly*, IV-2: 165–96.

Hix, S. (2001) 'Legislative behaviour and party competition in the EU: an application of Nominate to the EU', *Journal of Common Market Studies*, 39 (4): 663–88.

Huitt, R. (1961) 'The outsider in the Senate: An alternative role', *American Political Science Review*, 55 (3): 566–75.

Katz, R. (1999) 'Role orientations in parliaments', in R. Katz and B. Wessels (eds) *The European Parliament, the National Parliaments, and European Integration*, Oxford: Oxford University Press.

Moravcsik, A. (2001) 'Forum: A constructivist research program in EU studies?', *European Union Politics*, 2 (2): 219–49.

Navarro, J. (2009) *Les Députés Européens et leur Rôle. Sociologie des Pratiques Parlementaires*, Brussels: Editions de l'Université de Bruxelles.

Putnam, R. (1973) *The Beliefs of Politicians. Ideology, Conflict, and Democracy in Britain and Italy*, New Haven, CT: Yale University Press.

Sartori, G. (1965) *Democratic Theory*, New York: Praeger.

Schlesinger, J. (1966) *Ambition and Politics: Political Careers in the United States*, Chicago, IL: Rand McNally.

Scully, R. and Farrell, D. (2003) 'MEPs as representatives: individual and institutional roles', *Journal of Common Market Studies*, 41 (2): 269–88.

Searing, D. (1991) 'Roles, rules, and rationality in the new institutionalism', *American Political Science Review*, 85 (4): 1239–60.

Searing, D. (1994) *Westminster's World. Understanding Political Roles*, Cambridge, MA: Harvard University Press.

Strøm, K. (1997) 'Rules, reasons and routines: legislative roles in parliamentary democracies', in Müller and Saalfeld (eds) (1997) *Members of Parliament in Western Europe: Roles and Behaviour*, London: Frank Cass.

Viet, J. (1960) 'La notion de rôle en politique', *Revue Française de Science Politique*, 10 (2): 309–34.

Weber, M. (1968) *Economy and Society. An Outline of Interpretative Sociology*, vol. 1, New York: Bedminster Press.

Wessels, B. (1999) 'Whom to represent? Role orientations of legislators in Europe', in H. Schmitt and J. Thomassen (eds) *Political Representation and Legitimacy in the European Union*, Oxford: Oxford University Press.

11 Bringing parliamentary roles back in

Olivier Rozenberg and Magnus Blomgren

"Who will be my role-model now that my role-model is gone?"

Paul Simon

Hopefully, this volume has confirmed that roles are coming back into legislative studies. The studies included are highly diverse, but share the idea that in order to understand legislatures it is worth looking at how MPs see themselves, political representation and democracy. Roles are not distributed randomly; they can have their source in MPs' backgrounds and positions. Roles are not merely individual beliefs and tastes, but articulate collective norms and values, which might have consequences on MPs' behavior inside and outside the parliamentary chamber.

In this concluding chapter, we first propose a distinction between *legislative* and *representative* roles on the current state of role research as presented in this book. This brings us to the second section, in which we elaborate on the difficult issue regarding behavior and roles. This is followed by a third section on the equally significant question of human rationality and the role concept. The last sections deal with the emerging research agenda on parliamentary roles and the contemporary and future state of representative roles in advanced democracies.

Representative or legislative roles?

The contributions to this volume have confirmed how diverse the ways of defining and conceiving roles are. It is therefore illusory to call for a single conception of parliamentary roles. Yet the similarities and differences between these contributions enable us to distinguish two different approaches to the concept of roles. The first group is focused on the question of *whom* MPs represent. This approach is represented by a majority of the studies in this volume. The issues raised by these studies are concentrated on the loyalty of the MPs towards his/her diverse and potentially adversarial principals. The main focus in all these chapters is to establish the link between various explanations of why MPs adopt a certain role (**Ilonszki,**[1] **Zittel**), or show how the MPs' definition of their role have an effect on how they view their task (**Andeweg, Gauja**).

The second group of studies is focused on the question of *how* MPs organize their activity. The roles in this perspective are more connected with MPs' views of their activity (**Navarro**) or even directly with MPs' activity (**Jenny** and **Müller**). Therefore, this approach creates role concepts inductively compared to those mentioned above, which use a given set of roles and tries to measure these deductively. Here are two fundamentally different ways to approach the concept of roles even if some contributions, like **Best** and **Vogel**'s one, tend to adopt both perspectives by developing alternative measures.[2] In Table 11.1, we propose to call the first approach *representative roles* and the second *legislative roles*.

Regarding the first approach (representative roles), viewing the studies in this volume makes it clear that, albeit labeled slightly differently, three sets of roles are identified: the *local delegate*, the *party delegate* and the *trustee*. *Local* and *party delegates* are identified through MPs who seek to represent respectively their constituency, district, or town on the one hand, and their party, party supporters, or party voters on the other hand. The category of *trustee* often includes MPs who seek to represent the whole population and not their local voters or party supporters. This set of concepts obviously connects to Wahlke *et al.*'s legacy and have become mainstream. Yet, the traditional *trustee/delegate* cleavage has transformed into a threefold alternative. This is good news for role analysis: a coherent debate around three polarities (the constituency versus the party versus the independent politician) should make comparisons easier in the future. However, as Chapter 2 in this volume shows, these concepts have been heavily criticized. Therefore, **Andeweg**'s chapter tries to deal with this by following up Esaiasson and Holmberg's (1996) concepts of bottom-up and top-down representation.[3] This new distinction seems to be a fruitful way to proceed and this opens a constructive debate on how the conventional concepts of Wahlke *et al.* should be understood.

Legislative roles, on the other hand, do not use pre-defined role sets, which means that the roles may change from one study to another. In this volume, **Navarro** looks at the European Parliament and distinguishes between *animators*, *specialists*, *intermediaries*, *outsiders*, and *dilettantes*. In yet another study in this volume, **Jenny** and **Müller** identify five different kinds of MP in the Austrian chamber: *exemplary MPs*, *workhorses*, *showhorses*, *rapporteurs* and *spectators*. Although there is a link between some of these repertoires – e.g. *specialists* and *spectators* had already appeared in Searing's category – each repertoire appears highly specific to the parochial features of a given parliament.

Just as it is pointless to call for a single definition of roles, it does not make sense to determine between the search for representative or for legislative roles as to

Table 11.1 Two kinds of parliamentary roles

Names	Research question	Construction of roles	Typical repertoire
Representative roles	**Who** do the MPs represent?	Deductively	• Local delegate • Party delegate • Trustee
Legislative roles	**How** do MPs represent?	Inductively	High diversity

which is better than the other. Each approach has its merits and limitations. The positive thing about representative roles is their connection to the normative and philosophical debate on representation. There are indeed very few areas in contemporary social sciences where empirical case studies can help to answer classical questions such as "How should elected people make decisions in democracies?"

The stronger emphasis on political parties, when analyzing representative roles (in contrast with Wahlke *et al.*'s seminal study from 1962), makes this approach even more interesting. First of all, it makes the picture of the dynamics in parliaments more accurate and, second, it triggers the analysis to focus on cross-pressure and conflict regarding various principals. Furthermore, this kind of research may also be helpful in our understanding of how various institutional settings influence normative views of representation, e.g. electoral system, government formation rules, or the distribution of power between levels in a polity. Regarding legislative roles, this kind of approach is interesting since it helps to make sense of what really happens in parliament. For instance, after having read **Navarro**'s paper, we are better situated to identify the repertoire of MEPs like Martin Schultz, Daniel Cohn-Bendit or an obscure rapporteur of a draft directive. Legislative roles say something accurate about legislatures.

For sure, each approach suffers from not having the assets of the other. Legislative roles, as said before, are difficult to compare through time and space. More precisely, although comparisons are not impossible, they are costly, in all the meanings of the term. Legislative roles could also be criticized for being more descriptive than analytical. For instance, **Jenny** and **Müller** acknowledge that they could use the terms "roles" and "types" of MP interchangeably. By contrast, analysing representative roles (whom MPs think they should represent) sometimes leads these studies a bit far from the parliament's real world. For instance, modern legislatures are characterized by an increasing number of MPs who want to influence policy-making. These *policy advocates*, in Searing's terms (1994), are difficult to study through an approach based on representative roles. Their progression among British MPs during the second half of the twentieth century has been understood to result from improved access to secondary education on the part of Labour MPs (Norton 1997). Therefore, studying *policy advocates* only through the notions of loyalty and conflicts of representation would be to disregard a large part of the picture.

In that perspective, the problem is not so much the one noted by Searing – *trustees* and *delegates* as "constructs that existed in the minds of many social scientists rather than in the minds of many of the politicians we studied" (1994: 13) – but rather a tendency to exaggerate conflicts of representation. More precisely, studying whom MPs say they represent is not necessarily exaggerating conflict of representation; however, such exaggeration may be the result when MPs' views are used to create mutually exclusive categories. Representation, and more generally politics, is often about conciliating interests and views among society rather than selecting one against the others. By asking MPs if they follow their conscience, their voters or their parties, these studies often seem to argue that the three poles stand in contradiction. In so doing, such studies neglect not only the fact that these interests do not necessarily contradict each other, but also that adopting a role may be a strategy for MPs to conciliate between different interests. As indicated by **Gauja**, MPs develop articulated narratives for making sense of their representational choices. These narratives are worth studying without forcing artificial antagonism between principals.

In addition, from a more theoretical standpoint, the "*trustee* vs. *delegate*" categories can also be criticized for not being specific to studying Parliaments. Indeed, Rehfeld argues that whether collective choices should follow the will of the people or not, is a relevant question for any decision-maker – and not only for MPs:

> The casting of the "*trustee/delegate*" problem as particular to political representation thus constitutes a substantive error that fails to distinguish the tension between citizen preferences and normative ideals from professional obligations that *any* decision maker (whether monarch, representative, or citizen in a direct democracy) takes on when he or she takes on the role of making law or other decisions.
>
> (Rehfeld 2009: 216)

Knowing that MPs are less influential over public policies than executive members in most European democracies, we could even say that the "*trustee/ delegate*" dilemma weighs first and foremost on the shoulders of prime ministers. From the death penalty to nuclear energy, it is these top leaders who have to arbitrate between what they think is good for the country and what the people may think about it. At the backbencher level, being a representative hardly ever means being trapped by such a dilemma, but rather entails protecting and promoting a constituency day after day. In other political systems where legislatures are more powerful or legislators more independent, MPs' views on representation can impact more directly on their collective decisions and on legislative outputs. Therefore it could be said that the interest and relevance in studying representative roles vary from one country to another.

Roles and behavior

Another difference between various ways of approaching the concept of roles is in the way roles have been empirically assessed. Here, the majority of the studies in this volume capture roles through MPs' opinions. Those opinions may deal with issues such as conflicts of loyalty when MPs legislate (**Andeweg**), representation more generally (**Andeweg** again, **Zittel**), MPs "reasoning on pieces of legislation" (**Gauja**), even MPs' roles (**Navarro**) or a mixture of the above (**Best and Vogel**). This can be measured quantitatively (**Andeweg, Best and Vogel, Zittel**) or qualitatively (**Gauja, Navarro**). Yet, the design of these studies remains the same: MPs' views are collected and then compared to more objective data. If roles are treated as the dependent variable, the explanatory variables might be the electoral system, MPs' personal and political background and MPs' position in the parliament. If roles are analyzed as the independent variable, MPs' adoption of a certain role is compared with actual behavior, inside and outside the parliament, and in a few cases, with MPs' opinions on topics outside their job.

Two studies in this volume represent the obvious exemption to this. **Jenny** and **Müller** define roles on the basis of MPs' activities within the house (referring to the number of questions, bills, motions, reports and speeches). If this were the end of the story, one could ask if such an approach really uses the role concept. As mentioned in Chapter 2, for instance, Esaiasson (2000) opposed a task-based and a role-based approach. As roles refer to the norms attached to a given position, then those norms should be under study, which is not the case if the focus of the study is purely behavioral. **Jenny** and **Müller** actually avoid traps by comparing the behavior of a large number of Austrian MPs with opinion data based on in-depth interviews with them. The same can be said concerning **Ilonszki**'s longitudinal study of Hungarian MPs. She identifies three kinds of MPs – *party delegates*, *constituency members* and *newcomers* – on the basis of what could be called positional data, i.e. institutional data on the individual position of each MP: in the party (leadership or not), locally (holding multiple offices or not) and in the assembly (newcomers or not), as well as his/her type of seat (list mandate or not). Again, this typology is compared with the focus of representation among Hungarian MPs as identified by several quantitative surveys.

In the Austrian and Hungarian cases, the comparison between opinion data on the one hand, and behavioral or position data on the other hand helps to test the robustness of the categories of roles and to interpret their meaning. In the end, MPs' opinions about their job remain central to the study of roles; regardless of whether these opinions constitute the basis for identifying roles or for testing the robustness of a specific typology. Eventually, this may be regarded as an empirical result of this volume: *we can pretend to talk about parliamentary roles only if MPs' views about being MPs are considered in one way or another*. In empirical terms, it means that studies of legislatives roles require data about MPs' opinions.

From a methodological point of view, another striking feature of this volume is that several authors illustrate the adequacy of analyzing roles by using a comparative approach; either by comparing countries (**Gauja**), over time (**Andeweg, Best** and **Vogel, Ilonszki**), or institutional mechanisms such as electoral systems (**Zittel** among others). To a certain degree, this distinguishes modern analysis of roles from past studies, which often (but not always) suffered from parochialism. By contrast, the comparative method enables contributors to say something about the political system under study rather than only about roles. **Gauja**'s comparison of countries leads her to dismiss the influence of the electoral systems on MPs' behavior, whereas the comparison through electoral systems within a single country leads **Zittel** to the opposite conclusion. The long-term longitudinal approaches adopted by **Andeweg** (thirty-four years) and **Ilonszki** (eighteen years) highlight the relative stability of MPs' attitudes in a context of intense political changes – suggesting that legislatures can, under specific circumstances, be the locus of relative calm during electoral and partisan storms. Therefore, one conclusion of this book is that an important future strategy of role research is to make use of comparative methods in a more systematic way. For example, we are still missing quantitative comparisons of countries in terms of parliamentary roles.[4]

Furthermore, a number of studies in this volume present rather innovative methods in their study of roles. To study roles can be a strategy to understand legislators' cynicism or their knowledge about their voters (**Andeweg**). Furthermore, roles help to analyze the effect of institutional innovations, such as the right to hold multiple offices simultaneously (**Ilonszki**). Roles enable us to understand the subtle effects of institutional socialization through a large-n panel of legislators (**Best** and **Vogel**). They can even be granted with a relatively predictive effect by considering MPs' individual career paths according to their role (**Navarro**). In this respect, one of the most notable features of several chapters of this volume is the comparison between what legislators say on the one hand and what they do – and even where they stand (i.e. their position in the institution) on the other. In most cases, there is a good match between opinions, actions and positions. Hungarian MPs elected by a list system emphasize their party focus, more than their single-member district colleagues. MEPs who explained to **Navarro** that the European Parliament was first and foremost a place for discussion delivered more speeches in plenary than others.

This correspondence between politicians' values on representation and their actions is important in terms of validity. This tells us that legislators do not (always) lie and that it is worth asking them about their views. At the same time the correlation between self-reported views and behavior is far from perfect and the longstanding critique against research on roles has been specifically harsh concerning this problem. This is also shown in some of the chapters in this volume. For instance, while party discipline has increased in Hungary over the last twenty years, MPs have increasingly denied having a party focus; therefore **Ilonszki** talks about "role inconsistencies". Furthermore, **Jenny** and **Müller** grouped together half of the Austrian MPs under the label of *spectators* because they were almost inactive in more or less all the measurable activities within the assembly. When interviewed, the *spectators* explained that they spend their time in the two arenas where no quantitative measuring was possible: in committees and on party meetings. These kinds of inadequacy are perplexing. It is certainly important for the role research approach to test the veracity of what MPs say, yet it would be naïve to depict roles as lie detectors. The methodological problem of evaluating discrepancies between (f)acts and MPs' accounts of their activities is difficult to get around. Should we consider that MPs send "messages to the public" (**Ilonszki**) when they answer social scientists? Simply, that they lie to us? Or even that they lie to themselves? There is no general answer to this problem, other than it deserves our full attention in this line of research. It is also important to remember that discrepancies between what MPs tell researchers and their actions do not necessarily mean that roles are a faulty concept.

The tension between what legislators think is the "right" thing to say and what they actually do, tells us something about the overall estimate on what should be appropriate behavior. This is interesting in itself, because it reveals the value that a specific arrangement, political system or heritage bestows on MPs. If legislators fail to act accordingly, this may lead to interesting conclusions regarding the tension inherited within the concept of representation and in a politician's day-to-day life.

Roles and rationality

We argued in Chapter 2 that the comeback of legislative role research should be understood in the wake of the neo-institutionalist paradigm. The studies in this volume largely confirm this argument. When studied as dependant variables, roles are regarded as the products of different kinds of institutions, e.g. party affiliation or electoral rules. When studied as independent variables, roles are considered as a specific kind of institutions that can have an impact on MPs' behavior and attitudes – the specificity of roles as institutions being, as said above, their constitutive link with MPs' opinions on their job.

Even if neo-institutionalist views are mainstreaming, they cover different theoretical perspectives. The reference to Searing is common in all the chapters, which helps to unify the field of parliamentary roles research. Yet, what is taken from Searing is his rich empirical results and his eclectic approach, or his clear distinction between preference and position roles, rather than his theoretical views. None of the contributors in this volume develops an empirical design that would enable him/her to study and question the emotional implications of a single MP playing a role. Even **Navarro**, who most faithfully replicates Searing's approach, dissociates himself from Searing in theoretical terms, by applying Boudon's concept of cognitive rationality. As psychological explanations can 'pose a problem of homogeneity', he prefers to connect roles to legislators' evolving norms and values. Likewise, Blidook's (2010) recent study, on the role of the *policy advocate* in Canada, is more concerned with the strategic use of the Private Members' bills and motions, than with their motivations for playing such roles.

Dismissing a psychological understanding of parliamentary roles does not mean that a rational approach is unchallenged. In following up **Strøm**'s argument, **Zittel** approaches parliamentary roles from a rational perspective. Candidates to the Bundestag perceive themselves increasingly as *district delegates* (rather than *party delegates*) when they manage to be elected individually (rather than on a party list). The foundation for strategic role-taking is further strengthened by the absence of any relationship between length of tenure, the MP's position within a party and the choice of a specific role. Yet these results are challenged. As said before, in her three-country comparison, **Gauja** emphasizes the difference between parties in explaining role formation, and at the same time refutes electoral system variations as an explanation. **Best** and **Vogel** also study German MPs, using a larger sample than **Zittel**. Their regression models enable them to conclude that there is a "high significance of party in the processes of representative role-definition and role-taking". Among eight background criteria, party is the most successful predictor of representatives' roles whereas, in **Zittel**'s chapter, none of the tested party variables (party membership, party employment and party office at different levels) scores significantly.[5]

These mixed results about the rationality of adopting a specific parliamentary role call for three sets of remarks. First, the main proxy for demonstrating the rationality of role-taking rests on the pressure created by electoral incentives, which are often studied empirically through variations between electoral rules. The problem is that the effects of electoral rules on the selection of a given role appear to be extremely difficult to assess for one simple reason: there is no elected body that is completely unresponsive to voters. All legislators care about their voters – be they elected directly or from a list, from safe or contested constituencies. For instance, being elected on a list does not mean that a rational MP should not consider him/herself as representing a local district. A rational approach should only except to MPs identify themselves less as *district delegates* than legislators elected on single-member districts. This also means that the impact of the electoral system should be tested with care and subtlety. For instance, **Zittel** demonstrates that it is not being elected on a list rather than directly that matters to playing the *party delegate* role, but the reduced probability for candidates running in single-seat districts to win. Between two German MPs elected through lists, the one who has no chance of being elected in a single-seat district will emphasize his/her role as a *party delegate*.

Second, one of the great interests in the concept of roles is actually to question rational views rather than taking them for granted. Usually, rationality is not discussed in the rational choice approach: it is an axiom on which rational choice theories are based. By contrast, roles enable the limit and validity of this axiom to be tested. As said, **Zittel** demonstrates the greater validity of a strategic approach over a more sociological one. When explaining the local focus of Hungarian MPs, **Ilonszki** does not chose between norms-learning and rationality in terms of mutual exclusiveness, but rather as complementary. The reasons for the local focus of the representatives just after the Communist period have to be found in a coherent historical legacy and on stable social expectations. The further development of the territorial focus of representation during the two following decades is explained more by strategic considerations. With the consolidation of the political system, and especially with the right to hold multiple offices simultaneously, it became crucial for politicians to base their career on solid local grounds. Individual strategies took over social expectations.

Third, the differing results of the various chapters can be understood by considering that the level of rationality of a given role depends on the way it is interpreted. As indicated in the comparison between Strøm and Searing in Chapter 2, roles – as behavioral routines and patterns – can be regarded as strategic as long as they help MPs to save costs and therefore adopt an efficient method of working. Yet roles may also trap legislators in a process of repeating and reproducing collective patterns of behavior. The hypothesis can be raised that the alternative between these two views is a matter of MPs' individual understanding of their roles. Protecting interest and diffusing norms: roles could fill both purposes depending on how they are played. Legislators could actually be embedded within a dynamic equilibrium according to which underplaying a given role could be as risky strategically as overplaying it, as indicated in Figure 11.1.

The fact of underplaying a role – sometimes called "role distance" in the literature – refers to different possible situations. It can be the case when an MP is not credible in the role selected because he/she refuses to adopt some of the norms of behavior inherent to it. In some countries, we can think of a *ministerial aspirant* who refuses to abandon his or her regional accent. By contrast, a *local delegate* who would never use nor understand a local tongue could be in trouble. In all these cases, the strategic added value of a role can be deficient. It requires acting completely as a *ministerial aspirant* in order to become a minister or as a *local delegate* for being reelected.

Yet the strategic benefit of the role could decline if a role is overplayed. A role is overplayed when an actor follows its behavioral patterns to the point that this actor neglects his or her basic interest. A *ministerial aspirant* who would stop doing surgery work in his or her constituency, because of an obsession for a career, would be in such position. To take another example, a *specialist MP* who is openly interested only in one single policy area would lose credibility in the eyes of many voters and colleagues. A role can be overplayed by habits and by taste, because an MP is used to follow a behavioral pattern or because he/she likes to do so. The most extreme situation of overplaying is when an actor is no longer consciously playing a role, but feels that he/she *is* that role – neglecting therefore the basis for acting, namely simulation – according to Diderot's famous essay (2007).

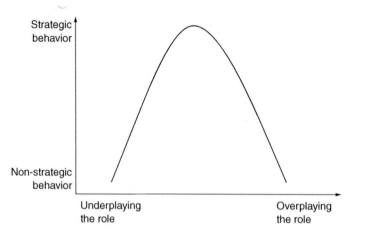

Figure 11.1 Variations in the rationality of roles according to their interpretation.

There is only room here to raise the hypothesis that legislative roles have differential strategic potential according to the way they are played – not to explore it fully. In order to verify the argument, MPs should be studied at the individual level rather than in aggregate. However, this does not mean that qualitative and ethnographic methods are the only strategy available, as indicated by the large-n panel study by **Best** and **Vogel**. Furthermore, such a strategy requires the conditions under which an MP might be pushed to overplay or underplay a role to be defined. Underplaying a role can express dissociation from the negative stereotypes associated with it, as Searing observed of *constituency members* in the Commons in the 1970s (1994: 398). Overplaying a role can result from psychological as well as institutional factors. On the psychological side, it has been shown that a majority MP in the Commons was so pleased to play the role of an *inquisitor* (against the cabinet) that he became marginalized in his Parliamentary Party Group (PPG) (Rozenberg 2009). On the institutional side, Searing explains that 'it is only the most demanding roles, in those of Ministers and perhaps Whips, that we see signs of character roles that require their players to think and feel the part' (1994: 397).[6] In their study, **Best** and **Vogel** confirm that German politicians holding leading positions in an assembly are strongly induced to present themselves as *trustees*, i.e. representatives of the whole of society. Yet, the potential for overplaying this role is circumscribed by the potential for role-conflict, as these parliamentary leaders might simultaneously hold leadership positions in the party and therefore be faced with radically different role expectations. These observations eventually suggest a trade-off in role involvement: higher positions in legislatures are associated both with stronger expectations and more potential for role-conflicts.

The emerging agenda for studying parliamentary roles

The come-back of legislative roles in political science is characterized by the idea that roles are less interesting to study per se, but that they say something of other phenomena. Five fields of research can be identified, either because they already use the role concept or because the potential of the concept appears to be particularly promising.

The first and most obvious field is electoral systems and electoral engineering. Even if the literature is full of contradictory results, it is established that the rules that transform votes into seats do have an impact on parliamentary roles. For instance, Wessels (1999) demonstrates that the smaller the district magnitude, the more MPs focus on their constituency. In this volume, **Zittel** establishes further introducing candidate-oriented electoral rules (i.e. mixed-member or flexible list proportional systems) would reduce the proportion of *party delegates* among MPs. However, the question remains open whether such change of MPs roles would impact party cohesion – as we know from **Andeweg**'s contribution, representatives' focus does not automatically transfer into actual behavior. The difficulty of assessing the impact of electoral rules on legislators' behavior through roles probably explains that, even if electoral rules are central to legislative roles studies, the contrary is not true. For instance, Norris neglects the concept of roles in her study of *Electoral Engineering* (2004). Yet, we believe that a comprehensive analysis of the electoral rules must consider also their impact on MPs' views about representation. The reason for this is that formal electoral rules do not impact mechanically on the types of relations between voters, MPs and parties. Among many other elements, parliamentary roles may spoil, in a way or another, their effects. Roles may delay or transform the excepted effects of any given electoral reform.

A second field of research is the question of what Pitkin (1972: 61) calls representation as *standing for something*, e.g. representation of women, ethnic minorities and even blue-collars workers, etc. To have reasonably representative assemblies is thought of as a good value in itself, and therefore these issues are discussed increasingly in the academic sphere, as well as in the public sphere. One result of this is the introduction of specific quotas. The growing literature regarding these questions indicates that there is no systematic correlation between the gender or the colour of a representative and his/her activities. For instance, in his study of the written questions asked in the UK House of Commons, Saalfeld (2011) concludes that MPs' belonging to ethnic minorities drew attention to minority issues if, and only if, their voters share massively the same ethnic background. In the absence of direct correlation, it is interesting to pose empirical questions regarding the notion of substantive representation through roles. In Searing's terms, is there something like a role of *group representative* aiming substantively to represent and protect historically discriminated groups (Celis and Wauters 2010)? In Strøm's terms, do MPs from minorities choose between different representational strategies like *ethnic entrepreneurs, bridge builders* or just *party delegates* (Saalfeld *et al.* 2011: 268)? **Best** and **Vogel**'s contribution to this volume expresses some doubts about substantive representation. The classic variables of elite studies – social origins, gender, and income – do have a very limited impact on the choice of roles in German assemblies compared to party affiliation. Yet it seems all the more relevant to address in terms of roles the question that representatives from different minorities increasingly face collective expectations about how they should behave. If, 'in response to the demand for more diversity in parliament, a "script" for parliamentary behaviour has been installed' (Celis and Wauters 2010: 382), then studies are needed to assess the degree to which this script is played.

Third, parliamentary roles can be useful for studying the transformation of party systems. To take one example, they offer a specific test for the cartel party thesis (Katz and Mair 1995). The idea of a multidimensional convergence between parties should be observed logically through the convergence of the representative roles between PPGs. The evidence collected in that volume stands rather in contradiction with such an expectation. For sure, there is no longer (if there ever has been) a clear distribution where liberals would be *trustees*, conservatives *local delegates* and left-wing MPs *party delegates*. Yet, party affiliation still matters for explaining role choice, as demonstrated by **Best** and **Vogel**. Several contributions indicate that the reference to party discipline is still a distinctive feature within left PPGs or more precisely within the "old left", as representatives from the Greens tend to adopt a *trustee* style (**Gauja**). The example of the cartel party thesis illustrates thus how relevant parliamentary roles can be for questioning the future of political parties.

A fourth field of study where roles can shed a new light is multi-level governance. As indicated already in Chapter 2, it is through European studies that the concept of roles came back into political science over the two last decades. Indeed, the development of a new level of governance multiplies the potential for conflicts of loyalty and justifies therefore studying the representative focus not only of legislators, but also of civil servants and executive decision-makers like Commissioners. The same is true of the empowerment of the sub-national level that most of the European countries have experienced for the last decades. Studies are needed in order to analyze the representative roles adopted at each level (Bradbury 2007) as well as the evolution from one level to another (Borchert 2011). In that perspective, **Ilonszki** regards the fact that so many Hungarian MPs are simultaneously mayors as a reason for the domination of a constituency focus among Hungarian legislators. This is also connected to the argument that the different levels within political parties are growing apart. If correct, the so called stratification thesis (Mair 1994; Carty 2004) should help in identifying how party representatives talk about their roles on different levels.

The last field where roles could be fruitful comprises the vast areas of MPs' non-legislative activities. Legislative activities are so strategic for the government that they are cautiously whipped. The institutional pressures put on the backbenchers' shoulders are so significant that it is not surprising to find that their views about their job do not impact on their votes. That is why roles have generally been disappointing for roll-call analysis (Jewell 1970). By contrast, day-to-day scrutiny activities offer more leeway to legislators. Parliamentary Questions may reveal more than MPs' votes about the attention they give to different issues and even their policy preferences. (Martin 2011). For instance, in the Swiss milita Parliament, the number of oral questions asked by MPs who claim to represent voters from National Party has increased, but it is stable for MPs who claim to represent voters from the Cantonal party, and for MPs claiming represent other groups it has declined (Bailer 2011). Those results indicate a close connection between representative roles and non-legislative behavior. **Navarro** and also **Jenny** and **Müller** offer several examples in the case of legislative roles.

The five fields developed do not cover all the areas where roles could bring additional scientific value. Other emerging or classic issues could be listed as well: the relations between parliamentary majority and opposition, the management of coalitions, parliamentary rituals, the questions of ethics and morality or legislators' careers. The contributions to this volume present several results regarding the influence of MPs' career patterns and invite further investigation. For instance, being a *policy advocate* MP can be regarded as a factor of voluntary legislative turnover distinct from electoral incentives: MPs who want "to make a difference" might decide not to run for the next elections as a result of frustration rather than because of the probability of an electoral defeat (Kerby and Blidook 2011).

The future of representative roles

To finish, the rich chapters making up this volume provide numerous and sometimes contradictory elements in the respective developments of the three main
representative roles: *party delegates, local delegates* and *trustees*. Table 11.2
presents a synthesis of these, by distinguishing between variables that are endogenous and exogenous to the political system.

Cartel-party delegates?

The crisis of "partyness" (Katz 1986) probably constitutes the most determinant
phenomena among those listed in Figure 11.3. This trend comprises dimensions
well-covered in the literature such as the decline of formal party membership,
the erosion of party identification among citizens or the convergence of policy
proposals. In terms of representative roles, and at a first level of analysis, this
multidimensional but coherent trend contributes to the decline of *party delegates*
in favour of any other kinds of representative focus. When parties become less
legitimate in politics, then it is more difficult for political actors to see themselves as faithful activists in charge of implementing a party platform or of following leaders' instructions. As a result, more MPs might favour the *trustee* or
local delegate types to the detriment of the *party loyalist*. From a more functionalist perspective, the decrease of partisan polarization also diminishes the capacity of parties to act as "broker" and cognitive "filters" between constituents and
representatives (see **Zittel**'s theoretical discussion). When Conservative MPs
tend to defend views that are close to those of their Social Democrat colleagues
than in the past, then the *party delegate* role becomes less distinctive at the MP
level and less useful at the legislature level.

The rise of parliamentary rebellion in some parliamentary chambers, for
instance in the Commons during Blair's years (Cowley 2005), or of party switching, for instance in Italy in late 1990s (Mershon and Shvetsova 2008), can be
seen as a consequence of the decline of partyness within parliaments. Katz and
Mair (2008) even hypothesize a situation where representation could either move
out of the electoral channel or be monopolized by non-governing parties.
Between pure office-seekers and *tribune MPs* (a specific role identified by Katz
and Mair to designate those who use the parliament as a tribune), the representative role of *party delegates* seems threatened. In addition, such a trend could
affect not only MPs roles but also the reliability of opinion surveys among legislators: it becomes less and less legitimate to present as party loyalists.

All this is still partly speculative. Party discipline is stable in many legislatures, in Germany, in France (Sauger 2009) and in the European Parliament (Hix
and Noury 2009). Party switching remains a marginal phenomenon in Europe
compared to for example the *transfuguismo* in Latin America. The recruitment
of political elites is still channeled by party gatekeepers. In sum, there are
reasons to think that *party delegates* will remain numerous among legislators.
Paradoxically, Katz and Mair's cartel–party thesis (1995) may help to understand

Table 11.2 The political and societal variables that may affect the development of representative roles

	Party delegates	Local delegates	Trustees
Political variables	• public parties financing • electoral volatility • full professionalization of politics	• decline of "partyness" • electoral volatility • decline of trust towards representatives • devolutions?	• decline of "partyness" • lengthening of parliamentary careers • emergence of new parties
Social variables		• Welfare State (retrenchment) • higher education • new technologies of communication	• post-materialist and individualist values • growing social heterogeneity

why the strengthening of *party delegates* within parliaments may result from the decline of partyness in society. The diagnostic of a fusion between governing parties and the state indeed constitutes the most empirically assessed part of their thesis.[7] The absorption of the parties into the state can be observed through the increasing of the public financing of politics. If parties transform themselves into a kind of public utility for representative democracy, then they are in a position where they can control their elected members more efficiently. For instance, reducing or banning the funding of political campaigns based on personal resources increases the dependence of legislators on their political parties. Electoral volatility could further strengthen the control exercised by party leaders over MPs by eroding their local roots. Beyond the cartel party thesis, the almost complete professionalization of legislators' positions and the growing social disconnection between them and the rest of the society (Best and Cotta 2007) give credence to the idea that loyalty to parties could survive at the legislature level, but decline among ordinary citizens.

Local delegates: an answer to the crisis of representation?

Local delegates could benefit from the decline of partyness. In addition, and in conformity with **Strøm**'s analytical framework developed in this volume, MPs could react to greater electoral volatility by trying to strengthen their position within their constituency. It makes sense to assume that a marginal electoral position is a major incentive for surgery work. More generally, putting the focus at the local level can be understood as a reaction of the legislators to what has been called the crisis of representation. Citizens' lack of trust towards politicians in general and parliaments in particular could induce MPs to withdraw to their constituency. As stressed by **Ilonszki**'s chapter, exalting their local connection is a way for MPs to send a message to the public by distinguishing themselves from national politicians as party leaders or ministers. From this perspective, the devolution that many countries have experienced calls for two opposite hypotheses. On the one hand, the devolved nature of the state may reduce connectedness between citizens and MPs, as it should direct citizens' claims towards subnational elected positions (Norton 2002). Yet devolution could also have the opposite effect: by creating a local and regional political market, it constitutes a potential threat to MPs' reelection and could therefore help to direct their activity towards constituency service (Russell and Bradbury 2007). In a way, the fact that nearly all French and Hungarian MPs are also elected locally expresses such a strategy of competition avoidance. **Ilonszki**'s conclusion as well as Costa and Kerrouche's French monograph (2009) warn us of the threat that lies in exacerbating the local focus in terms of attendance and participation to classic legislative activities.

The progression of *local delegates* could also result from exogenous variables. Several factors could indeed contribute to increasing the solicitations that constituents address to their MPs in order to obtain particular resources and advantages. Among them, the retrenchment of the Welfare State, the rise of education and the development of communication technologies can be listed. The development of the Welfare State has helped to multiply the opportunities for ordinary citizens to have something to ask of their representatives. With the relative retrenchment of the Welfare State (Pierson 1994) in the last decades, access to several kinds of public resources has become more competitive. As a result, the solicitations from citizens towards representatives could be more numerous. Increasing levels of higher education all over Western societies is another factor that may affect the development of the *local delegates*. People's general knowledge on what to expect as well as a more self-assured attitude among citizens might create a stronger activism towards representatives. Finally, the development of new technologies in communication such as the Internet has amplified the citizens' capacity to get in touch with their MPs. The impressive progression of the number of written questions asked by legislators all over Europe (Rozenberg and Martin 2011) indicates indeed that new technologies do have an impact on MPs' activities and probably on their connectedness to citizens. Thus several different factors may lead us to think that MPs, as other elected officials, are more solicited today by ordinary citizens. As a result, MPs may be better off emphasizing their local representative focus.

Towards a trustee representative world?

In most of the advanced democracies, the *trustee* style of representation is the most legitimate as indicated, for instance, by the article 27 of the French constitution, which stipulates that "no Member shall be elected with any binding mandate". This normative pressure explains that a relative majority of MPs generally adopt this focus. For instance **Best** and **Vogel** indicate that in 2003/04 as well as in 2007 one German legislator out of two claimed to represent the whole country. There are several reasons to believe that the number of *trustees* will increase further in the future. Again, the decline of partyness can result in legitimating the idea that MPs should follow their own conscience and views. The lengthening of parliamentary careers – observed in some legislatures as the US Congress but not everywhere – could also favor a *trustee* style. Patzelt for instance (1997: 73) had noticed a tendency of tenured German MPs to view themselves as *trustees* rather than *delegates*.

The emergence of new political parties has been one of the most striking political evolutions in Europe since the 1960s (Gallagher *et al.* 2011). The Hungarian and Dutch cases developed in this volume indicate that such a trend could increase the number of *trustees*. From 2001 to 2006, the Dutch political system experienced a political instability characterized by the emergence of new parties, cabinet instability and electoral volatility. **Andeweg** indicates that this period has been marked by a certain return of the *trustee* style of representation. While *trustees* had continuously decreased during thirty years (from 71 percent in 1972 to 40 percent in 2001), the tendency changed in 2006 with one MP out of two considering he/she should follow his/her own opinion rather the opinion of his/her party's voters. The trend is somehow similar in Hungary. **Ilonszki** indicates that from 2007 to 2010 the proportion of legislators claiming to represent all citizens of the country has increased. In greater numbers, newcomers see themselves as *trustees*, with nearly one out of two, compared to one out of three for the incumbents. **Ilonszki** explains that "modest local ties and less developed party organization" could account for the *trustee* focus as most of these newcomers originate from new political parties. This is the first explanation. The second one is focused on the ideologies of these new parties. Ironically, an ideological hypothesis can indeed be raised for two new parties with opposite tendencies: the populists and the Greens.

Regarding populist and/or extreme right movements, there could be a connection between nationalist views and a legislative focus based on the representation of the whole country. "*Forza Italia*", "*Le Mouvement pour la France*", "United Kingdom Independence Party", "*Perussuomalaiset*" (the True Finns party): these labels undoubtedly express a conception of a united polity that could impact on how elected members from these parties see their job as representatives. Regarding the Greens, as said before, several contributions to this volume indicate that they tend to adopt a *trustee* style despite their usual left position (where it seems that the reference to party loyalty is still more legitimate). This trend can be interpreted as a sign of the elective affinities between post-materialist views and a *trustee* representative focus. Beyond the Green case, the progress of individualist values helps to give credit to Burkean views among voters as well as representatives. The idea that elected members should follow instructions of a collective organisation whatever their own views is increasingly less compatible with principles of sincerity, self-autonomy, individual fulfilment or genuine deliberation.

The diffusion of individualist values brings us to the exogenous factors that may account for the development of *trustees*. The most significant one is probably the growing social heterogeneity. According to Wahlke and al. (1962), the likelihood of adopting a *trustee* or *delegate* role depended on the homogeneity of an electoral district. When constituencies are made of highly diverse groups and difficult to read socially, then legislators are induced to feel more independent and to take decisions according to their own views. As a result of a number of dynamics that cannot be listed here, our social world is becoming increasingly heterogeneous and complex. It is more difficult to identify blue-collar workers for instance and to distinguish them both from other clerical workers and from people out of work. As a result, legislators may give up feeling that they have to represent specific social groups directly or through parties. The standardisation of society calls for *trustee* legislators. For some, this trend will not really change the state of representation as the defence of specific social interests within Parliament has always suffered both from the inevitable diversity of their constituency, the physical remoteness of the representatives and their tendency to turn into oligarchies. The representative mandate has always been imaginary (Pizzorno 2008). Yet, the erosion of the imaginary power of the Parliament should be regarded as a serious issue. What may change with the higher complexity of modern society is the capacity of the Parliament to give specific social groups the feeling that they are represented and recognised as such. At the end of the day, the legislators' collective capacity to give a vision of what society is, and of where its relevant cleavages are, would be damaged with a completely *trustee-orientated* Parliament.

This last section has developed contradictory elements about the future of the three main representative roles. As there are reasons to think that legislators will increasingly behave as *party delegates, constituency MPs* or *trustees*, it cannot be predicted whether one kind of role will prevail in the future. Yet, if a prediction can be made from this discussion, it is that conflicts about whom MPs should represent will increase. As a result, this requires that social sciences study what values representatives attach to their task as representatives. In other words, there are good reasons for bringing parliamentary roles back in.

Notes

1 References to the contributions to this volume are in bold.
2 What they call "role requirements" and "role focus" can be regarded as representative roles and "role primacy" is closer to legislative roles.
3 After having developed elsewhere the distinction between ex-ante and ex-post accountabilities (Andeweg 2003; Andeweg and Thomassen 2005).
4 This is the ambition of the 'Partirep' research project coordinated by Kris Deschouwer. See: www.partirep.eu/.
5 The differences between their results can be explained both by the differences between their models (inclusion of electoral system or not in the regressions) and by the differences between their samples.
6 Alasdair MacIntyre (1984)'s notion of "character role" designs the fusion of a player's personality with a role (quoted from Searing 1994: 397).
7 The diagnostic of even an implicit collusion between governing parties being more controversial (Ignazi 2007).

References

Andeweg, R.B. (2003) "Beyond representativeness? Trends in political representation", *European Review*, 11: 147–61.

Andeweg, R.B. and Thomassen, J.J.A. (2005) "Modes of representation: Toward a new typology", *Legislative Studies Quarterly*, 30: 507–28.

Bailer, S. (2011) "People's voice or information pool? The role of and reasons for Parliamentary Questions in the Swiss Parliament", *Journal of Legislative Studies*, 17 (3): 302–14.

Best, H. and Cotta, M. (eds) (2007), *Democratic Representation in Europe: Diversity, Change, and Convergence*, Oxford: Oxford University Press.

Blidook, K. (2010) "Exploring the role of 'legislators' in Canada: Do Members of Parliament influence policy?", *Journal of Legislative Studies*, 16 (1): 32–56.

Borchert, J. (2011) "Individual ambition and institutional opportunity: A conceptual approach to political careers in multi-level systems", *Regional and Federal Studies*, 21 (2): 117–40.

Bradbury, J. (2007) "Introduction", *Regional and Federal Studies*, 17 (1): 3–22.

Carty, K.R. (2004) "Parties as franchise systems: The stratarchical organizational imperative", *Party Politics*, 10: 5–24.

Celis, K. and Wauters, B. (2010) "Pinning the butterfly. Women, blue collar and ethnic minority MPs vis-à-vis parliamentary norms and the parliamentary role of the group representative", *Journal of Legislative Studies*, 16 (3): 380–93.

Costa, O. and Kerrouche, E. (2009) "Representative roles in the French National Assembly: The case for a dual typology?", *French Politics*, 7: 219–42.

Cowley, P. (2005) *The Rebels: How Blair Mislaid His Majority*, London: Politico's.

Diderot, D. (2007) *The Paradox of Acting*, Whitefish, MT: Kessinger Publishing, 1st edn (1830).

Esaiasson, P. (2000) "How Members of Parliament define their task", in P. Esaiasson and K. Heidar (eds), *Beyond Westminster and Congress: The Nordic Experience*, Columbus, OH: Ohio State University Press.

Esaiasson, P. and Holmberg, S. (1996) *Representation from Above: Members of Parliament and Representative Democracy in Sweden*, Aldershot: Dartmouth.

Gallagher, M., Laver, M. and Mair, P. (2011) *Representative Government in Modern Europe*, London: McGraw-Hill, 5th edn.

Hix, S. and Noury, A. (2009) "After enlargement: Voting patterns in the Sixth European Parliament", *Legislative Studies Quarterly*, 34 (2): 159–74.

Ignazi, P. (2007) "The rise of the "state-centred party" and its questionable legitimacy", unpublished text.

Jewell, M.E. (1970) "Attitudinal determinants of legislative behavior: the utility of role analysis", in A. Kornberg and L.D. Musolf (eds), *Legislatures in Developmental Perspective*, Durham, NC: Duke University Press.

Katz, R. (1986) "Party government: A rationalistic conception", in F.G. Castles and R. Wildenmann (eds), *Visions and Realities of Party Government*, Berlin: de Gruyter.

Katz, R. and Mair, P. (1995) "Changing models of party organization and party democracy: The emergence of the Cartel Party", *Party Politics*, 1: 5–28.

Katz, R. and Mair, P. (2008) "MPs and parliamentary parties in the Age of the Cartel Party", paper presented at the ECPR Joint session of workshops, workshop on *Parliamentary and Representatives Roles in Modern Legislatures*, Rennes.

Kerby, M. and Blidook, K. (2011) "It's not you, it's me: Determinants of voluntary legislative turnover in Canada", *Legislative Studies Quarterly*, 36 (4): 621–43.

MacIntyre, A. (1984) *After Virtue*, Notre Dame, IN: University of Notre Dame Press, 2nd edn.

Mair, P. (1994) "Party organizations: From civil society to the state", in R.S. Katz and P. Mair (eds), *How Parties Organize*, London: Sage Publications.

Martin, S. (2011) "Parliamentary Questions, the behaviour of legislators, and the function of legislatures: An introduction", *Journal of Legislative Studies*, 17 (3): 259–70.

Mershon, C. and Shvetsova, O. (2008) "Parliamentary cycles and party switching in legislatures", *Comparative Political Studies*, 41 (1): 99–127.

Norris, P. (2004) *Electoral Engineering: Voting Rules and Political Behaviour*, Cambridge: Cambridge University Press.

Norton, P. (1997) "Roles and behaviour of British MPs", in W.C. Müller and T. Saalfeld (eds) *Members of Parliament in Western Europe: Roles and Behaviour*, London: Frank Cass.

Norton, P. (2002) "Introduction: Linking parliaments and citizens", in P. Norton (ed.), *Parliament and Citizens in Western Europe*, London: Frank Cass.

Patzelt, W.J. (1997) "German MPs and their roles", in W.C. Müller and T. Saalfeld (eds) *Members of Parliament in Western Europe: Roles and Behaviour*, London: Frank Cass.

Pierson, P. (1994) *Dismantling the Welfare State? Reagan, Thatcher and the Politics of Retrenchment*, Cambridge: Cambridge University Press.

Pitkin, H.F. (1972) *The Concept of Representation*, Berkeley, CA: University of California Press.

Pizzorno, A. (2008) "La sfera pubblica e il concetto di mandante immaginario", *Sociologica*, 3: 1–22.

Rehfeld, A. (2009) "Representation rethought: On trustees, delegates, and gyroscopes in the study of political representation and democracy", *American Political Science Review*, 103 (2): 214–30.

Rozenberg, O. (2009) "Présider par plaisir. L'examen des affaires européennes à l'Assemblée nationale et à la Chambre des Communes depuis Maastricht", *Revue française de science politique*, 59: 401–27.

Rozenberg, O. and Martin, S. (2011) "Conclusion: Questioning Parliamentary Questions", *Journal of Legislative Studies*, 17 (3), 393–404.

Russell, M. and Bradbury, J. (2007) "The constituency work of Scottish and Welsh MPs: Adjusting to devolution", *Regional & Federal Studies*, 17 (1): 97–116.

Saalfeld, T. (2011), "Parliamentary Questions as instruments of substantive representation: Visible minorities in the UK House of Commons, 2005–2010", *Journal of Legislative Studies*, 17 (3): 271–89.

Saalfeld, T., Wüst, A. and Bird, K. (2011), "Epilogue: Towards a strategic model of minority participation and representation", in K. Bird, T. Saalfeld and A. Wüst (eds), *The Political Representation of Immigrants and Minorities: Voters, Parties and Parliaments in Liberal Democracies*, London: Routledge.

Sauger, N. (2009) "Party discipline and coalition management in the French Parliament", *West European Politics*, 32 (2): 310–26.

Searing, D.D. (1994) *Westminister's World. Understanding Political Roles*, Cambridge, MA: Harvard University Press.

Wahlke, J.C., Eulau, H., Buchanan, W. and Fergusson, L.C. (1962) *The Legislative System: Explorations in Legislative Behaviour*, New York: John Wiley.

Wessels, B. (1999) "Whom to represent? Role orientations of legislators in Europe", in H. Schmitt and J. Thomassen (eds), *Political Representation and Legitimacy in the European Union*, Oxford: Oxford University Press.

Index

Page numbers in *italics* denote tables.